Small States and the European Union

This volume describes the economic structures of ten European small states with populations numbering some three million people or fewer, and discusses their performance.

The book covers seven small member states of the EU – Cyprus, Estonia, Latvia, Lithuania, Luxembourg, Malta and Slovenia, and two small states which are candidates for membership, namely Macedonia and Montenegro. Iceland is also included, given that this country is highly integrated into the EU and was itself, for a time, an EU candidate country.

The chapters, contributed by experts in their field, indicate that the main similarity of the small states covered in the volume is that they are all highly economically vulnerable, due to their high exposure to external economic conditions beyond their control. In spite of this, some of these states are economically successful, pointing to the fact that appropriate policies can enable small states to withstand economic vulnerability. However, the analysis presented clearly demonstrates that the ten small states discussed cannot be described as a homogeneous group. They differ in many economic aspects, most notably in their stage of development. The chapters also discuss the real and perceived benefits derived by these states as a result of EU membership, of which the most important relate to access to a large single market, given that the domestic market of these states is very small. For some states the transfer of funds from the EU is of major importance, while for others geopolitical factors or the upgrade of the economic regulatory frameworks are seen as the major benefits of EU membership.

Lino Briguglio is the Director of the Islands and Small States Institute of the University of Malta. He is known internationally for his seminal work on the 'Vulnerability Index', which led to a worldwide interest in and many quantitative studies on economic vulnerability. He has also pioneered work on the measurement of economic resilience.

Europa Economic Perspectives

Providing in-depth analysis with a global reach, this series from Europa examines a wide range of contemporary economic issues from areas around the world. Intended to complement the *Europa Regional Surveys of the World* series, *Europa Economic Perspectives* will be a valuable resource for academics, students, researchers, policymakers, business people and anyone with an interest in current world economic affairs.

While the *Europa World Year Book* and its associated *Regional Surveys* inform on and analyse contemporary economic, political and social developments, the Editors considered the need for more in-depth volumes written and/or edited by specialists in their field, in order to delve into a country's or a region's particular economic situation, or to examine economic theories in the context of current global economic affairs. Volumes in the series are not constrained by any particular template, but may explore any aspect of a country's recent economic issues in order to increase knowledge.

International Monetary Reform
A specific set of proposals
John Williamson

Small States and the European Union
Economic perspectives
Edited by Lino Briguglio

Small States and the European Union

Economic perspectives

Edited by
Lino Briguglio

Routledge
Taylor & Francis Group
LONDON AND NEW YORK

First published 2016 by Routledge

2 Park Square, Milton Park, Abingdon, Oxfordshire OX14 4RN
711 Third Avenue, New York, NY 10017

Routledge is an imprint of the Taylor & Francis Group, an informa business

First issued in paperback 2018

Europa Commissioning Editor: Cathy Hartley
Editorial Assistant: Eleanor Simmons

British Library Cataloguing in Publication Data
A catalogue record for this book is available from the British Library by Taylor & Francis Books

Library of Congress Cataloging in Publication Data
A catalog record for this book has been requested

ISBN: 978-1-85743-807-9 (hbk)
ISBN: 978-1-138-38642-6 (pbk)

Typeset in Times New Roman
by Taylor & Francis Books

Contents

List of illustrations

Figures

Tables

List of contributors

Serge Allegrezza possesses a PhD (Economics) from the University of Liège, Belgium. He served as research fellow at the CEPS/Instead (now LISER) between 1985 and 1991 and as Conseiller de gouvernement at the Ministry of Economics in Luxembourg between 1991 and 2003. Since April 2003 he has held the position of Director-General of the Institute of Statistics and Economic Studies (STATEC), Luxembourg. Dr Allegrezza also acts as head of the Competitiveness Observatory at the Ministry of Economy and Foreign Trade, Luxembourg. He is head of delegation at the Economic Policy Committee of the EU.

Lino Briguglio possesses a PhD (Economics) from the University of Exeter, United Kingdom. Professor Briguglio is the Director of the Islands and Small States Institute of the University of Malta. He is known internationally for his seminal work on the 'Vulnerability Index', which led to a worldwide interest in and many quantitative studies on economic vulnerability. He has also pioneered work on the measurement of economic resilience. He has acted as consultant, mainly on matters related to small states, to various international organizations, including the Commonwealth Secretariat, the United Nations Environment Programme (UNEP), the United Nations Conference on Trade and Development (UNCTAD), and the World Bank.

Aleksandrs Cepilovs is a junior research fellow at Ragnar Nurkse School of Innovation and Governance, Tallinn University of Technology and a senior expert at the Ministry of Finance, Latvia. His main research interests lie in innovation policy with a focus on demand-side innovation, as well as innovation and development policies in small states. His recent work has covered issues relating to public procurement as an innovation policy instrument, demand-side innovation policies more generally, innovation in the public sector, as well as the role of bureaucracy in fiscal and financial policymaking.

Hilmar Þór Hilmarsson is a Professor at the University of Akureyri, School of Business and Science, Iceland. He teaches courses on international business and macroeconomics. Professor Hilmarsson holds a PhD in Public Administration and Economic Development from the American University in Washington, DC. He served as a Specialist and Co-ordinator with the World Bank Group in Washington, DC from 1990 to 1995, at the World Bank office in Riga from 1999 to 2003 and at the World Bank office in Hanoi from 2003 to 2006. From 1995 to 1999 he served as a Special Adviser to the Minister for Foreign Affairs in Iceland. Professor Hilmarsson has published over 60 scholarly articles and book chapters. In 2014 he published a book entitled *Small States in a Global Economy: Crisis, Cooperation and Contributions.*

Branimir Jovanovic is a Visiting Researcher at the University of Turin, Department of Economics, Italy. Before that, he worked at the Research Department of the National Bank of the Republic of Macedonia from 2007–2015. He is also a Visiting Professor at the University American College Skopje, Macedonia. He has carried out research on monetary economics, exchange rates, forecasting, financial crises and other topics from the area of monetary-international-macroeconomics. His current research is focused mainly on income inequality and poverty. He won the annual award of the National Bank of the Republic of Macedonia in 2007, and the Olga Radzyner award of the Austrian National Bank in 2013.

Tarmo Kalvet is senior research fellow in the field of technology governance at the Ragnar Nurkse School of Innovation and Governance, Tallinn University of Technology, Estonia. He was for many years the founding head of the Innovation Policy Research Programme at the Praxis Centre for Policy Studies, Estonia's leading policy think tank, as well as one of its board members. Previously he worked for Archimedes Foundation (1999–2001) and for the Phare Public Development Programme in Estonia (1997–1998). He has published more than 80 research and policy analysis papers, especially in the fields of enterprise, economics, research and innovation, and Information and Communication Technology (ICT) policies, often with a focus on small states.

Milorad Katnić is Professor at the University of Donja Gorica, Montenegro and President of the Board of Directors of the Societe Generale Montenegro Bank. Previously, he served as Minister of Finance (2010–2012). During his career he was a member of the Administrative Council of the Development Bank of the Council of Europe (2006–2008), Governor at the World Bank and the European Bank for Reconstruction and Development (2010–2012). Dr Katnic was involved in the design and implementation of numerous important projects related to public finance, economic development and structural reforms. He is a member of the Mont Pelerin Society.

Algidras Miskinis holds a doctorate in Economics. He is Vice-Dean for Masters Studies at the Faculty of Economics of Vilnius University, Lithuania. He is also Head of the Department of Economic Policy at the same

University. Professor Miskinis is currently President of the Lithuanian Economic Association and Editor-in-chief of the journal *Ekonomika* published by Vilnius University. His main areas of expertise are international trade, foreign direct investments and competitiveness of nations.

Mojmir Mrak is a full-time Professor and a Jean Monnet Chair holder at the Faculty of Economics, University of Ljubljana, Slovenia. He has also been a regular visiting Professor at the Wirtschaftsuniversität in Vienna, Austria. Professor Mrak's main research areas include international capital flows, national and European Union (EU) public finances, and EU accession. He is author, co-author and editor of numerous books and journal articles, and also serves as a member of editorial boards and/or reviewer for several international journals. Professor Mrak has had numerous consultancy assignments on public finance and EU accession issues for the government of Slovenia as well as for international organizations and governments of several countries in the region of South Eastern Europe.

Lauma Muižniece is a PhD candidate at Ragnar Nurkse School of Innovation and Governance, Tallinn University of Technology and a project manager, senior expert at the University of Latvia. Her main research interests are in innovation policy with a focus on science-industry linkages, university technology transfer as well as related government incentives in small countries. Her recent work is related to commercialization of publicly funded research and the impact that EU funds allocated for research and development have on technology transfer processes.

Marjan Petreski is an Associate Professor at the University American College Skopje, Macedonia. He also chairs the University Research Committee, which is in charge of steering research work. Dr Petreski specializes in research and teaching in applied macroeconomics. His narrow research focus is exchange-rate regimes and monetary policy and strategy, with particular reference to developing countries. For his research he was awarded the Young Scientist Award 2009 by the Macedonian Academy of Sciences and Arts, the Olga Radzyner Award 2010 by the Austrian National Bank and the Japanese Award for Outstanding Research on Development 2013 by the Government of Japan.

Aušytė Rastenienė is an Associate Professor in the Department of Theoretical Economics at Vilnius University, Lithuania and is a deputy editor-in-chief of the magazine *Ekonomika*. She is an expert in the Centre for Quality Assessment in Higher Education (SKVC), Lithuania. Dr Rastenienė completed her PhD at Vilnius University. From 1997–2002 she worked as a senior economist at the Bank of Lithuania, Department of Monetary Policy. Her fields of interest also include emigration and sustainable development.

Tijana Stanković is adviser to Deputy Prime Minister for Economic Policy and Financial System, Montenegro. She is national co-ordinator for the

Economic Reform Programme of Montenegro and has also co-ordinated strategically important documents including the National Development Plan of Montenegro, preparation of public–private partnerships (PPP) law and structural reform plans. During the period 2011–2013 she served as Deputy Minister of Finance for economic policy and development. Her background in academic expertise is institutional economy, specifically pension system reforms. She is the member of the Gender Diversity and Governance Network in the Mediterranean and UNECE (United Nations Economic Commission for Europe) PPP Team of Specialists.

Andreas Theophanous obtained his MA and PhD degrees in Economics from Pennsylvania State University, USA in 1985 and 1988, respectively. He served as Economic Adviser to the President of the Republic of Cyprus from 1990–1993. He is currently Professor of Political Economy, President of the Center for European and International Affairs and Head of the Department of European Studies and International Relations, University of Nicosia, Cyprus. As a Visiting Professor, Senior Fellow and/or Guest Speaker, he has visited several universities and think-tanks, including the London School of Economics and Political Science, the Brookings Institution, the Woodrow Wilson International Center for Scholars, the Australian Institute of International Affairs, the Centre for European Integration Studies (University of Bonn) and the Hebrew University of Jerusalem. Professor Theophanous has published several books and numerous articles on the Cyprus problem and its economic aspects, Cyprus–European Union relations including the current economic crisis, issues of governance in bi-ethnic and multi-ethnic societies, European integration and European Union–Turkish relations.

Igor Velickovski holds a doctorate in Economics obtained from Staffordshire University, UK and is a Manager of the Payment Systems Department at the National Bank of Macedonia. His previous work experience was closely related to monetary policy implementation and foreign reserve management as he has been a Head of the Open Market Operations Division and Deputy Manager of the Financial Market Operations Department. He is also Associate Professor of Economics at the School of Business Economics and Management, University American College Skopje, Macedonia. His teaching area covers monetary economics and international and corporate finance, while his research focus includes monetary, trade and financial integration processes. He has been engaged in several research projects and received the Dr Dragoslav Avramović award by the National Bank of Serbia for the best research paper in macroeconomics and finance in 2012.

Acknowledgement

The editor would like to acknowledge the helpful suggestions by the following reviewers: Gordon Cordina (E-Cubed consultants), Diana Panke (University College Dublin), Goran Petreski (Saints Cyril and Methodius University, Malta), Jadranka Kaludjerovic (University of Donja Gorica), Matjia Rojec (University of Ljubljana), Ian Taylor (University of St Andrews), Anders Wivel (University of Copenhagen), Vincentas Giedraitis (Vilnius University), Riaz Tayob (Tallinn University of Technology), Ringa Raudla (Tallinn University of Technology), Roderick Pace (University of Malta), Sladjana Pavlovic, Ministry of Finance, Montenegro.

Abbreviations

AIC	Actual Individual Consumption
CAP	Common Agriculture Policy
CBI	Central Bank of Iceland
CEE	Central and Eastern Europe
CEFTA	Central European Free Trade Agreement
CFP	Common Fisheries Policy
CIS	Commonwealth of Independent States
EBRD	European Bank for Reconstruction and Development
EC	European Community
EEA	European Economic Area
EEC	European Economic Community
EFTA	European Free Trade Association
ERDF	European Regional Development Fund
EU	European Union
EU27	European Union (of 27 countries, between 2007 and the accession of Croatia in 2013)
EU28	European Union (of 28 countries)
FDI	Foreign Direct Investment
FEI	Financial Engineering Instruments
GCI	Global Competitiveness Indicators
GDP	Gross Domestic Product
GNI	Gross National Income
HDI	Human Development Index
IMF	International Monetary Fund
IEF	Index of Economic Freedom
NATO	North Atlantic Treaty Organization
NYH	Non-income HDI
OECD	Organisation for Economic Co-operation and Development
OSCE	Organization for Security Co-operation in Europe
PPP	Purchasing Power Parity
PPS	Purchasing Power Standard
QMV	Qualified Majority Voting
SAA	Stabilization and Association Agreement

SFRY	Socialist Federal Republic of Yugoslavia
UNCTAD	United Nations Conference on Trade and Development
UK	United Kingdom
UN	United Nations
UNDP	United Nations Development Programme
WEF	World Economic Forum
WGI	Worldwide Governance Indicators
WTO	World Trade Organization

Introduction

Small states and the European Union

Lino Briguglio

1 The purpose of this book

The purpose of the book is mainly to describe the economic structures of ten European small states and to discuss their performance, referring to the benefits or disadvantages that European Union (EU) membership has offered or is likely to offer to these states.

In this publication country size is measured in terms of population size, and, as defined here, small states are those with a population of about three million persons or fewer. According to this definition seven EU member states qualify for inclusion in this group, namely Cyprus, Estonia, Latvia, Lithuania, Luxembourg, Malta, and Slovenia. The book also includes two small states which are candidates for membership, namely Macedonia and Montenegro. Iceland is also included in view of the fact that it is highly integrated in the EU and was itself, for a time, an EU candidate country.

This introductory chapter is organized into five sections. Section 2 presents and discusses some statistics relating to major common features of or differences between the ten small states covered in this publication. Section 3 summarizes the views expressed by the authors of country chapters regarding the advantages and disadvantages of EU membership. Section 4 deals with the economic prospects of each of the ten countries. Section 5 concludes this introductory chapter by summarizing the main arguments in the previous sections.

2 Some characteristics of the EU small states

2.1 Characteristics of small states

Small states face special disadvantages in view of their small domestic market, their limited natural resource endowments and their economic diversification constraints. Due to these characteristics, these states tend to be highly dependent on international trade, and are therefore exposed to external shocks. In spite of these constraints, the seven small member states of the EU register relatively high gross domestic product (GDP) per capita and have fitted satisfactorily into the EU family of states, side-by-side with larger states, including Germany, Italy, the UK and Spain.

The small EU member states had to transpose EU directives and abide by regulations set for all EU members, large and small. It is well known that small states tend to suffer from the problem of overhead cost indivisibility, due to the fact that such costs cannot generally be downscaled in proportion to the population. It is therefore to be expected that the transposition of these directives and regulations into the body of laws of the respective countries results in higher relative costs for these small states.

Another factor worth discussing, when considering small states, is their voice in an organization dominated by much larger states. There is the possibility that the interests of small states could be side-lined in view of their limited ability to influence decision making in the organization. This matter is discussed in most of the chapters in this book. As we shall argue below, this reality poses disadvantages for small states, with the mitigating factor being that the voice of these small states within the EU is much stronger inside than it would have been had they decided to stay out.

2.2 *Common features*

2.2.1 High degree of trade openness

All the country chapters in this publication refer to the characteristics of small states, notably the high degree of economic openness. The fact that small states have a small domestic market means that they cannot rely on their own market for a critical mass of production of many goods and services. In addition, small states tend to be poorly endowed with natural resources and consequently they often depend highly on imports of food, fuel and industrial supplies. This renders them highly economically vulnerable to external economic shocks.

The ten small states considered in this book are all characterized by trade openness, with Luxembourg, Malta and Estonia being the most open economies, as can be seen in Figure 0.1. Indeed all the ten small states have an openness ratio higher than the average of the 28 EU member states (EU28). The implication of this is that their economic performance is influenced by external factors.[1]

2.2.2 The 2009 growth dip

Due to the fact that these countries export a large proportion of their goods and services to the EU, which was itself highly impacted by the global recession of 2008/2009, they inevitably also experienced a decline in their GDP. This 2009 dip is clearly visible in Figure 0.2, for all the states considered in this book.

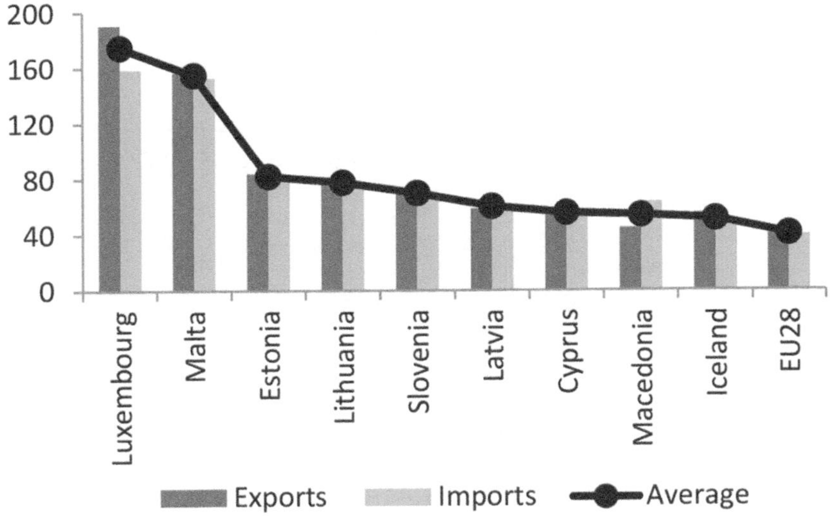

Figure 0.1 Exports and imports of goods and services as a ratio of GDP (%)
Source: Eurostat database.

2.3 *Disparities*

However, the ten small states considered in this book are not a homogenous group in many economic aspects. In this section we shall contrast and compare a number of statistics pertaining to these states.

2.3.1 Population, country size and population density

To start with, although the ten states are all small, they have different populations and different land areas, leading to different population densities, as can be seen in Figures 0.3a, 0.3b and 0.3c. It can be seen that Iceland occupies the largest land area (over 100 thousand km^2) but has the lowest population in the group (326 thousand) leading a population density of 3 persons per km^2. At the other extreme there is Malta, with a land area of 315 km^2 and a population of 425 thousand, so that its population density is over 1,300 per km^2. Luxembourg and Cyprus have relatively high population densities, but by far lower than that of Malta.

Interestingly, some of the ten small states covered in this book are not that small when measured in terms of land area, with, for example, Iceland having an area almost as large as that of England.

2.3.2 GDP per capita and GDP growth

The GDP per capita of the ten small states also differs markedly, as can be seen in Figure 0.4. Luxembourg is by far the highest income generator, with

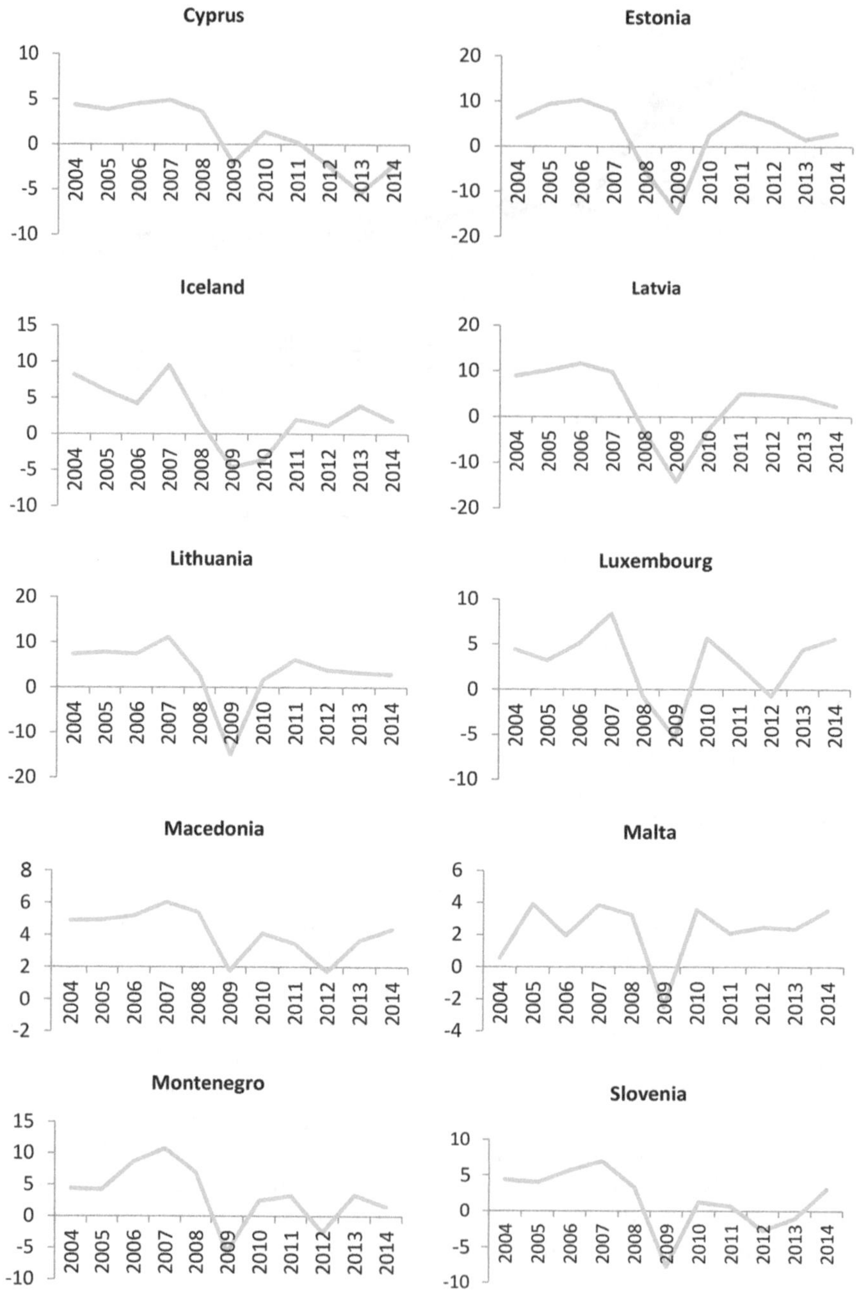

Figure 0.2 The 2009 dip
Note: The vertical axis measures GDP real annual growth rates (%).
Source: International Monetary Fund (IMF) Outlook database: www.imf.org/external/pubs/ft/weo/2015/02/weodata/index.aspx.

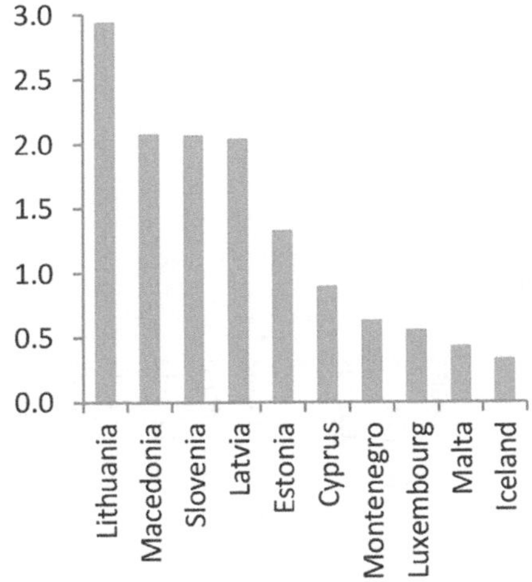

Figure 0.3a Population (thousand, 2014)
Source: http://data.worldbank.org/indicator/SP.POP.TOTL.

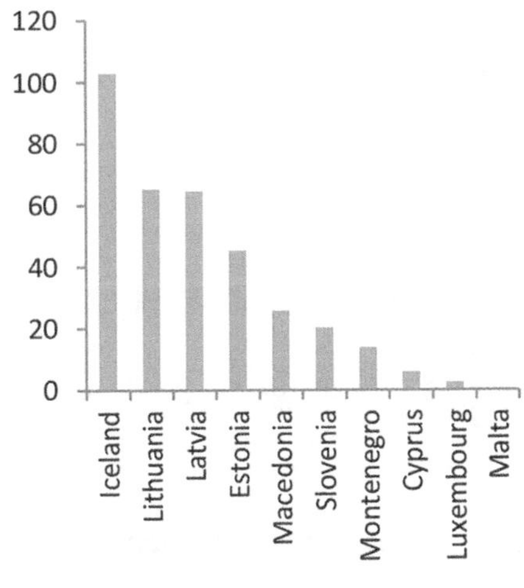

Figure 0.3b Land area (thousand km^2)
Source: http://data.worldbank.org/indicator/AG.LND.TOTL.K2.

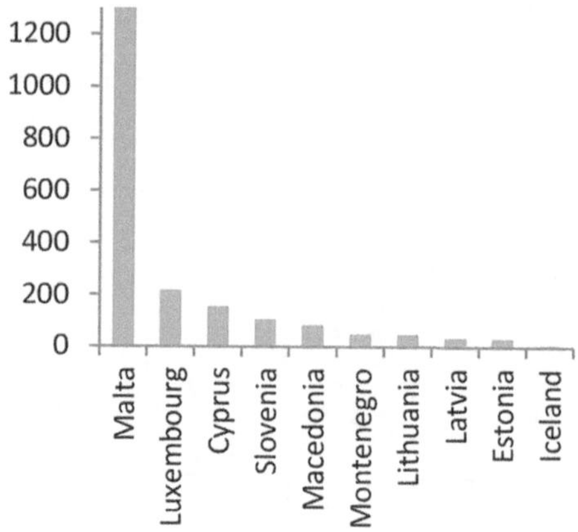

Figure 0.3c Population density (2014, per km^2)
Source: http://data.worldbank.org/indicator/EN.POP.DNST.

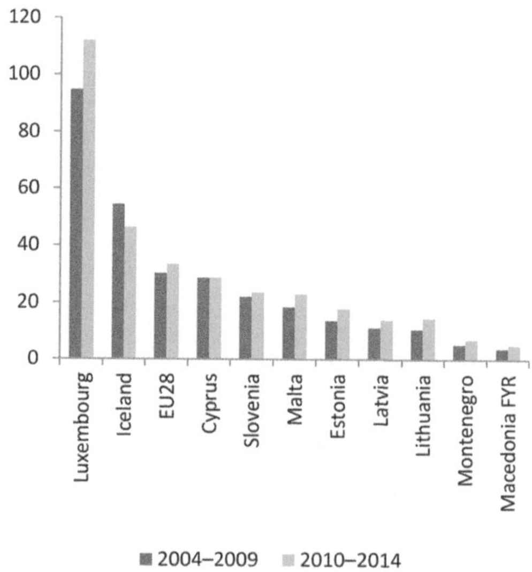

Figure 0.4 GDP per capita (thousand US$)
Source: IMF Outlook database: http://www.imf.org/external/pubs/ft/weo/2015/02/weodata/index.aspx.

over US$100 thousand per capita (averaged between 2010 and 2014).[2] Iceland follows with over US$40 thousand per capita.[3]

Next in line are Cyprus, Malta and Slovenia, generating more than US$20 thousand per capita. It can be noted that all countries, except Cyprus, increased their GDP per capita between 2010 and 2014 when compared to the earlier six years.

The ten small states also differ in their rate of growth, as can be seen in Figure 0.5, which presents the annual change in real GDP between 2004 and 2009 and 2010 and 2014. The fastest growing EU member state between 2004 and 2009 was Latvia. Iceland, Montenegro and Macedonia also registering very rapid growth rates during this period. Growth rates between 2010 and 2014 were generally slower when compared to 2004–2009, particularly for Cyprus, which experienced a rapid decline in its real GDP. Iceland, Latvia and Slovenia, which experienced serious financial difficulties in recent years,[4] also registered relatively slow growth rates during the 2010–2014 period. During this period, the fastest growing economies were those of Estonia, Lithuania and Luxembourg.

2.3.3 Indebtedness, balance of payment deficits and unemployment

Indebtedness, balance of payment deficits and unemployment are considered as indicators of macroeconomic stability or otherwise.

The ten small states discussed in this chapter differed markedly in their rate of debt to GDP ratios, as can be seen in Figure 0.6, with Cyprus, Iceland, Malta and Slovenia registering relatively high rates of indebtedness between

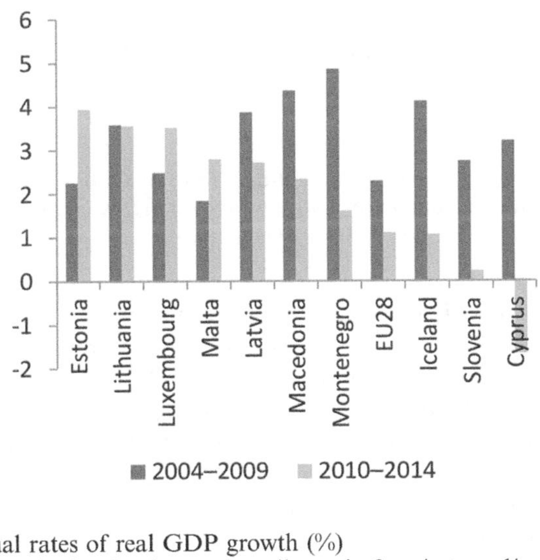

Figure 0.5 Annual rates of real GDP growth (%)
Source: IMF Outlook database: http://www.imf.org/external/pubs/ft/weo/2015/02/weodata/index.aspx.

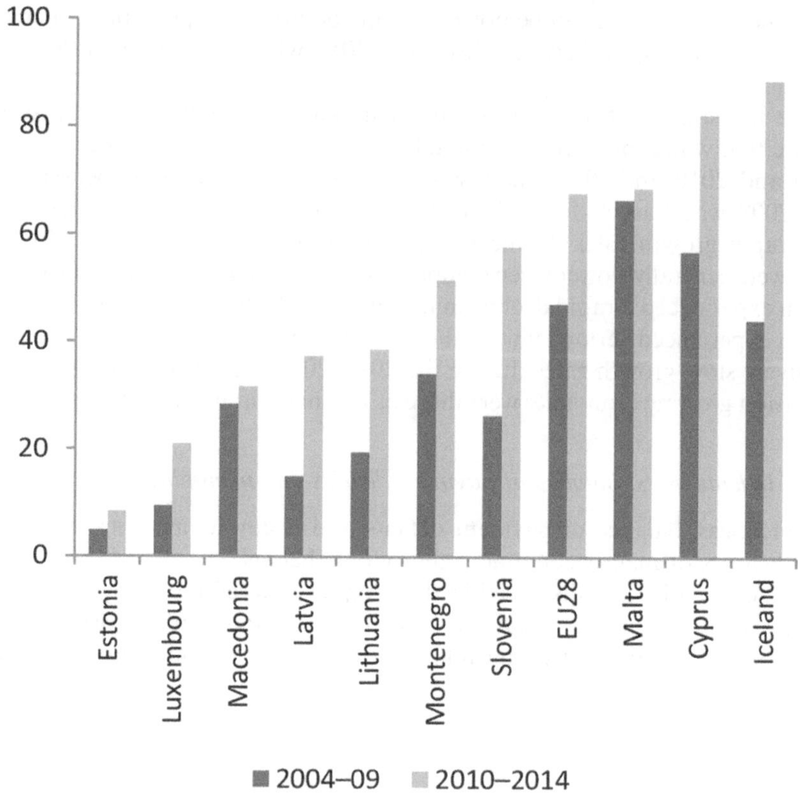

Figure 0.6 General government gross debt as a ratio of GDP (%)
Source: IMF Outlook database: http://www.imf.org/external/pubs/ft/weo/2015/02/weodata/index.aspx.

2010 and 2014, while Estonia and Luxembourg were characterized by low debt to GDP ratios. The other four states (Latvia, Lithuania, Macedonia and Montenegro) were moderately indebted. It should be noted from Figure 0.6 that in all countries, the debt ratio increased after the global recession.

Cyprus, Slovenia and Iceland passed through difficult times and all three faced the threat of insolvency, as discussed in the chapters on these three small states. Malta did not face a financial crisis, mostly because its core banks were to a high extent isolated from external contagion, but subsequent governments could not effectively reign in their deficits between 2010 and 2014 so that the debt averaged about 70% of GDP between 2010 and 2014.

With regard to the balance of payments, eight of the ten small states, Luxembourg and Slovenia being the exception, registered negative balances in the current account between 2010 and 2014. The highest deficits were those of Montenegro and Cyprus, as can be seen from Figure 0.7.

The unemployment rate in these states also differed markedly with Macedonia being by far the country with the highest rate (Figure 0.8). In most countries the unemployment rate increased on average between 2010 and 2014, compared to the preceding six ears. After the global recession, the Baltic States and Cyprus registered the highest unemployment rates among the small EU member states.[5]

2.3.4 *Wage rates and competitiveness*

Another major difference between the ten states relates to their wage levels, as can be seen in Figure 0.9, which shows the average wage per hour in the private sector for the ten countries. The pattern is very similar to the GDP per capita of the respective countries, with Luxembourg and Iceland paying the highest wage rates and the Baltic States and the two candidate countries the lowest.[6]

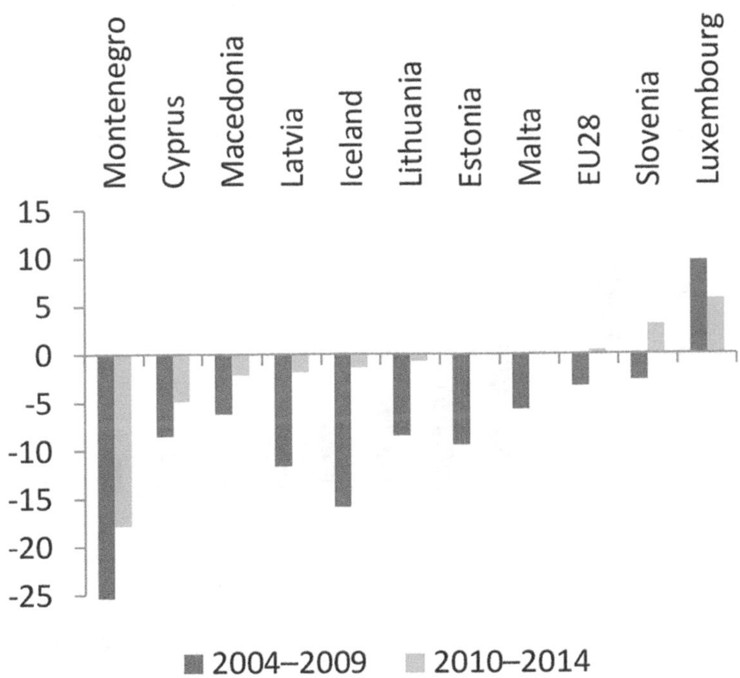

Figure 0.7 Current account as a ratio of GDP (%)
Source: IMF Outlook database: http://www.imf.org/external/pubs/ft/weo/2015/02/weodata/index.aspx.

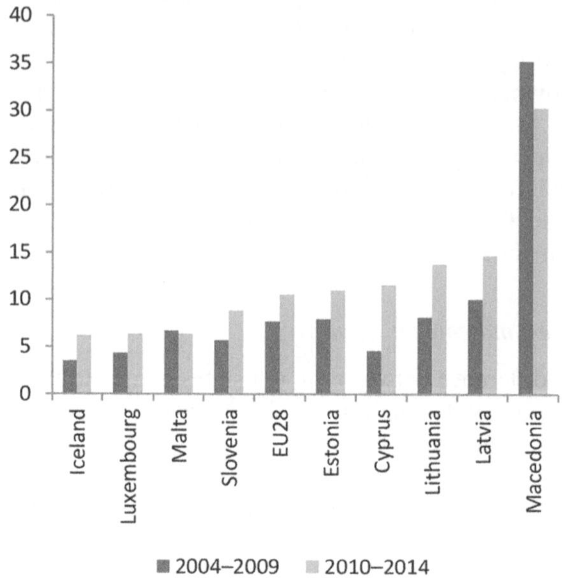

Figure 0.8 Unemployment rate (%)
Source: IMF Outlook database: http://www.imf.org/external/pubs/ft/weo/2015/02/weodata/index.aspx.

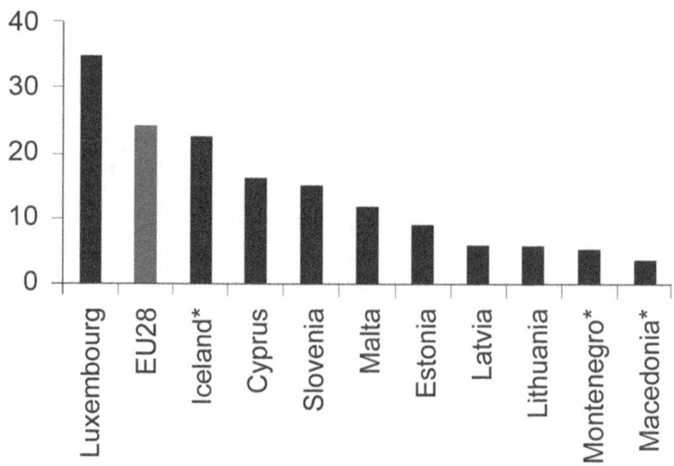

Figure 0.9 Wage levels (€ per hour, 2012–2014)
Note: *Data for Iceland, Montenegro, Macedonia estimated (see footnote 6).
Source: Eurostat database.

The competitiveness scores for the ten small states are shown in Figure 0.10. The scores are mostly based on the perceptions of the respondents to an annual survey used to compile the Global Competitiveness Indicators (GCI).[7] The overall scores range between 1 and 7, with 7 being the highest possible degree of competitiveness.[8] It can be seen that Luxembourg and Iceland received markedly higher scores than the EU average. The remaining small states' scores are below the EU average.[9]

It is to be noted that in spite of the fact that the wage rates of Luxembourg and Iceland are relatively high, they still exceed the other small states' scores in terms of competitiveness, indicating that labour productivity can more than offset wage costs in fostering competitiveness.

The GCI assume that developing economies are mostly factor-driven and that they generally rely on their factor endowments, primarily unskilled labour and natural resources. With economic development, countries move into the stage labelled efficiency-driven, where more efficient production processes will be developed leading to improvements in the product quality and to higher wages. At this point, competitiveness is likely to be increasingly driven by efficient goods, labour and financial markets and the ability to harness the benefits of existing technologies. Finally, countries will move into the innovation-driven stage when relatively high wages are sustained due to increased labour productivity through technological advance. According to the latest report[10]

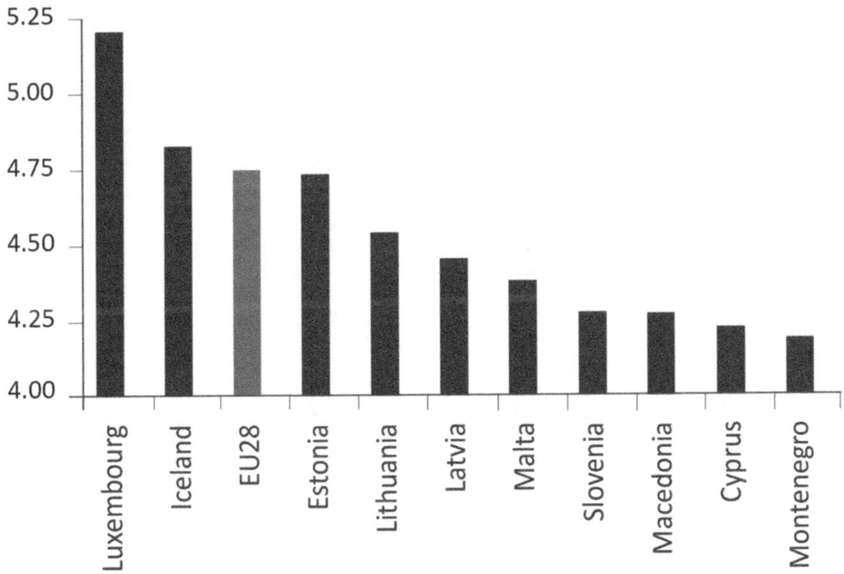

Figure 0.10 Competitiveness Index scores
Source: Schwab (2015).

Estonia, Iceland, Malta, Luxembourg and Slovenia are at the innovation-driven stage, Latvia and Lithuania are on their way there, and Macedonia and Montenegro are still in the factor-driven stage.

2.3.5 The importance of the financial sector

The importance of the financial sector in each country can be measured by financial depth, which relates to a country's size of banks, other financial institutions, and financial markets, taken together and compared to GDP. The World Bank measures financial depth as private credit relative to GDP.[11]

The importance of the financial markets in a country may reflect economic sophistication but it may also enhance the vulnerability of the country to financial contagion, as happened in the case of Cyprus and Iceland.

Figure 0.11 shows that the degree of financial depth in Cyprus, Luxembourg and Malta, was very high and exceeded the EU28 average. The Iceland and Slovenia ratios were also relatively high. Although Malta and Luxembourg have a relatively large financial sector, they did not face a banking crisis as the other three small states just mentioned. In the case of Malta this was mainly due to the fact that the core banks were not highly exposed to external contagion. In the case of Luxembourg, the reason could be that

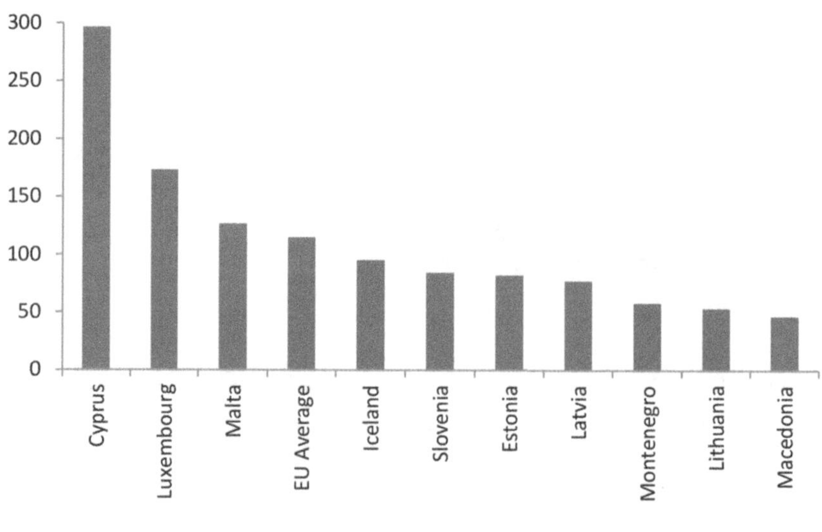

Figure 0.11 Financial depth (2010–2013) measured as private credit relative to GDP (%)

Source: World Bank (2015).

the banks in that country held a high proportion of liquidity (Standard and Poor's Rating System, 2013).

2.3.6 Problematic factors for doing business

The Global Competitiveness Report asks the respondents of the survey to identify the most problematic factors in doing business in their respective countries. In Table 0.1, the perceived problematic factors, as reported in Schwab (2015) are ranked in terms of the average score for the ten small states. It appears that taking the ten countries together, the most problematic factors are access to financing, inefficient government bureaucracy and tax rates.

Access to financing of business was perceived to be the most problematic factor for Cyprus, Macedonia and Montenegro (shown by numbers in bold). Inefficient government bureaucracy is perceived to be the most problematic factor for Lithuania and Malta. In the case of Estonia and Luxembourg, the most problematic factor is perceived to be inadequately educated workforces. Restrictive labour regulations is the most problematic factor for the Slovenian respondents and foreign currency regulations for the Icelandic respondents.

The numbers in italic in Table 0.1 show the second-most problematic factor for each country, according to the perceptions of the respondents.

2.3.7 Social and political governance

Although the present publication focuses on economic aspects, it is worth examining the state of social and political governance in the ten small states under consideration. We have used two indices for this purpose, namely the Worldwide Governance Indicators for political governance and the non-income components of the Human Development Index for social governance. Although the latter is not strictly a governance index, it is related to educational and health outcomes which are themselves related to policy measures.

The Worldwide Governance Indicators (WGI)[12] has six dimensions of political governance, namely (1) voice and accountability (2) political stability and absence of violence (3) government effectiveness (4) regulatory quality (5) rule of law and (6) control of corruption. The scores assigned to each country range from approximately −2.5 to 2.5, with higher values corresponding to better governance.[13] A simple average of the six dimensions for 2013 was computed for the purpose of this study.

The data for the WGI scores, pertaining to the ten small states covered in this chapter are shown in Figure 0.12. It can be seen that Luxembourg, Iceland, Estonia and Malta have relatively high scores, higher than the EU28 average. Cyprus, Lithuania, Slovenia and Latvia have lower scores than the EU average, but their scores are still relatively high by international standards. Montenegro and Macedonia have relatively low governance scores and markedly lower than those of the rest of the eight states, although they are still positive scores, indicating that they are higher than the world average.

Table 0.1 The ten most problematic factors for doing business

Areas of concern	*Avg*	*CYP*	*EST*	*ICE*	*LAT*	*LIT*	*LUX*	*MAC*	*MAL*	*MON*	*SLO*
Access to financing	14.4	**24.6**	11.0	*12.0*	11.5	7.4	10.9	**18.4**	*16.1*	**18.0**	14.0
Inefficient government bureaucracy	13.8	*18.9*	10.3	9.2	*14.5*	**16.6**	13.1	9.4	**18.5**	*11.8*	*15.9*
Tax rates	10.4	2.5	*18.3*	12.0	**15.1**	*14.8*	6.8	4.5	4.9	9.5	15.7
Inadequately educated workforce	9.5	2.4	**19.7**	1.3	9.2	9.3	**21.0**	*10.7*	12.3	7.2	2.1
Restrictive labour regulations	7.7	6.1	4.4	1.6	4.4	13.5	*18.4*	2.3	4.9	5.1	**16.5**
Insufficient capacity to innovate	7.2	9	9	3.2	8.2	3	8.8	7	13.9	7	2.8
Complexity of tax regulations	6.1	1.1	5.3	5.0	10.2	10.2	4.4	7.7	3.7	5.1	6.3
Inadequate supply of infrastructure	6.0	5.9	7.6	2.4	4.7	3	5.9	6.1	12.1	10.1	2.5
Corruption	5.5	10.1	1.6	1.8	5.4	8.8	0	7	6.1	8.2	0
Poor work ethic in labour force	5.0	3.9	7.4	1	5.6	3.8	4.8	10.1	3.4	7.8	2.4
Foreign currency regulations	3.3	2.3	0.3	**28.7**	0	0.3	0	0.9	0	0.9	7.9

Source: Schwab (2015).

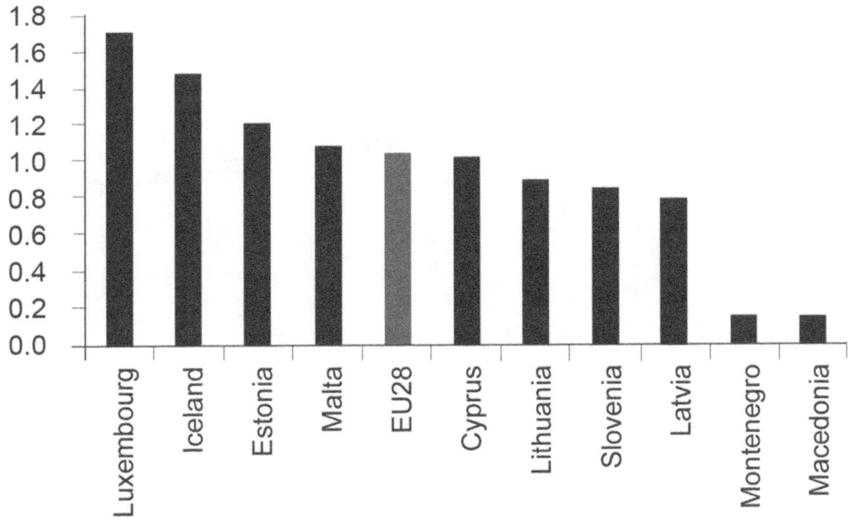

Figure 0.12 World Governance Indicators, 2014
Source: http://info.worldbank.org/governance/wgi/index.aspx#home.

The Human Development Index (HDI)[14] measures the average achievements in a country in three basic dimensions of human development, namely health (measured by life expectancy), education (measured by the average of years of schooling and expected years of schooling)[15] and the standard of living, measured by the log of gross national income (GNI) per capita (PPP $). The HDI is an average of the rescaled values of the three dimensions.[16]

The Non-income HDI (NYH), used in the study, consists of two of the three HDI components namely (a) the health and (b) the education components. These two components are thought to be policy induced and closely related to social governance. The NYH was measured by assigning a weight of 50% to the health component and 25% to each of the educational components (the same procedure used by the HDI compilers), and the result was again rescaled using the Min-Max formula so that the NYH index took values ranging between 0 and 1.

Figure 0.13, graphically shows the data for the NYH scores pertaining to the ten small states. It can be seen that Iceland and Slovenia have higher social governance scores than the EU28 average. Luxembourg, Cyprus, Estonia, Malta and Lithuania have very similar scores, which are slightly lower than the EU28 average.

It can also be seen that the educational scores of Estonia and Lithuania are higher than the EU28 average, while the health scores of Luxembourg, Cyprus and Malta are higher than the EU average. Montenegro, Latvia and Macedonia have the lowest scores in both education and health.

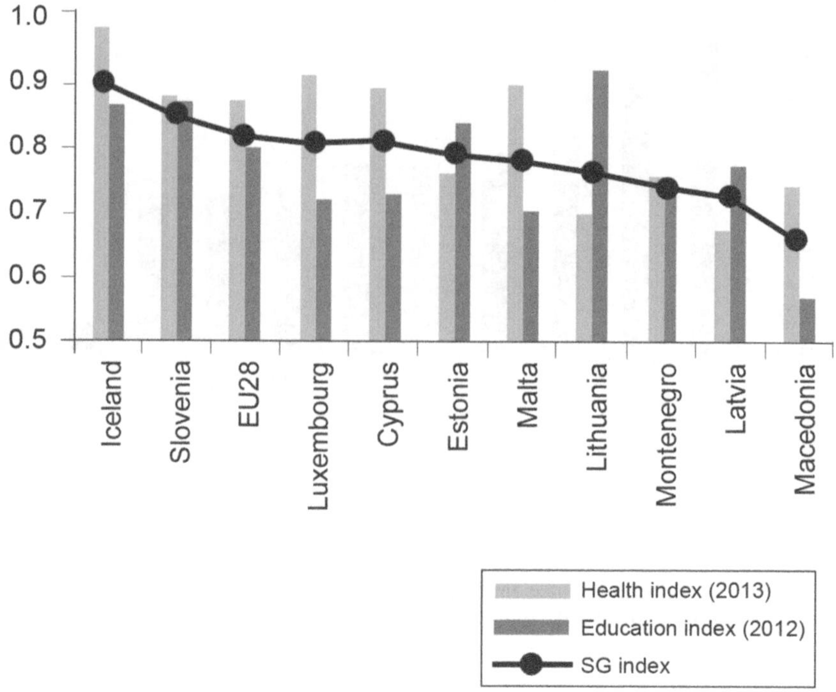

Figure 0.13 Education, health and social governance indicators (rescaled)
Source: UNDP (2014).

In general the HDI scores of the seven small EU member states (that is excluding the candidate countries), with the exception of Latvia, were relatively high by international standards. The worst performing state among the ten small states, namely Macedonia, ranked 84th among 187 countries, but even this country had an NYH score that was above world average.

2.4 Commonalities and disparities

As indicated above, the major common feature of the small states covered in this book relates to their high degree of trade openness and hence their exposure to external shocks. Even here the degree of openness is not the same for all countries, as has been shown in Figure 0.1, with Luxembourg and Malta being the most open among the ten countries.

In other matters, the ten small states *varied* considerably, broadly in line with the difference in their level of development, as measured by their GDP per capita. In general, the ten countries can be grouped into four categories in terms of their economic, political and social governance. Luxembourg's and Iceland's features render them the most developed, Malta, Cyprus and Slovenia the second-most developed, and the Baltic states the third-most developed. Macedonia and Montenegro, the two candidate countries are the least developed among the ten countries considered in this publication.

3 Small states in the EU

An issue discussed in most chapters of this book relates to the advantages and disadvantages of joining the European Union from a small state perspective. Several considerations are made in the chapters that follow, ranging from the benefits of accessing a large single market to the downsides of losing a portion of their sovereignty. The chapters on the Baltic States, Luxembourg and Malta seemed to be highly favourable to EU membership, with the least favourable being those of Iceland and Cyprus.

3.1 The advantages of being an EU member state

The major advantages mentioned in the chapters are the freedom of movement of goods, capital, services, and people, often referred to as the 'four freedoms' between the member states. As already explained, small states tend to depend highly on exports due to their small domestic markets and therefore the fewer the barriers to trade the better it is for them. Such a situation permits them to enjoy the benefits of economies of scale. In addition the intense competition that such a situation brings about is likely to also improve the allocation of resources in these states.

Another advantage mentioned in most chapters, especially the chapters on the Baltic economies, is that the emphasis by the EU Commission on research and innovation has stimulated and enabled these countries to upgrade their productive capacity. In the case of small states, with the human resource as their main asset, improvement in labour productivity that could result from innovation is of major importance.

Small states have also been eligible for EU regional and other funds, which have, among other things, enabled these states to successfully transpose the EU regulations and directives. Nine of the ten small states covered in this publication, Luxembourg being the exception, received more than they contribute to the EU budget.[17] (See Figure 0.14.)

The highest net recipients of EU funds, as a percentage of GNI, were the Baltic States. In Lithuania, the net flows amounted to about 4.5% of its GNI in 2013. Montenegro and Macedonia, the two candidate countries, also receive considerable pre-accession funds.

Although the Baltic States receive considerable EU funding, a highly regarded benefit mentioned in the chapters relating to these states is associated with the geo-political realities of the region, where peace, political stability and freedom are of major importance, given their location and their recent past history.

In the case of Luxembourg, which is a net contributor, a major benefit mentioned in the chapter on that country, is that a number of EU institutions

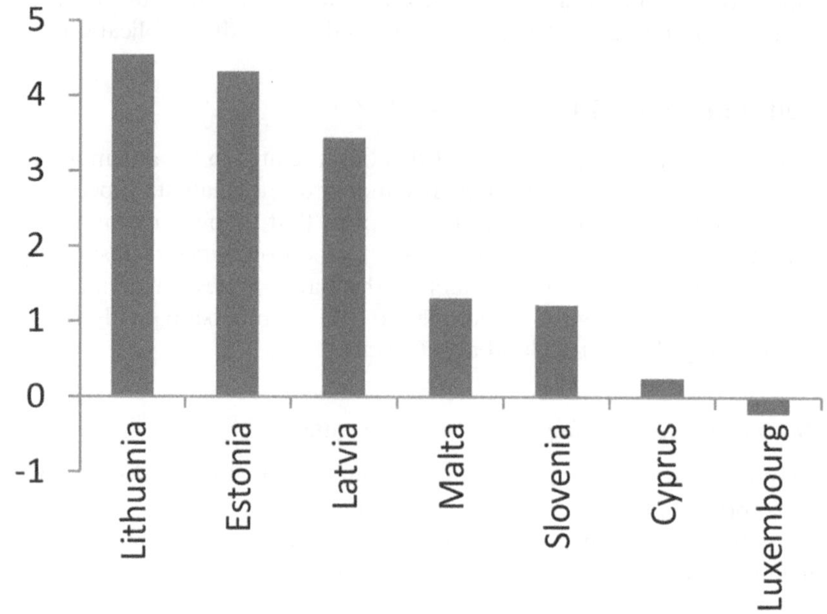

Figure 0.14 Net receipts from the EU budget as % of the country's GNI (2013)
Source: http://ec.europa.eu/budget/mycountry/EE/.

are based in this country, including the Court of Justice, the Court of Auditors, the European Investment Bank, the General Secretariat of the European Parliament and some Commission services.

3.2 The downsides of EU membership

As expected, the most important downside of EU membership is loss of sovereignty. There are various studies on the so-called democratic deficit of the EU, with some authors criticizing the economic governance of the EU during the euro crises, arguing that the austerity policies imposed on countries, *were* authoritarian and may have threatened democracy (Giannone, 2015; Mabille, 2012). The chapter on Iceland, the government of which withdrew the application for EU membership, and the chapter on Cyprus, the government of which was compelled to undertake austerity measures following the 2012–2013 financial crisis, assign particular importance to this matter. In the case of Cyprus, an issue that is stressed in this regard is that the Troika[18] imposed measures that may have greatly harmed the banking sector of Cyprus.

Another disadvantage identified by most authors is the weak voice that the EU small member states have within the EU institutions. Although small member states benefit from degressive proportionality, which gives them a stronger voting weight in the institutions than they are entitled to when their population size is considered, they do not generally have the political clout to influence major decisions on their own. This issue is considered by Panke (2012) as a disadvantage the small EU member states face. Panke identifies three main reasons for this (a) line-Ministries of small states are small and they do not have enough specialists to engage effectively in international negotiations – sometimes what are normally two or more line Ministries in a large state fall under one Ministry in some small states (b) their delegations during negotiations are generally small and (c) they are politically and economically weak to pose credible threats in their persuasion strategies.[19]

In addition, as noted by Keating, McEwen and Harvey (2014) big states sometimes make side-deals outside the formal decision-making process, something that small states cannot do persuasively as they have less to offer in return.

In some areas which are still subject to unanimity, small states can in theory exercise a veto. These areas include matters relating to taxation, the finances of the Union, aspects of the common foreign policy and of the common security and defence policy, citizenship as well as certain institutional issues, notably the revision of the treaties and EU enlargement. In reality, however, small states rarely use the veto as this would incur a high political price, including the possibility of being isolated (Thorhallsson, 2000; König and Junge, 2009).

In some chapters there is reference to the Qualified Majority Voting in Council decisionmaking, suggesting that this would seem to be detrimental to small states as they can easily be outvoted. The seven small EU member states covered in this publication, taken together, have less than 3% of the EU population whereas for a decision to be adopted the backing of member states needs to represent at least 65% of the total EU population, together with the assent of at least 16 member states. The blocking minority requires at least four Council members representing more than 35% of the EU population.[20]

However, according to Thorhallsson and Wivel (2006), the consensus culture in the Council of Ministers means that the voting method is of little importance in many cases, and a vote very rarely takes place.[21] This means that, in practice, when a consensus is sought, the voice of the small states could be important, particularly when alliances are formed to push a decision forward. On this matter, Thorhallsson (2015) argues that whereas the veto threat of the larger state is taken seriously, the veto threat of smaller states is not, and for this reason small states tend to 'prefer bargaining in the form of package deals where they can give priority to a few issues of importance, setting aside others.'

3.3 The perceptions of EU citizens

Some authors in this publication refer to the perceptions of the citizens of the EU small states when discussing the pros and cons of EU membership. The opinions of the citizens of the seven EU small states vary considerably with regard to the benefits they derive from the EU. Table 0.2 summarizes the answers to six questions in response to a 2015 Eurobarometer survey (European Commission, 2015).

The six questions were chosen by the present author because they were considered to capture the attitudes of respondents towards the EU, and relate to (1) whether the respondent trusts the EU, (2) whether the voice of the respondent counts in the EU, (3) whether the EU conjures up for the respondent a negative or positive image, (4) whether the respondent feels a citizen of the EU, (5) whether the interests of the respondent's country are well taken into account in the EU, and finally (6) whether the country of the respondent could better face the future outside the EU.

Table 0.2 shows all the percentage scores in response to these six questions. The table also shows the rank of each score among the seven small EU member states and the rank of each score among the 28 member states.

The EU small states that appear to look at the EU membership most favourably in terms of these six aspects of EU membership just mentioned are Malta, Luxembourg, Lithuania and Estonia in that order, with a ranking among the highest eight in the EU. Latvia and Slovenia ranked relatively low at 18th and 21st respectively among the EU28, while Cyprus emerged as the country that looks at the EU least favourably among the seven small states and among the EU28.

The attitudes of the Cypriot respondents were to be expected, given the austerity and punitive measures imposed by the EU and IMF on the Cypriot people in 2013, possibly the only country expected to rely to a very high extent on a 'bail-in'[22] method to unravel the solvency problems of its banks.

4 Prospects

All the chapters in this publication present the views of the author on the economic prospects of their respective country, often referring to the projections produced in the IMF article IV consultation or to the European Commission country reports.

From what emerges in the chapters relating to Estonia, Latvia and Lithuania, it appears that the economic prospects of these Baltic States are not bleak, although the geo-political tensions in that area and the ensuing uncertainty, as well as the Russian economic problems, may negatively affect their export performance. It appears that Estonia's economy will continue to grow in the medium term as the country improves its export performance. The country is characterized by solid public finances, with public debt expected to remain below 10% of GDP. In the case of Latvia, growth is also likely to be sustained, mostly by domestic demand, but the country's sour relations with Russia may have an impact on the domestic economy. A major problem with Latvia is its shrinking labour force. Lithuania's economy is also likely to remain on course in the medium term, again with domestic demand

Table 0.2 Perceptions of EU citizens

EU 28 and EU 7 small states	*Do you tend to trust the EU or tend not to trust it?*			*My voice counts in the EU*			*Does the EU conjure up for you a negative or positive image?*			*Do you feel you are a citizen of the EU*		
	Tend to trust			*I agree*			*Positive image*			*Yes*		
	Score %	*Rank SS 7*	*Rank EU 28*	*Score %*	*Rank SS 7*	*Rank EU 28*	*Score %*	*Rank SS 7*	*Rank EU 28*	*Score %*	*Rank SS 7*	*Rank EU 28*
EU28 Avg	40			42			44			67		
Cyprus	23	7	28	19	7	28	24	7	28	50	7	26
Estonia	55	3	8	27	5	33	49	4	8	79	3	5
Latvia	51	4	9	23	6	26	39	5	16	69	5	16
Lithuania	68	1	1	34	4	20	55	1	3	78	4	6
Luxembourg	49	5	11	50	2	9	52	2	6	88	1	1
Malta	62	2	3	60	1	4	51	3	7	84	2	2
Slovenia	41	6	20	42	3	16	37	6	20	65	6	19

Source: Eurobarometer results, Retrieved from: http://ec.europa.eu/public_opinion/archives/eb/eb83/eb83_anx_en.pdf.

Table 0.2 continued Perceptions of EU citizens

EU 28 and EU 7 small states	*The interests of our country are well taken into account in the EU*			*My country could better face the future outside the EU*			*Average score and rank of the six questions*		
	I agree			*I disagree*					
	Score %	*Rank SS 7*	*Rank EU 28*	*Score %*	*Rank SS 7*	*Rank EU 28*	*Score %*	*Rank SS 7*	*Rank EU 28*
EU28 Avg	43			58			49		
Cyprus	17	7	27	44	7	26	30	7	28
Estonia	48	4	12	66	4	7	54	4	11
Latvia	31	6	25	55	5	18	45	5	18
Lithuania	57	2	3	74	1	2	61	3	7
Luxembourg	59	1	2	70	2	3	61	2	6
Malta	51	3	6	69	3	6	63	1	5
Slovenia	33	5	24	44	6	27	44	6	21

Source: Eurobarometer results, Retrieved from: http://ec.europa.eu/public_opinion/archives/eb/eb83/eb83_anx_en.pdf.

likely to be the major contributor to growth. A worrying possible development in these states is that the increases in wage rates, partially caused by the economic recovery itself, could negatively affect the competitiveness of these countries.

The prospects of the two Mediterranean states, namely Malta and Cyprus, are very different. Malta's economic growth is projected to be sustained in the medium term, driven by strong domestic and external demand, leading to an increase in the number of gainfully employed persons and a reduction in unemployment. In the case of Cyprus, the effects of the 2013 financial crisis and recession are still being felt, and the chapter on Cyprus in this publication sheds doubt as to whether the structural reforms and austerity measures imposed on it will lead to sustained growth. However, some projections indicate that the Cypriot economy is set to stabilize itself and even expand gradually in 2015/2016 after a number of years in recession. Stability of the banking system has also improved. However, there is the possibility that economic stabilization may occur at an unacceptable low level of economic activity and high unemployment.

Luxembourg's economic growth rate is expected to be robust in the coming years, driven by domestic and foreign demand. This country is characterized by solid economic fundamentals, but its reputation was somewhat tarnished by the tax rulings aimed at reducing tax liability through a secret corporate tax avoidance scheme for a large number of multinational companies located in Luxembourg.

Economic growth in Slovenia is also expected to be sustained in the medium term but public finances are likely to remain problematic. The two candidate countries considered in this publication, namely Macedonia and Montenegro, are both likely to remain on the growth path driven by investment, notably in the infrastructure, although both countries may experience public finance constraints. In the case of Macedonia, the increase in income inequality in recent years is likely to have negative social impacts. In addition, the political crisis that Macedonia has been going through since the end of 2014 could adversely affect all segments of living and undermine the European perspective in the country. Even the latest EU accession report has conditioned the recommendation to open accession negotiations with Macedonia on the continued implementation of the political agreement reached in June and July 2015, which has been jeopardized several times.[23]

Iceland is still recovering from its devastating 2008 financial crises which led to a severe economic downturn in the following two years and to political unrest. The economy has since recovered, mainly due to increased domestic demand and a rapid rise in tourism inflows. Wage rates in Iceland are relatively high and are likely to be further pushed upwards with increased demand for labour. Problems have also arisen with regard to government debt, although measures are being taken to reduce its ratio to GDP.

More detailed analysis of the ten small states are presented in the country chapters. The overall impression one obtains from these chapters is that the worst is over and that a period of recovery beckons. It remains to be seen whether these projections materialize.

5 Conclusion

This introductory chapter has given an overview of the economies of the ten small states covered in this book. A number of similarities and differences were identified. The main similarity is that they are all highly economically vulnerable, due to their exposure to external economic conditions beyond their control. In spite of this some of these states are highly successful in terms of their level of GDP per capita and their economic growth, pointing to the fact that appropriate policies can enable vulnerable states to withstand their economic vulnerability. However, the analysis presented in this chapter clearly shows that the ten small states cannot be described as a homogenous group. They differ in many aspects, most notably in their stage of development.

The real and perceived benefits derived by these states as a result of EU membership also converge in some ways, while in others they vary considerably. All these states benefit from free access to a single large market, in view of the fact that their domestic market is very small. Most of them also benefit from transfer of funds from the EU. However, in the case of the Baltic States geo-political reasons are seen as the major benefits derived from EU membership, in view of their experiences as part of the Soviet Union and their proximity to Russia. Luxembourg, though a net contributor of funds to the EU budget, benefits greatly by hosting a considerable number of EU institutions. Malta benefitted greatly from transfer of funds, enabling the island to significantly upgrade its infrastructure. Cyprus stands out as an EU member state where the majority of its people think that the EU did not really help Cyprus in times of need, as evidenced by the responses to the 2015 Eurobarometer.

The chapters that follow will take a deeper look into the economies of these ten countries. It will be noticed that different chapters place different emphases in their approach. For example the chapter on Cyprus and Iceland assign importance to political factors more than other chapters, whereas the chapters on the Baltic States pay more attention to innovation. Malta and Luxembourg, which both have a relatively large financial sector, make reference to this sector when discussing the structure and performance of their economies.

What therefore emerges from this publication is that we are dealing with a group of countries which are heterogeneous in many aspects, and what mostly binds them together is their small domestic market and their high exposure to external economic conditions as well as their relatively weak voice in the EU institutions.

Notes

1 However, as Briguglio (2014) has shown, this does not necessarily result in economic backwardness as a number of resilience policy options are available for these

states in order to mitigate the harmful effects of external economic shocks. The resilience index proposed in Briguglio (2014) consisted of five components namely (a) macroeconomic stability; (b) market flexibility; (c) political governance; (d) social development; and (e) environmental management. The index was scaled to have a value of between 0 and 1. The index showed that the very highly open economies of Luxembourg and Malta were also characterized by relatively high scores.

2 One reason why Luxembourg has a very high GDP per capita is that many workers who contribute to the GDP do not live in Luxembourg, but in the neighbouring countries of Belgium, France, and Germany.

3 A similar pattern emerges when income per capita is measured by GNI per capita in terms of purchasing parity standards (PPS), but the income disparities are reduced due to price differences across the ten countries. GNI in $PPS is one of the pillars of the Human Development Index and is available at: http://hdr.undp.org/en/data.

4 The Icelandic financial crisis occurred as a result of the default of the country's three major privately owned commercial banks in late 2008. The Slovenian financial crisis in 2012–2013 was mostly as a result of the banks' bad debts. Latvia was severely hit by the global financial crisis and lost about 25% of its GDP between 2008 and 2010 mostly due to an overheated economy before the crisis. The Cypriot financial crisis 2012–2013 was to a large extent due to the exposure of Cypriot banks to overleveraged local property companies, the Greek government-debt crisis – at the same time both the state and most households spent beyond their means.

5 The unemployment rate for Montenegro was not available on the IMF website. But it was possibly about 15% in 2014 (see http://www.tradingeconomics.com/montenegro/unemployment-rate).

6 The average wage rates of Montenegro and Macedonia were estimated by taking the ratio of their minimum wage rate in relation to the minimum wage rate of Luxembourg. Data for minimum wage rates is available at: http://ec.europa.eu/eurostat/tgm/table.do?tab=table&init=1&language=en&pcode=tps00155&plugin=1. The average wage rates of Iceland were estimated from http://www.salaryexplorer.com/hourly-wage.php?loc=99&loctype=1.

7 The scores are derived from the Global Competitiveness Indicators (2015–2016). The compilers of this index define competitiveness as 'the set of institutions, policies, and factors that determine the level of productivity of a country.' The overall index is a weighted average of many different components, each measuring a different aspect of competitiveness. These components are grouped into three subindices, with 12 pillars. Data available at http://reports.weforum.org/global-competitiveness-report-2015-2016/downloads/ and is published as part of the Global Competitiveness Report (Schwab, 2015). The data for the index produced in 2015 contained many variables with most of the data pertaining to 2014.

8 However no country actually gets a score of 7. The highest placed country, Switzerland, was given a score of 5.76.

9 It should be noted that one of the components of the Global Competitiveness Indicators is country size, with smaller countries being given a lower score, albeit with a relatively low weight. This means that GCI are slightly biased against small states.

10 www3.weforum.org/docs/gcr/2015-2016/Global_Competitiveness_Report_2015-2016.pdf

11 This index is available at: http://data.worldbank.org/data-catalog/global-financial-development. The data was averaged over four years 2010 to 2013 (the last available date for which data was available). The index forms part of World Bank (2015).

12 The Worldwide Governance Indicators 2013 scores are available at: http://info.worldbank.org/governance/wgi/index.aspx#home. The indicators are based on the views of persons involved in business, ordinary citizens and expert surveys, with sources derived from various institutes, think tanks, non-governmental organizations, international organizations, and private sector firms.

13 A detailed description of the WGI methodology is available at: http://info.worldbank.org/governance/wgi/index.aspx#doc-reading.
14 The data for this study was sourced from the 2014 HDI, available at http://hdr.undp.org/en/data. The index formed part of UNDP (2014).
15 Mean of years of schooling for adults aged 25 years and expected years of schooling for children of school entering age.
16 A description of the HDI methodology is available at: http://hdr.undp.org/sites/default/files/hdr14_technical_notes.pdf.
17 The EU budget is mostly based on three kinds of sources: customs duties on imports from outside the EU and sugar levies, a small portion of the value added tax (VAT) levied in the EU, and contributions from each member state according to the share of its gross national income (GNI) in the EU GNI, which form the largest source of income to the EU budget (74 % in 2013). Other sources of revenue include taxes on EU staff salaries, fines on companies for breaching competition laws and bank interest.
18 Troika refers to the European Commission, the International Monetary Fund, and the European Central Bank.
19 See also Thorhallsson and Wivel (2006).
20 In some cases the assent of 72% of the member states and 65% of the EU population are needed when a proposal does not need a Commission initiative (this arrangement is called Super Qualified Majority), such as when a new Commission is being appointed and when the European Council elects its permanent President. See http://www.consilium.europa.eu/en/council-eu/voting-system/qualified-majority/.
21 However, during a meeting of the EU interior ministers in September 2015, the consensus approach was uncharacteristically abandoned on the issue of emigration, when the majority voting method was used to adopt a plan to relocate 120,000 refugees across the EU, with four eastern European countries (Hungary, Slovakia, Romania and the Czech Republic) being outvoted
22 The so-called 'bail-in' is a method to make the local depositors and the local banks provide for the recapitalization of the banks, *instead of* outside sources.
23 See http://europa.eu/rapid/press-release_MEMO-15-6038_en.htm.

References

Briguglio, L. (2014) 'A Vulnerability and Resilience Framework for Small States', in *Building the Resilience of Small States: A Revised Framework*. London: Commonwealth Secretariat: 10–55.

European Commission (2015) *Public Opinion in the European Union: First Results.* Standard Eurobarometer 83 (Spring). Available at: http://ec.europa.eu/public_opinion/archives/eb/eb83/eb83_first_en.pdf (accessed 23 January 2016).

Giannone, D. (2015) 'Suspending Democracy? The Governance of the EU's Political and Economic Crisis as a Process of Neoliberal Restructuring', in Demetriou, K.N. (ed.) *The European Union in Crisis*: 101–119. Available at: http://link.springer.com/chapter/10.1007/978-3-319-08774-0_6#page-1 (accessed 23 January 2016).

Keating, M., McEwen, N. and Harvey, M. (2014) *The Role of Small States in the European Union: Lessons for Scotland.* Evidence Presented to the Scottish Parliament Europe and External Affairs Committee. Available at: www.centreonconstitutionalchange.ac.uk/sites/default/files/papers/The%20Role%20of%20Small%20States%20in%20the%20European%20Union_SP%20Submission.pdf (accessed 23 January 2016).

König, T. and Junge, D. (2009) *Why Don't Veto Players Use Their Power?* University of Mannheim, Germany. Available at: http://lspol2.sowi.uni-mannheim.de/Lehrstuhlinhaber/Publikationen/2009_Koenig_Junge_VP.pdf (accessed 23 January 2016).

Mabille, P. (2012) 'Draghi Buries European Social Model', *La Tribune*, Paris, 27 February. Available at: http://www.voxeurop.eu/en/content/article/1555361-draghi-buries-european-social-model (accessed 23 January 2016).

Panke, D. (2012) 'Dwarfs in International Negotiations: How Small States Make their Voices Heard', *Cambridge Review of International Affairs*, 25(3): 313–328. Available at: http://www.tandfonline.com/doi/abs/10.1080/09557571.2012.710590 (accessed 23 January 2016).

Schwab, K. (2015) *The Global Competitiveness Report, 2015–2016*. Geneva: World Economic Forum. Available at: http://www3.weforum.org/docs/gcr/2015-2016/Global_Competitiveness_Report_2015-2016.pdf (accessed 23 January 2016).

Standard and Poor's Rating System (2013) *Small Countries, Big Banking Systems: How Malta and Luxembourg Differ from Cyprus*. Available at: https://0d2d5d19eb0c0d8cc8c6-a655c0f6dcd98e765a68760c407565ae.ssl.cf3.rackcdn.com/c006451c3f14d9e10f9c4853c6b56e8b2915694074.pdf (accessed 23 January 2016).

Thorhallsson, B. (2000) *The Role of Small States in the European Union*. Aldershot: Ashgate.

Thorhallsson, B. (2015) 'How Do Little Frogs Fly? Small States in the European Union', Norwegian Institute of International Affairs Policy Brief, No. 12/2015. Available at: http://brage.bibsys.no/xmlui/bitstream/handle/11250/284448/3/NUPI+Policy+Bief+12-15-Thorhallsson.pdf (accessed 23 January 2016).

Thorhallsson, B. and Wivel, A. (2006) 'Small States in the European Union: What Do We Know and What Would We Like to Know?' *Cambridge Review of International Affairs*, 19(4): 61–668. Available at: http://www.cesruc.org/uploads/soft/130311/1-130311111352.pdf (accessed 23 January 2016).

UNDP (2014) *Human Development Report*. Available at: http://hdr.undp.org/sites/default/files/hdr14-report-en-1.pdf (accessed 23 January 2016).

1 Cyprus

From an economic miracle to a systemic collapse and its aftermath

Andreas Theophanous

1 Introduction

The objective of this chapter is to provide an analytical description and assessment of how Cyprus reached a systemic collapse in March 2013 following more than three decades of a remarkable socio-economic record. The chapter examines the characteristics and the dynamic changes of the economy since the 1970s including the current crisis.[1]

The Republic of Cyprus is a small island state located in the eastern Mediterranean. The population in the government-controlled areas of the Republic of Cyprus was about 858,000 in 2013. In the occupied northern part of Cyprus it was estimated that the population was about 280,000; more than 50% are settlers from Turkey. It is the third largest island in the Mediterranean after Sardinia and Sicily with an area of 9,251km^2. Since 1974 the Republic of Cyprus has controlled only 59.5% of the island's territory; 35.2% is under the control of the Turkish troops of occupation, while 2.6% is a buffer zone. The two British bases established in 1960, located in the southern part of the island, constitute 2.7% of the territory of Cyprus. The island has a rich history, going back to antiquity, as evidenced by its archaeological heritage. Cyprus obtained its independence from Britain in 1960 and joined the European Union in 2004 and the eurozone in 2008.

As a small island state, Cyprus shares similar characteristics with many other small states, in that the country is highly dependent on international trade and on a narrow range of exports, including tourism. It is therefore highly exposed to economic forces outside its control. The high exposure to external economic conditions was a main reason why the island underwent serious economic crises in 2013, although, as explained in this chapter, internal factors exacerbated the negative effect of economic vulnerability.

The discussion contained in the chapter takes place within a particular political context. While this applies to all countries, in the case of Cyprus the political aspects are especially important, particularly because in 1974 Cyprus experienced the Turkish invasion which led to the loss of territory and ethnic cleansing. The serious socioeconomic and political repercussions of this event are felt to this day.

This chapter is organized as follows. In Section 2 the major characteristics of what was described as an 'economic miracle' and its broader implications are outlined. We also explain why this description is appropriate. Section 3 outlines the reasoning for advancing a customs union with the European Community and subsequently accession to the EU and adoption of the euro. We also describe the country's socioeconomic record and the structural weaknesses of the economy which at the time were underestimated. Section 4 examines how Cyprus found itself on a fatal path leading to what may be described as a systemic collapse. We assess the record of the banking sector and how it became problematic leading the economy *to an unprecedented crisis.* Section 5 describes and assesses the Eurogroup's decisions in March 2013, relating to Cyprus' financial crisis and the fallout since then. In the last section we put forward some concluding remarks as well as policy recommendations and suggestions for further research.

2 Understanding the economic miracle

2.1 The Turkish invasion of 1974

When Cyprus acquired its independence in 1960 it was a poor, undeveloped and essentially an agrarian country. With a philosophy of a mixed economy and a high work ethic, Cyprus managed to achieve high growth from 1960 to 1973, on average about 7% annually in real terms. This remarkable record was abruptly interrupted by the Turkish invasion of 20 July 1974. Military operations continued until 16 August 1974 when there was a final cease-fire. In addition to the immense loss of human life, wounded and missing persons, Cyprus lost about 38% of its territory and also suffered ethnic cleansing. Almost 200,000 Greek Cypriots who lived in the northern part of Cyprus were displaced. Turkish Cypriots who lived in the southern part of the island were gradually moved to the area under the control of the Turkish occupation troops.

Cyprus lost its international airport in Nicosia, its major port in Famagusta, most of its tourist infrastructure (Famagusta and Kyrenia) and 70% of its productive resources. The economy was severely dislocated and dismantled as the occupied territories included most of the citrus growing areas, the best agricultural land and the most developed tourist areas (Whitaker, 1980; Bamber, 1982; Theophanous, 1991). Many Greek Cypriots were so shocked by the events that they sought refuge and opportunities for a new beginning in foreign lands.

Consequently, ever since, economic activity has been taking place in the light of these events and the political fallout associated with them. Yet the country survived, the economy was successfully revived, the pace of emigration was gradually reduced and, eventually, after 1980, reversed. It is under these circumstances that the change of perceptions and psychology took place as well as the consolidation of law and order, the attraction of foreign investment, the recovery of the economy and indeed the survival and continuity of the Republic of Cyprus.

2.2 The economic recovery

The Cypriot economic recovery and the subsequent process of growth, modernization and development were so successful that they were described as an 'economic miracle' (*Economist*, 1977; Christodoulou, 1992). Although exogenous factors played a role in the immediate recovery and subsequent modernization and further development of the area under the control of the Republic of Cyprus, it was the endogenous dynamism of the Cypriot economy and society which mostly led to the 'economic miracle' (Christodoulou, 1992; Theophanous, 1995). Gross Domestic Product (GDP) dropped sharply by 32.7% during the period 1973–1975 and unemployment rose to almost 30% during the same period, but the government managed to reverse the situation. By 1979, the GDP of Cyprus recovered in real terms, and was 61.8% higher than in 1975. Furthermore, unemployment was reduced to about 2%. By the beginning of the 1980s, Cyprus, for the first time, began to experience a net-inflow of people who had emigrated in 1974 or even before.

The economic structure of the country went through a major transformation. Cyprus recovered and embarked on a path of a remarkable growth and development. What has been achieved was comparable with the achievements of West Germany after the Second World War.

Greek Cypriots had understood, after the military defeat and the occupation of a substantial portion of Cyprus territory by Turkey that if they did not succeed in the domain of the economy the future of Cyprus would be bleak. Economic recovery and subsequent development would keep the population and also guarantee the continuity of the Republic of Cyprus. It was also considered that the economy would constitute a major pillar in the peaceful struggle for the solution of the Cyprus problem in an integrationalist manner.

During this process there was a radical socioeconomic transformation, as can be seen from Tables 1.1 and 1.2.

Table 1.1 shows that during the period under consideration the primary sector (mostly agriculture and fishing) declined from about a fifth of GDP in the 1960s to just about 7% in 1990. On the other hand, the secondary sector (mostly manufacturing) and the tertiary sector (mostly tourism and market services) increased their share of GDP. These structural changes were also reflected in the composition of gainful employment.

Table 1.2 shows that during the period under consideration, GDP per capita increased rapidly, whereas unemployment decreased considerably. There was a remarkable growth in tourist arrivals and in the revenue from tourism.

The bulk of growth in the period from 1980 to the early 1990s originated in services, particularly those associated with tourism, rather than secondary activities. The share of the services sectors in gross value added rose from 55% in 1980 to 67% in 1990. Tourist related sectors such as restaurants and

Table 1.1 Economic structure (1960–1990)

	1960	*1968*	*1973*	*1975*	*1978*	*1984*	*1990*
Composition of GDP by sector (%)							
Primary sector	21.0	23.5	15.7	18.0	12.6	9.5	7.2
Secondary sector	19.4	20.0	28.0	25.9	31.4	28.5	26.0
Tertiary sector	59.6	56.5	56.3	56.1	56.0	62.0	66.8
Composition of the gainfully occupied population by sector (%)							
Primary sector	46.8	43.6	38.4	27.5	22.8	17.9	14.2
Secondary sector	23.1	24.0	25.8	25.6	32.5	31.7	28.8
Tertiary sector	30.1	32.4	35.8	46.9	44.7	50.4	57.0

Source: Cyprus 1960–1990, Time Series Data, Department of Statistics and Research, Ministry of Finance, Republic of Cyprus.

Table 1.2 Key economic and social indicators (1973–1992)

	1973	*1975*	*1978*	*1990*	*1991*	*1992*
Population (thousands)*	634	502	500	571	577	585
Gross Domestic Product (current prices million Cyprus pounds)	341	271	527	2,574	2,709	3,100
Per capita GDP (current prices Cyprus pounds)	538	540	1,054	4,506	4,695	5,303
Average Exchange Rates (USD/CYP)	0.349	0.368	0.373	0.431	0.512	0.465
Unemployment rate (%)	2.5	16.2	2.0	1.8	2.3	1.8
Government budget/GDP (%)	−3.7	−7.9	−5.7	−2.3	−4.4	−3.4
Tourist arrivals (thousands)	265	47.1	213.9	1,566.1	1,385.2	1,991
Tourist per Cypriot	0.42	0.09	0.43	2.74	2.40	3.40
Revenue from tourism/GDP (%)	6.9	2.0	6.3	22.3	17.6	22.4
Trade balance/GDP (%)	−22.7	−21.6	−23.3	−25.3	−25.4	−28.2

Source: Economic and Social Indicators 1992, Planning Bureau, Annual Report 1993, Central Bank of Cyprus.

* The population in 1973 included 18.4% Turkish Cypriots. Thereafter the population refers only to the government-controlled areas of the Republic of Cyprus.

hotels and transport storage and communication also saw their distribution shares rise significantly. Tourist receipts rose more than tenfold, from €123 million in 1980 or 9.5% of GDP, to €1.3 billion or 22% of GDP in 1990. The tourist related sector of hotels and restaurants was growing at an average pace of 13.9% annually in value added terms in the 1980s and provided the foreign exchange needed to fund imports and finance considerable infrastructural works.

Manufacturing activity also contributed considerably to growth in the 1980s driven by export demand for low value added goods mainly from Arab countries. However, manufacturing activity which was based on cheap labour and low value added goods peaked in the middle of the decade and declined thereafter. Lack of change in the techniques of production and innovation rendered the Cypriot manufacturing sector virtually unable to compete in the EU and internationally.

This successful outcome was brought about by various factors, including that:

1. The government achieved social cohesion and also inspired the people. On the one hand, it encouraged entrepreneurship and, on the other, persuaded the unions to agree to a 25% reduction of salaries for three years. Furthermore, the government continued and enhanced its indicative planning through five year plans.
2. The government also encouraged tourism in Paphos, Limassol, Larnaca, Agia Napa and Protaras; prior to 1974 there was little or no tourist activity in those areas. Tourism soon developed to be a major sector and pillar of the economy.
3. There was a massive expansion of the public and broader public sector; new jobs were created as well as new institutions.
4. The government adopted a policy of sustained fiscal and monetary expansion to stimulate the economy. It also provided specific incentives to encourage economic activity. This included an especially low tax rate of 4.5% to encourage offshore business activity.
5. The vast expansion of the construction industry and related business sectors were particularly important for the recovery. The government financed and/or subsidized the building of housing at various levels for the refugees. Likewise, there was heavy building of infrastructure including hotels and other tourist facilities.
6. Cyprus also encouraged light industries. From 1974 to 1984 there was a modest expansion of exports of agricultural and light industrial goods especially to the Arab World.
7. There was also a modest amount of foreign aid especially after the invasion. Nevertheless, this was not the decisive factor for survival and recovery.

The economic miracle had some shortcomings: a sizable portion of jobs initially created were of low added value, while the expansion of tourism was anarchic and on several occasions without respect for the environment. Be that as it may, it is essential to understand what the miracle was all about: the fast economic recovery and above all the survival and continuity of the Republic of Cyprus. During this process there was a radical socioeconomic transformation (see Tables 1.1 and 1.2).

During this period there was a fast process of urbanization which was related to the post-war realities: most Greek Cypriots who left their villages in the northern part of Cyprus eventually were relocated in the towns. Furthermore, gradually the primary sector decreased and the tertiary sector grew.

With the remarkable growth rates there were major changes in the social norms and broader attitudes. The massive expansion of tourism had its impact as well.

With the economic recovery advancing, cases of nepotism were observed as well as the deepening of patron-client relations at various levels. Furthermore, with the growing affluence, the strength of the trade unions especially in the civil service, the broader public sector and the banking sector became a major characteristic of the economic structure; these excesses would constitute major contributing factors for the crisis which culminated in 2013.

3 Accession to the EU and the adoption of the euro

3.1 The political context

The Republic of Cyprus was first linked with the Common Market in 1973 by means of an Association Agreement. The progress of the relationship was impeded – but not thwarted – by the Turkish invasion and occupation of 38% of the territory of Cyprus in 1974. With the economic recovery, further growth and subsequent modernization of Cyprus and with the appropriate political will, the country was successful in completing a Customs Union Agreement with the European Community in 1987 which became effective on 1 January 1988. In addition to its economic aspects, this agreement had important political implications; its provisions referred to the Republic of Cyprus as a whole and not only to the area under the control of the government. Furthermore, on 4 July 1990, Cyprus submitted an application for membership, joined the EU in May 2004 and adopted the euro in January 2008.

When Cyprus applied for membership of the EU on 4 July 1990 it was expected that the accession process and accession itself would contribute to a fair settlement of the Cyprus problem. Furthermore, at a time of major changes in the European and international environment, most Cypriots believed that it was time for such an option (Theophanous, 2004).

Within this new political framework, two vital objectives of the Republic of Cyprus were (a) accession to the EU and the solution of the Cyprus problem in an integrationalist manner; and (b) the further modernization of the economy and the harmonization with the EU standards and norms.

Cypriot policymakers did not realize that despite the overall successful economic record and metamorphosis of the society, major socioeconomic problems existed and that if these were not adequately addressed, what was achieved could be undermined (Christodoulou, 1995). It was a time of enthusiasm and high expectations.

Accession negotiations started in 1998. During the accession negotiations an international effort supported by the UN, the EU, the USA and NATO was taking place for the solution of the Cyprus problem. Cypriot policymakers who felt that accession to the Union was a top priority and knew that the stalemate in the Cyprus question could cause problems, overlooked details in the accession negotiations. Consequently, negotiation chapter after chapter was being closed without much analysis regarding the consequences. For example, Cyprus, given its small size, did not raise the issue of regulating the free movement of workers from EU countries to this island-state. To the contrary Malta was more careful with the relevant issues.

Cyprus also opted to adopt the euro after accession to the EU, and entered the Exchange Rate Mechanism II in 2005 at the same exchange rate parity at which subsequently, in January 2008, it converted to the euro.[2] Joining the eurozone was one of the obligations of the Republic of Cyprus on joining the EU, although in some new member states this was postponed to later years and some have not joined the euro as yet. It was expected to serve the interests of Cyprus to belong in the eurozone as this constitutes perhaps the most integrationalist pillar. In addition, participation in the eurozone was thought to serve as an extra incentive to further streamline the public finances, the banking and the overall financial system. Moreover, there was the expectation that the adoption of the euro could also contribute toward a solution of the Cyprus problem.

Obviously the strategic decision to adopt the euro entailed political objectives. Nevertheless, the prerequisites for a successful participation in such a monetary union were not fully understood. Likewise the faulty pillars and rules of the architecture of the eurozone were not fully assessed.

3.2 The economic and social record

During the period under consideration Cyprus was transformed into a service-based economy with sizeable tourist and trade sectors, and subsequently with a rising financial services sector. Income variability declined but exposure to exogenous shocks increased as the degree of economic openness and the international expansion of the banking sector advanced considerably. The country failed to adjust to the consequences of the global economic crisis of 2008/2009, the debt crisis in Greece and its own structural weaknesses.

Finance, insurance, business and real estate services made a considerable contribution to growth. In the latter part of the 1990s offshore business activity started to pick up giving impetus to banking and finance. The start of accession negotiations in 1998 ushered in a period of profound change, financial liberalization and economic transformation that ultimately put finance and business services at the centre of economic activity.

The financial sector of Cyprus performed relatively well behind protective walls; it continued to grow as the country was approaching accession to the EU. In the period from 1995 to 2009, the Cyprus economy achieved considerable growth and managed to narrow the gap with the eurozone.

The process of harmonization and adjustment prior to accession, the removal of exchange rate risk once the Cyprus pound was fixed to the euro, the lower interest rate environment that resulted from the process, and the lower tax regime following the tax reform of 2002 led to considerable growth. Real GDP growth between 1995 and 2009 averaged 3.3% a year. The economic structure changed significantly in the process turning Cyprus into a distinctly service economy with a large and growing financial and business services sectors, as can be seen from Table 1.3.

Subsequently, the economy enhanced the international banking activities which accounted for a considerable part of recorded growth. However, it was this particular sector which was to prove fatal. Tourism that once was the growth engine of the economy declined in relative importance; receipts dropped below 10% of GDP in 2010 compared with more than 20% in the late 1990s. Cyprus was affected by the global economic crisis of 2008 with a one-year lag as it entered into recession in the second quarter of 2009.

3.3 Strategic failures

A major chronic problem in Cyprus was the growing structural budget deficit and public debt. The problems were bigger than the numbers would indicate over time given the heavy intergovernmental borrowing. Consequently, while for example the budget deficit in 1998 was estimated to be 4.3% and the public debt 61% of the GDP, if intergovernmental borrowing and intergovernmental debt were taken into consideration the figures would be higher than 10% and 98% respectively.

There was also an inefficiently run civil service, characterized by overstaffing, low efficiency, red tape and a lack of flexibility. These ailments resulted from a clientelist intrusion by the political parties based on nepotism. A similar situation existed in significant sections of the quasi-public sector in which some of the public companies were experiencing losses. Furthermore, there was a positive differential in salaries in Cyprus, the overall benefit package and the working terms and conditions, between the public, the quasi-public sector and the banking sector on the one hand, and the other sectors of the economy on the other. Over time, this created serious socio-political and economic problems. For example, nepotism as well as a 'patron and client' relationship system between citizens and the political parties influenced appointments at various levels, directly and indirectly. This state of affairs led to the loosening of the climate of understanding, cooperation and overall social cohesion which prevailed in the aftermath of 1974 (Christodoulou, 1995). This was one of the failures of the political system. The unions of the broader public sector and of the banking system had their share of responsibility as well. Little attention was paid to the need for action to promote meritocracy and above all of a paradigm shift which was imperative if Cyprus were to address the new challenges successfully.

During the accession negotiations, the major structural problems of the economy did not receive their fair share of attention given the particular political circumstances. This was so especially in the banking and broader financial sector and related activities. Furthermore, the theoretical and

Table 1.3 Gross Domestic Product by activity (percentages) (NACE Rev. 2)

	1995	*1998*	*2003*	*2008*	*2009*	*2010*	*2011*	*2012*	*2013**
Primary sector	4.7	4.0	3.1	2.3	2.3	2.3	2.4	2.3	2.4
Agriculture, forestry and fishing	4.4	3.8	2.8	2.0	2.0	2.1	2.2	2.2	2.3
Mining and quarrying	0.2	0.3	0.3	0.3	0.3	0.2	0.2	0.1	0.1
Secondary sector	20.1	19.2	18.0	17.9	16.1	14.9	13.5	12.4	10.5
Manufacturing	9.7	9.1	7.5	5.6	5.5	5.3	5.0	4.6	4.5
Electricity, gas, steam and air conditioning supply	1.4	1.5	1.5	1.1	1.4	1.5	1.6	1.9	1.7
Water supply, sewerage, waste management and remediation activities	0.4	0.5	0.6	0.6	0.6	0.7	0.8	0.9	0.9
Construction	8.6	8.2	8.4	10.7	8.6	7.4	6.1	4.9	3.4
Tertiary sector	67.1	70.2	69.8	68.9	72.4	73.8	75.8	76.9	79.2
Wholesale and retail trade; repair of motor vehicles and motorcycles	12.7	12.6	12.6	12.9	12.7	12.9	12.9	12.6	13.0
Transport and storage	9.4	8.8	6.9	5.8	6.3	6.1	5.7	5.7	6.1
Accommodation and food service activities	7.8	7.7	6.6	5.3	5.0	5.1	5.4	5.8	6.2
Information and communication	2.5	3.4	3.9	3.3	3.3	3.5	3.6	3.7	4.0
Financial and insurance activities	4.1	5.1	4.9	6.0	6.6	6.7	7.2	7.8	8.4
Real estate activities	7.1	7.6	7.7	9.2	10.4	10.6	10.6	10.8	10.8
Professional, scientific and technical activities	4.3	4.7	5.0	5.1	5.1	5.6	6.3	6.6	6.6
Administrative and support service activities	0.9	1.0	1.1	1.0	1.0	1.0	1.0	1.1	1.1

	1995	*1998*	*2003*	*2008*	*2009*	*2010*	*2011*	*2012*	*2013**
Public administration and defence, compulsory social security	8.3	8.4	9.5	9.0	9.8	9.8	10.0	9.6	9.6
Education	4.1	4.6	5.1	4.8	5.3	5.4	5.6	5.8	6.0
Human health and social work activities	2.8	3.0	3.2	3.0	3.3	3.3	3.5	3.5	3.6
Arts, entertainment and recreation	1.0	1.2	1.2	1.0	1.1	1.3	1.5	1.4	1.3
Other service activities	1.9	1.7	1.6	1.7	1.6	1.5	1.5	1.4	1.5
Activities of households as employers	0.3	0.4	0.6	0.7	0.8	0.9	1.0	1.0	1.0
Total Gross Value Added	**91.8**	**93.5**	**90.9**	**89.1**	**90.8**	**91.0**	**91.7**	**91.6**	**92.1**
Plus: Import duties	3.9	2.3	2.0	1.4	1.0	0.8	0.7	0.5	0.4
Plus: Value added tax	4.3	4.3	7.2	9.5	8.2	8.2	7.6	8.0	7.6
Gross Domestic Product	**100.0**	**100.0**	**100.0**	**100.0**	**100.0**	**100.0**	**100.0**	**100.0**	**100.0**

Source: Statistical Service of Cyprus, Statistical Abstract 2013, Economy and Finance.

Note: * Provisional

practical implications of accession to the eurozone may not have been fully understood.

Perhaps the greatest shortcomings of Cyprus were the lack of strategic thinking and complacency. Successive years of economic growth and low unemployment created the illusion that no matter what, there would be sustained growth. Under such circumstances, the state as well as most households systematically spent beyond their means.

3.4 Cyprus as a small EU member state

When the Republic of Cyprus applied for membership to the EU in 1990 there was great euphoria. The vast majority of Cypriots expected that participation in the Union would enable the country to further modernize and also address successfully various socioeconomic structural problems. Moreover, it was expected that, in one way or another, the EU could act as a catalyst for the resolution of the Cyprus problem. In addition, it was widely believed that the value system of the Union and the *acquis communautaire* would be incorporated in the framework of the solution.

Furthermore, the initial perceptions of most Cypriots about the Union were overoptimistic and included various exaggerations. For example, the EU was viewed as a benevolent entity in which national antagonisms were not the norm but the exception. Likewise, Cypriots paid much attention to the declared values of the Union and especially to the principle of solidarity.

Retrospectively Cypriots realized that there is a great gap between expectations and reality. In addition, the EU did not prove to be the catalyst for the Cyprus problem. Instead, on several occasions pressures were directed toward the Republic of Cyprus rather than toward Turkey, a non-member state. This was done to accommodate Ankara. In other words, Cyprus as a small state was not treated fairly.

Last but not least, when Cyprus found itself in a major economic crisis, the prescriptions from the EU were more of a punishment than a recipe for the rationalization of the economy and reconstruction. In addition, Cypriots felt that they were unjustifiably and unnecessarily used as an experiment with the bail-in prescription. Furthermore, the Gini coefficient[3] increased from 0.29 in 2008 to 0.34 in 2014. In this context, participation in the eurozone was associated with an increase in inequality.

4 Toward the systemic collapse

4.1 Theoretical issues and forgone opportunities

Following accession to the EU and entry into the Exchange Rate Mechanism, efforts to consolidate the public finances intensified. As a result, the historically large budget deficits turned into surpluses in 2007 and 2008. Nevertheless, this was not achieved by structural reform; there was restraint in those years but the improvement was the outcome of a tax amnesty for repatriated capital as well as tax revenues from the sale of overvalued real estate. Obviously, these factors could not be sustainable. Furthermore, during the Christofias administration (February 2008 to February 2013) there was a fast deterioration of the fiscal situation (Orphanides, 2014). Exposure to exogenous shocks also increased as the degree of economic openness and the international expansion of the banking sector advanced considerably.

The banking sector posed risks due to its size (eight times the GDP), concentration (three banks dominated the sector) and its large exposure in Greece. Obviously, problems in the banking sector could quickly escalate to systemic proportions with serious economic repercussions. Credit expansion after 2008 was further supported by an inflow of non-resident deposits and an expansionary fiscal policy. The overheating of the economy gave rise to additional vulnerabilities – a major structural problem was the high private indebtedness.

In October 2011, the big domestic banks, with considerable assets in Greece, were negatively influenced by the private sector involvement in the country's debt restructuring. As a result Cypriot banks faced significant capital needs to meet the requirements of the European Banking Authority. In this context the government promoted an equity rights issue in favour of the country's second biggest bank, Laiki/Popular Bank, for up to €1.8 billion or about 10% of GDP in June 2012. The disastrous effects of the private sector involvement in Greece's debt restructuring on the banking system of Cyprus and the economy were not fully assessed. This, in conjunction with the intensification of the debt crisis in Europe and the adverse shocks to world trade and fiscal adjustment, had a severe impact on Cypriot banks with spill-overs on the real economy.

The debt and the banking crisis created a new set of realities; the model that Cyprus had pursued successfully for years required a major overhaul. Cyprus had to address structural problems and issues. For example, the composition of the labour market has drastically changed. A major dimension of this change is the fact that in the last 25 years the number of young Greek Cypriots seeking higher education had doubled so that today more than two out of three hold degrees at various levels. There were high expectations in relation to their employment prospects which the existing model could not satisfy. The government also had to reduce the relative weight of the payroll of public employees and better target social outlays. It had also to revisit the social security and the public pension system. Nevertheless, it failed to do so for ideological reasons and lack of understanding of the situation.

4.2 The economic realities on the ground

The economy had many distortions and there was mismanagement at almost all levels. The banking mismanagement and crisis and the outdated economic paradigm contributed to the downfall. As already explained, the broad public and banking sectors had been offering superior terms of employment compared to the rest of the economy. This led to overstaffing and inefficiencies in these sectors. Furthermore, the economic model of Cyprus, highly based on services, led to the decreasing competiveness and neglect of the secondary and primary sectors. In addition, the economy could not create enough high value-added jobs for the growing number of Cypriot professionals with higher qualifications. The political system proved incapable to confront these problems. In short, what took place was a major systemic failure.

The Cypriot crisis peaked as a result of the excesses of the banking sector which took place simultaneously with the deterioration of fiscal indicators. The housing bubble and the surge of loans to the private sector which reached approximately 300% of the GDP by the end of 2012 were related with these developments. These figures indicated that the society lived beyond its means. Furthermore, there was insufficient understanding of the rules of a monetary union in which the leading country, Germany, believed in a very austere fiscal and monetary policy.

The interconnection of the Cypriot economy with that of Greece proved to be fatal. The impact of the Greek debt haircut in October 2011 was devastating for the Cypriot economy. The two biggest banks lost approximately €4.5 billion (more than 25% of GDP).

The private debt to GDP ratio exposed the superficial prosperity of Cypriot enterprises and households while they piled up huge amounts of debt. As Table 1.4 shows, during the period 2008–2011 there was an increase in the debt of the private sector by about 50% of GDP; in 2013 it reached 352.9% of GDP.

Table 1.4 also shows that the public debt followed a downward trend from 2004 reaching 45.3% of GDP in 2008. Thereafter, the public debt shot up reaching 107.5% of GDP in 2014.[4] Although the public debt of Cyprus was less than the average public debt of the EU countries, the important element was its rate of growth, as within just four years the public debt increased by 38% of GDP. This was the outcome of fiscal expansion as well as of borrowing to cover the increasing balance of payments deficit. Indeed, Cyprus was spending beyond its means. The table also shows the increase of the fiscal deficit that started in 2009 and peaked in 2011 when it reached 6.3% of GDP.

Table 1.4 also shows the plight of Cyprus in relation to the trade balance and balance of payments. Cyprus had always maintained trade deficits. These were covered by the services sector. In the last few years, though, the eroding competitiveness of the Cypriot economy led to sustained deficits on the current account of the balance of payments as well.

4.3 The Mari Incident and the haircut of the Greek debt

The destruction of the major electricity generating station in Mari on 11 July 2011, due to an explosion of ammunition held nearby, led to a tragic loss of human life and was symbolic of an imminent collapse. The infrastructural

Table 1.4 Selective indicators

	2004	*2005*	*2006*	*2007*	*2008*	*2009*	*2010*	*2011*	*2012*	*2013*	*2014*
Population	727.5	738.5	751	767.1	786.6	808	829.4	862	865.9	858	847
Private debt/ GDP (%)	163.5	200.4	199.1	219.6	236.6	256.2	273	283.4	300	352.9	n.a.
Public debt/ GDP (%)	64.7	63.4	59.3	54.1	45.3	54.1	56.5	66.0	79.5	102.2	107.5
Fiscal balance/ GDP (%)	−4.1	−2.4	−1.2	3.5	0.9	−6.1	−5.3	−6.3	−6.3	−5.4	−5.3
Trade balance/ GDP (%)	−29	−28.7	−30.5	−33.3	−36	−28	−30.9	−27.3	−21.8	−17.2	−15.5
BoP Current Account/GDP (%)	−4.6	−5.4	−6.4	−10.8	−14.3	−9.8	−9.0	−3.1	−6.3	−1.7	−1.9

Source: Eurostat (http://ec.europa.eu/eurostat/data/database) and International Monetary Fund (IMF – http://www.imf.org/external/pubs/ft/weo/2015/02/weodata/index.aspx).

damage associated was estimated to be more than €2 billion. If we also assess the broader repercussions, such as the increasing costs in all sectors of the economy, the damage would have been much higher. According to the Report by Polyviou (2011) this terrible incident was the outcome of systemic failure. The message was clear: in the absence of major structural changes, Cyprus was going to face additional setbacks.

Four months later, in October 2011, the Cypriot government agreed to the decision of the Eurogroup for a haircut of the Greek debt, underestimating the effects that this was to have on the Cypriot banking system and the economy. The damage to the Cypriot banks amounted to 25% of GDP. The Cypriot government could have asked for support from the EU in order to recapitalize its banks as a precondition of accepting this decision. It did not. The required communication between the Presidency, the Central Bank and the Ministry of Finance was lacking. Furthermore, the government did not want a deal with the Troika for ideological reasons. And the opposition expected that the deterioration of the situation would provide political gains in the then forthcoming presidential elections of February 2013. Cyprus was moving towards a disaster; yet political expedience, party interests and ideology prevailed over the public interest.

5 The decisions of the Troika and their consequences

5.1 The context

Cypriots were aware of the serious economic problems and that the inevitable bailout agreement – which turned into a bail-in as well – was going to be austere (Theophanous, 2013). There was a willingness by the Cypriot public to address these problems substantively. Fiscal rationalization had essentially started in December 2012 and the people were prepared for a gradual paradigm shift. Furthermore, the new government which took over on 2 March 2013 had expected the solidarity of the Eurogroup and of Berlin.

The March 2013 actions and decisions of the Eurogroup came as a shock. On 16 March 2013, the European partners, the IMF and the Cypriot government reached an agreement for a Cyprus programme. As part of the deal, a one-time bank deposit levy of 6.75% for deposits less than €100,000 and 9.9% for greater sums was considered. These measures were estimated to raise about €6 billion. The deal was rejected by the Cypriot Parliament on 19 March 2013. A final agreement was reached on 25 March; this involved the closure of the most troubled Laiki/Popular Bank while the country's largest bank, the Bank of Cyprus, was to be restructured. The rescue package of the Bank of Cyprus included a deposit haircut for accounts over €100,000. The final amounts of the haircut were subsequently defined – amounting to around 50%, and the absorption of good assets and deposits below €100,000 of Laiki/Popular Bank and its Emergency liquidity assistance obligations.

Furthermore, all Cypriot banking operations in Greece were sold at low prices at the request of the Troika.[5] The objective was to reduce the systemic influence of Cyprus in Greece (due to the possibility that the problem could spread in the Cypriot banks operating in Greece; subsequently this could have immediately negatively affected the Greek banking system). The agreement also provided for a loan of €10 billion for the period 2013–2016; the remaining €7.5 billion were to be raised from Cyprus. Nevertheless, the way this was done created more damage than good. The policies pursued, in retrospect, should not be judged by the alleged benefit of trying to protect taxpayers, but by the effects on the ground, including the fact that the comprehensive package left Cyprus with less liquidity and more uncertainty.

The Cyprus programme was characterized by the participation of the depositors in the rescue package for the first time. According to the EU, the 'deposits' haircut' had to be implemented to make foreign investors (mainly Russians), who benefited from the high interest rates provided by the Cypriot banking sector and the favourable regulation scheme, contribute to the rescue package. The EU and especially Germany considered it as unacceptable that their taxpayers had to pay in order to save Russian deposits. However, the reality is that Cyprus was used as an experiment for subsequent bank rescues.[6]

Over time, several misperceptions had been created about Cyprus. For example, that it was a money laundering centre, a casino economy, and that it was a state that caused the EU recurring headaches. The reality is that Cyprus had passed relevant legislation and had made a systematic effort to control illegal activities around money laundering; and Cyprus was in a better position than most European countries, including Germany, in relation to the anti-money laundering (AML) index.[7] Some quarters in the EU had – quite remarkably – held a grudge that in 2004 the Greek Cypriots had rejected the UN plan for the solution of the Cyprus problem. Cyprus was also a victim of its own inability to adjust and position itself to withstand a very difficult political and economic environment.

5.2 The Memorandum of Understanding and its philosophy

In the case of Cyprus, the Troika's philosophy introduced the 'bail-in' arrangement to complement the 'bail-out'. The idea was that apart from the money that the Troika would lend, the country would also 'participate' in its rescue effort. This was associated with a shock approach in the financial system, fiscal discipline and strict austerity. The Troika's policies had cataclysmic effects, such as loss of wealth, higher unemployment, reduction of wages, increased taxes, reduced social benefits and the shrinking of the welfare state.

The Troika considered the banking sector as the main culprit of the Cypriot economic model. The domestic banking sector represented about 550% of GDP in 2013. On 22 March 2013 under the mandate of the Troika,

Parliament voted legislation which provided for the carve-out of the Greek operations of all Cypriot banks as well as the resolution of Cyprus Popular Bank,[8] and the absorption of selected assets and liabilities by the Bank of Cyprus. It also provided for the recapitalization of the Bank of Cyprus through a debt to equity conversion, without the use of public money (the so called 'deposits' haircut'). As a result of these actions the Cypriot banking sector was downsized immediately and significantly to 350% of GDP. Moreover, it suffered a severe blow from which it cannot be predicted when the sector will recover.

In relation with the Memorandum agreed on 23 November 2012 with the previous government, the Troika requested additional measures for the state budget of 2013 worth approximately €351 million (2.1% of GDP): these included the property taxation of at least €75 million, increase of the statutory corporate income tax rate to 12.5% and an increase of the tax rate on interest income to 30%. Moreover, the provisions of the Memorandum included a series of new measures to reduce government expenditure on various housing schemes by at least €36 million. There was also a scaled reduction in emoluments of public and broader public sector pensioners and employees.

The target set by the partners of the Cypriot support programme was to achieve a primary surplus[9] of 3% of GDP in 2017, 4% of GDP in 2018 and maintain at least such a level thereafter. The Troika also erased the amount of €7.2 billion that the state owed to the social security fund. The implementation of this measure will have a very serious negative effect on pensions in the near future.

Furthermore, the Memorandum demanded the privatization of state-owned enterprises. The objective was to improve economic efficiency through enhanced competition and encouragement of capital inflows and to help in restoring debt sustainability. The privatization plans in consultation with the Troika are expected to raise €1.4 billion by 2018. Nevertheless, privatization will lead to private monopolies, reduce, if not eliminate, the social role of these enterprises and may also cause social turmoil.

5.3 Implementation of the Troika philosophy and the forgone alternative

Cyprus is not likely to get out of the deep recession within the framework of the philosophy of the Memorandum and the current architecture of the eurozone. To the present day this seems untenable. In reality what happened was an unprecedented attack on Cyprus' financial sector that took the country back decades. The Eurogroup decisions seriously damaged the banking system of the country.

The banking system of Cyprus was cut to pieces and its public robbed with a viciousness that raises serious questions about the existing value system in the EU. Despite two recapitalizations of the banking system, from March 2013 to November 2014 there are still fundamental problems. The non-performing loans increased from about 25% in March 2013 to almost 50% in June 2015.

Inevitably there are serious disruptions in all aspects of life. The euphoria that existed in Cyprus before the accession to the EU has therefore turned into deep bitterness.

The Troika's decisions pushed the country into a chaotic situation from which it will be difficult to exit. Inter alia, the implementation of the Memorandum caused a huge increase in unemployment, demographic outflows, deep and persistent wage cuts, tax increases, untamed public and private debt and above all misery and social disintegration. The high public debt and the growing indebtedness of households and businesses will lead to property divestment and social fabric dissolution. This inevitably will lead to social, economic and political discontent.

The strategy chosen by the Troika to promote balanced budgets does not differ from the rest of the troubled European periphery. This revolves around the imposition of extreme fiscal austerity. The deficit reduction is expected to be achieved gradually not through growth but through reductions in wages and pensions (internal devaluation), cuts in benefits, tax increases and unprecedented pressure on society. It is doubtful whether this objective will be achieved even with these draconian measures.

Despite the reduction of prices, the purchasing power of wages decreased as salary cuts were greater. In addition there are many unemployed workers. Interest rates have been reduced gradually and will move in line to the ones existing in the northern euro area countries over time.

The adoption of the Memorandum had dramatic repercussions on GDP, which shrunk substantially, mirroring the devastation of economic production. The reduction of the GDP in 2013 led to the increase of private debt to GDP ratio of Cyprus to 353% and the public debt to GDP ratio to 102% in the same year.[10] The implementation of the Memorandum is having a devastating impact on businesses and households as many of them are bankrupt. Inevitably the deep recession is leading to a situation where it will be impossible for both the public and the private debt to be served. While the crisis originated in the banking and the public sector the cost on the other sectors of the economy in terms of unemployment and salary cuts is much higher.

Under the framework of the Memorandum there was an improvement in the index of the trade and current account balance basically due to the deep recession. These developments also led to a reduction on the balance of payments deficit. With the Memorandum policy Cyprus cannot anticipate relative improvements of these indicators under conditions of social prosperity. The improvement in these indicators has essentially been the outcome of the deep recession and the loss of wealth.

More than two years after the disastrous Eurogroup decision of March 2013, Cyprus is still in a recession. Despite repeated and sustained announcements of the government that the implementation of the Troika's philosophy is contributing to the rationalization of the economy and that growth is around the corner, the harsh realities on the ground point to a different situation. Unemployment is high, there is a serious demographic outflow, many small firms are closing down, and poverty is increasing.

Although the old model, and especially the banking sector, has been destroyed, there is still no new paradigm. The government has repeatedly claimed that this harsh package was the least costly under the circumstances. Nevertheless, what happened was the worst-case scenario. The government should not have accepted the haircut of deposits. The option of adopting, at least on a temporary basis, a national currency in conjunction with additional policy tools could have offered better results (Krugman, 2013; O'Brien, 2013; Theophanous, 2013).

Resorting to the national currency could have been supported at least by Britain; this could have limited the depreciation that the new currency would have suffered. Such a policy could have been pursued in conjunction with an accommodative fiscal and monetary policy. Ideas could have been utilized from various historical records such as Roosevelt's New Deal and Reagan's Supply Side Economics. Furthermore, a national currency would have led to a change in the terms of trade. Last but not least, the potential of the energy sector could have been taken into consideration in terms of growth prospects.

6 Concluding remarks

For years Cyprus took pride in the 'economic miracle' that it had achieved after the Turkish invasion. Yet Cyprus found itself in a deep crisis in 2013. The successful record since the post invasion years had led to complacency and to the illusion that the positive path would always be sustained. The endogenous structural problems that accumulated over time were largely the result of the inadequacy of the wider economic, social and political system. Furthermore, the international economic crisis, the euro debt crisis and the interconnection of the Cypriot and the Greek economy worsened the situation.

By 2012 Cyprus was facing a huge banking crisis, serious fiscal imbalances and a real estate bubble. Admittedly Cypriot policy-makers and other stakeholders had engaged in imprudent practices with devastating results. When finally Cyprus requested the support of the EU it was treated in an irrational, brutal and punitive way in March 2013. According to the ex-Foreign Minister of Spain, Miguel Angel Moratinos (2013), the EU acted myopically by not helping Cyprus address the crisis; on the contrary, with the dictated austerity policies it deepened the crisis.

The decisions of the Eurogroup were influenced by other considerations as well: these included the timing of the then upcoming German elections, the objective to contain Russian presence in Cyprus, to use Cyprus as an experiment for future crises and to send particular messages to other, bigger, more troublesome countries. Cyprus did not deserve this treatment. With such attitudes and practices the EU will not move towards deeper integration. Apart from the solidarity deficit, there are deep institutional, structural and cultural differences between the member states. Increasingly, several countries see Germany as hegemonic, while the Troika is facing problems of legitimacy as its economic philosophy both in theory and practice lacks reason and sensitivity.

More than two years after the disastrous Eurogroup decisions of March 2013 the Cypriot economy remains in a situation of structural stagnation with the country suffering its worst demographic outflow since the Turkish invasion of 1974. The banking system has been seriously damaged with no new economic paradigm in sight. The Cypriot government and the Troika have repeatedly expressed their satisfaction for 'the progress made despite great obstacles ahead'. The harsh reality though is that the economy was still shrinking. Stabilization, if it comes, will be at a low level (Theophanous, 2014).

While Cyprus has to move to a new model, it is essential to change the pursued economic policy of austerity: it is important to reduce taxes, to enhance targeted spending and to encourage more liquidity. Reducing taxes will stimulate economic activity, enhance consumption and investment and indirectly mitigate the situation of the non-performing loans. Serving private and public debt cannot effectively take place while economic activity is receding; foreclosures will not get rid of non-performing loans. The implementation of the suggested policy will not worsen the fiscal situation; tax rates will be cut, but revenues will increase because of a dynamic process which will lead to reduced unemployment combined with a new approach of high penalties for non-compliance.

In relation to banking practices, while in the past there were imprudent practices, after March 2013 strict procedures have effectively limited the granting of loans. Indeed we have passed from a state of great imprudence to that of suffocation. This should be reversed. Furthermore, given that Cyprus lost about €4.5 billion during the Greek private sector involvement and had a negative wealth effect around €20 billion during the bail-in in March 2013, which was harsh and unnecessary, the EU should find ways to compensate Cyprus with a specific (mini) Marshall-type plan. Last but not least, rationalization plans should also take into consideration institutional arrangements.

Cyprus aside, the economic conditions in other countries exposed to the Troika treatment are also problematic to say the least. In the case of Greece the socioeconomic conditions are harsh and the country is facing the 'depression of the century'.

Cyprus' ability to pursue discretionary fiscal and monetary policy after the invasion enabled the country not only to recover but also to achieve an economic miracle. Today, however, Cyprus as a member of the eurozone cannot pursue discretionary policies to address the serious recession. Given the eurozone's faulty architecture in effect we have a situation of automatic destabilizers (Feldstein, 1997). Cyprus' efforts to rationalize the economy and also move to a new paradigm are constrained by the rules of the eurozone and the prevailing philosophy of the Troika/Institutions. Consequently, Cyprus has to convince the Institutions to relax the conditions of the Memorandum. It is also important to promote new engines of growth and to create high value-added jobs. These should include the energy sector as well the promotion of Cyprus as an academic and medical centre.

Furthermore, one cannot underestimate the economic issues and the challenges of reunification in the event of a solution to the Cyprus question. These range from the issues of governance, socioeconomic convergence, legal harmonization and property arrangements (Theophanous, 2008). Moreover, it is essential to assess whether and how a federal structure can function within the framework of the eurozone architecture.

Notes

1 The analysis and the data before 1974 refer to the entire area and population of the Republic of Cyprus. Following 1974 we only examine developments as well as data in the area under the control of the government of the Republic of Cyprus.

2 The national currency was the Cyprus pound. The central exchange rate parity of the pound was 0.585274 per euro.

3 The Gini coefficient is a measure of dispersion or inequality, often used to measure income distribution of a nation's residents.

4 It is noted that at the end of 2012 the public debt was roughly equally split between domestic and foreign debt.

5 Memorandum of Understanding on Specific Economic Policy Conditionality, 12 April 2013 available at http://www.mof.gov.cy/mof/mof.nsf/final%20MOUf.pdf. The Troika was made up of the European Commission, the European Central Bank and the International Monetary Fund.

6 As the German Finance Minister Wolfgang Schäuble said on 21 April 2013 in an interview in the business magazine *WirtschaftsWoche*: 'The model of participation of shareholders, creditors and unsecured deposits should be the usual practice where a financial institution presents problems.' The interview is available at: www.wiwo.de/politik/europa/reaktionen-schaeuble-interview-in-wirtschaftswoche-schockt-boerse/8098476.html.

7 It is noted that the AML regime of Cyprus received an overall positive evaluation in the 2011 MONEYVAL Report (available at: https://www.coe.int/t/dghl/monitoring/moneyval/Evaluations/round4/CYP4_MER_MONEYVAL(2011)2_en.pdf). Furthermore, research from the Basel Institute on Governance indicates that Cyprus has a lower risk rating than many European countries such as Germany which is in 89th place on the list for the AML index while Cyprus is in 110th place among 152 countries, with higher rankings indicating lower risks (Basel AML Index 2015 available at: https://index.baselgovernance.org/sites/index/documents/Basel_AML_Index_Report_2015.pdf).

8 The resolution of Cyprus Popular Bank (also known as Laiki Bank) involved the sale of the bank's branches in Greece and its business in Cyprus to other Banks. More information is available at: http://www.centralbank.gov.cy/nqcontent.cfm?a_id=12631&lang=en.

9 The primary budget surplus arises from the subtraction of public expenditure from public revenues excluding interest payments on government debt.

10 It should be noted that the European Statistical Service in September 2014 changed the way the GDP is calculated so that this figure would appear higher. With this methodology some indicators such as the budget deficit and the public debt appear better (i.e. lower).

References

Bamber, D. (1982) 'Cyprus – A Survey', *Euromoney* (Supplement).

Christodoulou, D. (1992) *Inside the Cyprus Miracle: The Labours of an Embattled Mini-Economy.* Mediterranean and East European Monographs, Minneapolis: University of Minnesota.

Christodoulou, D. (1995) 'Where the "Miracle" Has not Reached' (in Greek). Nicosia: Intercollege Press.

Economist, The (1977) 'Cyprus: Miracle in Half an Island', 264(6991): 50–51.

Feldstein, M. (1997) 'EMU and International Conflict', *Foreign Affairs,* 76(6): 60–73.

Krugman, P. (2013) 'Cyprus Seriously', *The New York Times,* 26 March.

Moratinos, M. (2013) 'En defense de Chipre', *El Pais,* 28 March.

O'Brien, M. (2013) 'Cyprus Is Doomed: Why the Country Must Leave the Euro Immediately', *The Atlantic*, 28 March.

Orphanides, A. (2014) 'What Happened in Cyprus? The Economic Consequences of the Last Communist Government in Europe', MIT Sloan Research Chapter No. 5089–14.

Polyviou, P. (2011) 'Mari – Findings of the Single-member Investigative Committee to Conduct an Investigation into the Explosion of 11 July 2011 at the Naval Base "Evangelos Florakis"', Nicosia, Cyprus.

Theophanous, A. (1991) 'Economic Growth and Development in Cyprus, 1960/1984', *Modern Greek Studies Yearbook*, 7: 105–132.

Theophanous, A. (1995) 'An Anatomy of the Economic Miracle 1974–1994', in N. Persitianis and G. Tsangaras (eds). *20 Years After: An Anatomy of a Metamorphosis.* Nicosia: Intercollege Press.

Theophanous, A. (2004) 'The Cyprus Question: The Challenge and the Promise', Nicosia: Intercollege Press.

Theophanous, A. (2008) 'The Political Economy of a Cyprus Settlement: The Examination of Four Scenaria', Nicosia: PRIO Cyprus Centre.

Theophanous, A. (2013) 'The Way out of the Cyprus Economic Crisis', Policy Chapter 96 Notre Europe – Jacques Delors Institute.

Theophanous, A. (2014) 'Troika Fixes Fail: How to Fix the Troika', *Friends of Europe,* 4 December.

Whitaker, D. (1980) 'The Economy', in F. Bunge (ed.). *Cyprus: A Country Study.* Washington DC: The American University, pp. 105–151.

2 The Estonian economy

Structure, performance and prospects[1]

Tarmo Kalvet

1 Introduction

Estonia, with a population of 1.3 million, is a Baltic country in Northeast Europe. The country became politically and economically independent from the Soviet Union in August 1991. Since then, Estonia has undertaken large-scale liberalization in its trade and capital markets, and by 1995, most companies were privatized. Estonia joined the European Union (EU) in May 2004 and adopted the euro in January 2011.

Estonia has often been considered by many as one of the successful, if not the most successful, Eastern European EU member state in its catching up achievement (Laar, 2008), although there is some doubt on this claim (e.g. Tiits et al., 2008).

This chapter presents an account of the structure and performance of the economy since the year 2000, focusing on its key aspects. Special consideration will be given to competitiveness and innovation, which are considered of major importance for the Estonian economy as well as for the EU.

The chapter will also discuss the impact of EU accession, again assigning special consideration to the competitiveness and innovation perspective. It will be argued that there are many advantages in being a member of the European economic block, but there are some downsides as well.

Another theme to which reference will be made in this chapter relates to the special economic characteristics of Estonia as a small state. A characteristic which Estonia shares with other small states is its very high dependence on international trade, a result of its small domestic market, and this renders it very important for the country to be competitive and innovative.

This chapter is organized as follows. Following this brief introduction, Section 2 presents an account of the structure and performance of the Estonian economy since 2000, referring to research and innovation aspects. Section 3 discusses the advantages and disadvantages of Estonia's membership of the EU, again referring to the innovation perspective. Section 4 deals with the prospects for Estonia's economy. Section 5 concludes the chapter with some comments.

2 Structure and performance of the economy

2.1 Economic structure

The Estonian economy has undergone considerable changes since the 1990s (Table 2.1). The share of primary activities, especially of agriculture, forestry and fishing has decreased markedly. The share of manufacturing industries has also declined, caused mainly by the developments in North-East Estonia, a region that was industrialized after the Second World War with a focus on heavy industries, a legacy of the Soviet era. To satisfy the increased labour force needs, large-scale immigration took place during the Soviet period, resulting in a population with a very high proportion of non-Estonians. Since the 1990s, rapid deindustrialization of the region has taken place, while the creation of new jobs has been limited. As a result the North-East region is characterized by relatively low income per capita and low employment rates, leading to relatively high unemployment and poverty rates. In turn this has resulted in outward migration from that region (see Kalvet, 2013; Raagmaa, Kalvet and Kasesalu, 2013).

Overall, the Estonian economy has become more services oriented since the 1990s and many new types of services have been developed. The emergence of the modern information and communications technology (ICT) industries as well as the spreading of the ICT into many other domains, most notably into banking and public administration, has made Estonia famous in this regard (see, e.g., Kalvet, 2012).

However, the Estonian economy has been and remains structurally dominated by traditional sectors with relatively low levels of value added on average, including transportation, furniture, and paper products (see Table 2.2). These sectors dominate in terms of both employment and exports and are also the ones wherein Estonia is most specialized compared to the average employment profile of other European economies (Christensen et al., 2012: 9). Although manufacture of computer, electronic and optical products could be considered as medium or high technology production, much of it in Estonia consists of lower value-added subcontracting activities.

In Estonia, large enterprises and especially branches of multinational corporations, are very important actors in the economy. The largest companies in Estonia are heavily dominated heavily by owners from the Nordic countries in some cases with 100% foreign ownership (Kalvet, 2010).

A specific feature of Estonia, similar to most small states, is its openness (Figure 2.1). Estonia is more dependent on trade than most other EU member states and therefore more exposed to forces outside its control. Estonia shares other characteristics with other small states, notably a high degree of dependence on strategic imports, namely fuel and food, and a high degree of export concentration (Briguglio, 2014).

Table 2.1 The main sectors of Estonian economy (share in value added at current prices, %)

	1995	*2000*	*2005*	*2010*	*2012*	*2014*
Agriculture, forestry, fishing, mining and quarrying	7.6	6.0	4.4	4.6	5.3	4.9
Manufacturing	19.8	17.3	16.6	15.7	16.1	15.7
Construction	6.6	5.9	8.6	5.9	7.2	6.5
Wholesale and retail trade; repair of motor vehicles and motorcycles	12.0	12.6	14.4	11.8	12.4	12.2
Transportation and storage	8.4	10.5	8.5	9.0	9.0	8.7
Information and communication	4.5	5.2	4.7	5.3	5.0	5.3
Financial and insurance activities	2.8	4.0	3.9	4.1	3.8	3.8
Real estate activities	6.4	11.6	9.8	9.8	9.8	10.1
Public administration and defence, education, health and social work	19.8	14.5	13.4	16.2	14.2	14.8
Other service activities	12.1	12.4	15.9	17.7	17.0	17.8

Source: Statistics Estonia 2015 available at: http://www.stat.ee/statistics.

Table 2.2 Proportion of industrial production

	2005	*2010*	*2013*
Manufacture of computer, electronic and optical products	5.1	10.8	15.6
Manufacture of wood and wood products	15.6	13.0	12.9
Manufacture of food products	12.5	11.8	11.3
Manufacture of fabricated metal products	9.5	9.4	8.0
Electricity, steam and hot water supply	6.1	8.8	7.6
Manufacture of electrical equipment	3.0	4.5	4.7
Manufacture of chemicals and chemical products	4.8	4.0	4.5
Other manufacturing	43.4	37.7	35.4

Source: Statistics Estonia 2015, available at: http://www.stat.ee/statistics.

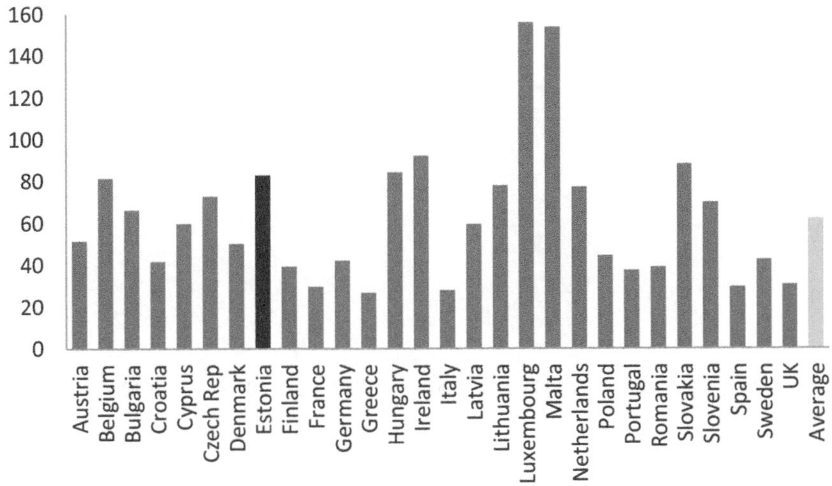

Figure 2.1 Trade openness in the EU (average of exports and imports as a percentage of GDP, 2009–2014)
Source: UNCTAD Statistics (Trade Openness Indicators), available at: http://unctadstat.unctad.org/wds/ReportFolders/reportFolders.aspx.

2.2 Economic growth

Estonia has made considerable economic progress since its political and economic re-independence. The country achieved rapid economic growth of real gross domestic product (GDP) between 2000 and 2007, but it started to slow down in 2008, in the course of the global financial crisis, and was followed by one of the most severe contractions of an economy in the world, as can be seen in Figure 2.2.

The very rapid economic growth demonstrated by Estonia between 2000 and 2007 was based on the massive inflow of foreign capital. The record low interest rates in Western Europe and in the USA in combination with the EU enlargement led to a significant inflow of foreign direct investment to Central and Eastern Europe (CEE). In per capita terms, Estonia was one of the particularly attractive locations for foreign direct investment. In Estonia, the majority of the foreign capital came in the form of the reinvested profits rather than new export oriented greenfield investments.

In addition to the inflow of foreign direct investments, there was a remarkable inflow of debt financing. A significant share of the inflow of the debt financing was provided by the Scandinavian banks, which were competing for their market shares in Estonia. Such inflow of capital, which came at record low interest rates, triggered major asset and consumption booms in Estonia. The latter contributed, in turn, to the emergence of a large and widening current account deficit. Domestic consumption fuelled growth which in turn triggered very rapid wage inflation (Tiits, Tamm and Tõnnisson, 2010).

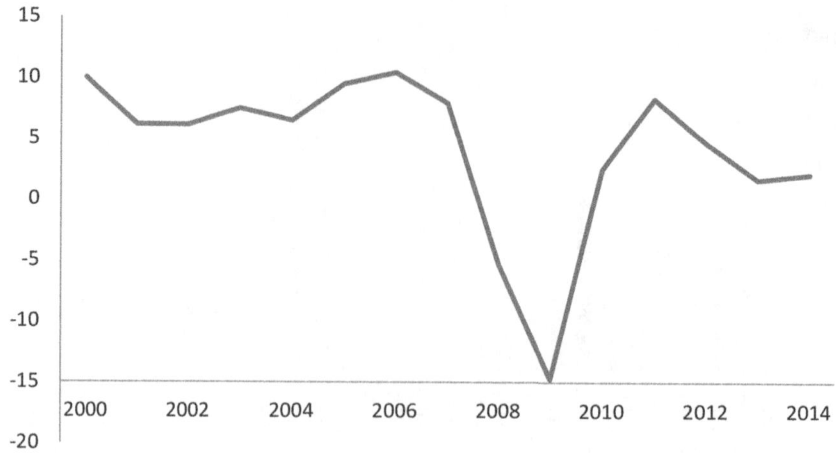

Figure 2.2 Real GDP growth (%), Estonia, 2000–2014
Source: International Monetary Fund (IMF) World Economic Outlook Database (2015), available at: http://www.imf.org/external/pubs/ft/weo/2015/update/02/.

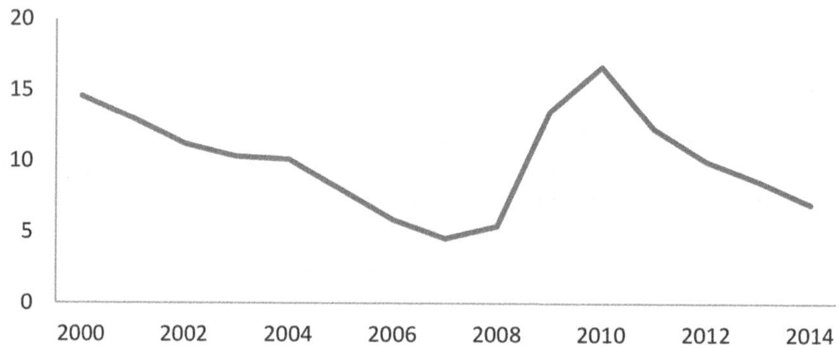

Figure 2.3 Unemployment rates as a percentage of the labour force (%)
Source: IMF World Economic Outlook Database (2015) available at: http://www.imf.org/external/pubs/ft/weo/2015/update/02/.

2.3 The labour market

The period after the Russian crisis of 1998 had major negative effects on the Estonian labour market, particularly on agricultural and food processing enterprises due to the loss of their main Eastern market. With the overall development of the economy and the restructuring – the closing of 'old era' industries and the emergence of a more modern economy – unemployment decreased quite rapidly in the early 2000s and kept decreasing, until the global economic crisis, as can be seen in Figure 2.3.

For a number of years, wage increases significantly outpaced the productivity growth in industry. The rapid increase in wage rates was to a large extent caused by the non-tradable sectors such as real estate, renting and business activities, wholesale and retail, trade, transport and communications, financial services, and construction, which led to the overheating of the economy.

Another main issue relates to structural mismatches in the labour market particularly due to differences in what was produced by the education system as compared to the companies' employment requirements. Both higher education and public research suffered during the transition in the 1990s, due to a highly fragmented system of higher education which to this day continues to be unable to provide the sufficient numbers of engineering workers that are needed by industry (Tiits, Kalvet and Mürk 2015).

A problem that has emerged since Estonia joined the European Union in 2004, is an increasing number of people and companies that have emigrated abroad, especially to Finland (Laakso et al., 2013). In particular, the outflow of high-skilled individuals (such as medical workers) has caused major gaps in the Estonian labour market.

2.4 Government finances

Government stability, coupled with sizable fiscal reserves (accumulated during the boom years), a very low level of public debt, and fiscal adjustment measures taken in 2008 and 2009, helped the government avoid funding problems during and immediately post the global recession (see, e.g., International Monetary Fund, 2009) and, as a result, the Estonian government avoided borrowing from outside sources during the global crisis. Estonia was, as a

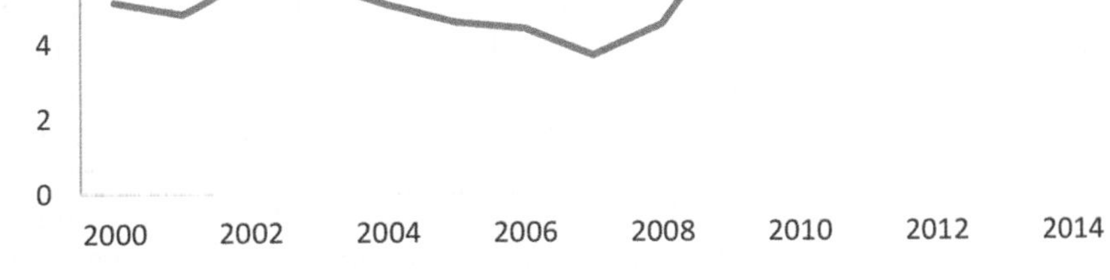

Figure 2.4 Debt as a percentage of GDP
Source: IMF world Economic Outlook Database (2015), available at: http://www.imf.org/external/pubs/ft/weo/2015/update/02/.

result, able to adopt the euro in 2011 as a result. The Estonian debt burden continues to be among the lowest in Europe (see Figure 2.4).

2.5 Competitiveness and innovation

The key document in Estonian research and development (R&D) and innovation policy is *Knowledge Based Estonia – Estonian R&D and Innovation Strategy 2007–2013* (Ministry of Education, 2007), which is a follow-up to the Estonian R&D Strategy of 2002–2006. The strategy sets out three main objectives:

1. *Competitive quality and increased intensity of R&D.* This objective foresees the need for an increase in the supply of top-level specialists, an increase of R&D intensity and quality, the advancement of research management, and a major upgrading of the R&D infrastructure.
2. *Innovative enterprises creating new value in the global economy.* This objective emphasizes internationalization, inward technology transfer, and foreign investments focusing on developing innovative products and services.
3. *Innovation friendly society aimed at long-term development.* This objective addresses a number of broader institutional and social issues, including the development of a legislative and business environment conducive to R&D as well as increasing political and social awareness of the challenges facing the Estonian economy and society, as well as the role of R&D in overcoming these challenges.

According to the World Economic Forum's Global Competitiveness Index (Schwab, 2015), which ranks countries in terms of their competitiveness scores, Estonia has throughout the recent decade retained a relatively stable ranking being among the 20–30 most competitive economies. Estonia's relative strengths have been transparent and efficient institutions and a low burden of government regulation, a solid macroeconomic environment, a low level of corruption, ease of starting new businesses and the success of government in the promotion of ICT. The up-take of ICT, both in the public and private sector, is an area where Estonia has really excelled. However, low sophistication of business organization and low level of clustering remain major weaknesses. In addition, the limited availability of qualified labour and low levels of business R&D investments remain major hindrances to further development.

The Innovation Union Scoreboard (2015) positions Estonia as a moderate innovator, that is with a group of the EU member states where the innovation relative performance rates is between 50% and 90% of the EU average. In Estonia the public sector is well endowed to perform R&D activities, and the availability of risk capital for private firms to develop new technologies is not lacking. As a result, companies invest in innovation activities both for science-based R&D activities and non-R&D innovation activities, including investments in advanced equipment and machinery. Estonia performs also well above average on international scientific co-publications. However, innovation

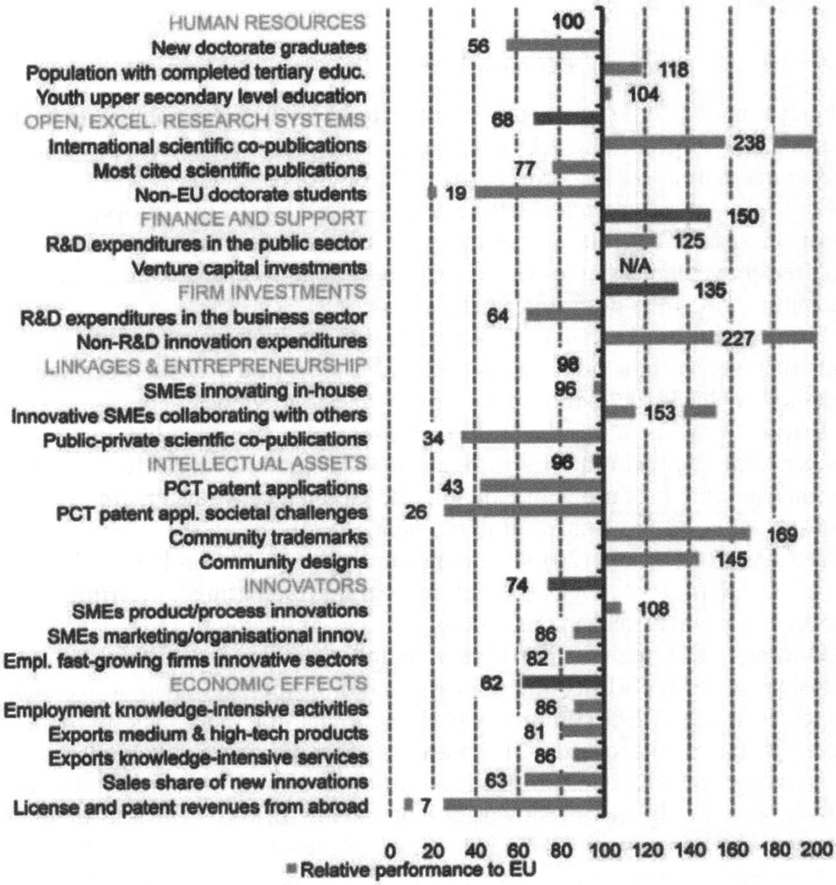

Figure 2.5 Estonia in the Innovation Union Scoreboard
Note: PCT – Patent Cooperation Treaty.
Source: European Commission, Innovation Union Scoreboard (2015): 50.

outcomes both in the level of the companies as well as on the national level remain below the EU averages (Figure 2.5).

In Estonia, the acquisition of equipment and machinery remains the most important source of innovation (Statistics Estonia, 2015). The number of world-class or close-to-world-class research-intensive companies is rather small. Out of all the Estonian sectors, only the ICT industry has strong linkages with other related sectors, including software developers, telecommunications, banking, wholesale and retail trade, and governmental structures (Kalvet, 2012). The R&D personnel employed in financial intermediation (where innovations in Estonia are largely ICT-based) and in ICT-related activities have accounted for half of the total business-sector R&D personnel over the last years, making ICT a knowledge and development-intensive sector (Statistics Estonia, 2015).

3 Estonia and the EU

3.1 General support for EU membership

The Estonian people are consistently found to be leading supporters of the European Union among EU citizens, as indicated by opinion polls, notably the Eurobarometer. According to a Eurobarometer survey carried out in 2015,[2] 79% of respondents felt that they are citizens of Europe. The three most important benefits associated with EU membership were identified as (1) free movement of goods, services and capital, (2) peace and security in Europe, and (3) the adoption of the euro.

Support among Estonians for the EU can be interpreted as an indication that they see various advantages in Estonia being an EU member state and see the benefit of the common European rules and values.

Estonia has, as a result of EU membership, considerably increased its influence in European affairs through its participation in the European institutions, notably its European Council, the Council of Ministers, the European Commission and the European parliament. According to the Ministry of Foreign Affairs of Estonia (2014), joining the European Union has made Estonia far bigger than it has ever been before, without increasing its territory, due to the free movement of persons, goods, services and capital.

However, EU membership has a number of disadvantages, and in the Eurobarometer report just mentioned, a small proportion (8%) of respondents indicated that the EU conjures a negative image for them. The most problematic issue in this regard is the issue of loss of sovereignty and the interference by the EU Commission in internal affairs. According to Veebel (2014), one of the major downsides of having Brussels intrude in internal affairs is the lack of transparency in terms of member states' joint obligations.

Although small countries like Estonia have some influence in EU affairs, greater than they would have had if they had stayed out of the EU, their voice remains relatively weak in major European decisionmaking, and this in spite of the fact that their representation in EU institutions in general is scaled higher than the proportion of their population.[3]

3.2 Estonia and the euro

Estonia joined the Exchange Rate Mechanism (ERM II) on 28 June 2004 with a central rate of 15.6466 kroon to the euro and standard fluctuation margins of ±15%. The go-ahead for Estonia's adoption of the euro was given by the EU in July 2010 and the actual adoption took place on 1 January 2011.

In general, the changeover was very smooth and successful. According to the Estonia *Ex-Post Citizen Survey*[4] the vast majority of Estonians (87%) thought that the changeover happened smoothly and efficiently, while only 8% thought the contrary.

As already mentioned, the majority of Estonians view the adoption of the euro as a positive development. For the business community, this is possibly because the introduction of the euro ushered in a number of advantages for trade, notably lower transaction costs and lower exchange rate risks for exporters and importers. In addition, the introduction of the euro reduced costs for Estonian tourists in their travels within the euro area as this meant no cost in currency exchange. The adoption of the euro also permitted Estonia to join a group of countries enjoying high economic prestige, although the recent euro crises have dented this advantage.

A downside often associated with the euro adoption is that it tends to generate inflationary pressures. One reason for this includes that in its early stages changeover is costly for business due to so-called menu costs, and this leads business firms to raise prices to compensate for such costs. Another factor in this regard relates to the rounding up of prices upwards around the time of the changeover. These are one-off changes. A possible recurrent effect on prices could be that buyers tend to keep on calculating prices in terms of the old currency and rely on approximate rather than exact calculations when interpreting euro prices. This may encourage firms to increase prices, taking advantages of this confusion. However in a study by Rõõm and Urke (2014), it was found that in the case of Estonia the inflation effect was negligible.

Another downside of the adoption of the euro is that being a member of the euro zone does not permit exchange rate alignment and this reduces the policy flexibility of the country in adjusting its balance of payments. There is considerable debate about the advantages or otherwise of such policy flexibility, with one argument being that the inability to devalue the currency will necessitate the reduction of wage costs, an internal devaluation which is more difficult to achieve than currency devaluation (Lanzavecchia and Pavarani, 2015). In the case of Estonia, after 2011 the country did not experience major problems relating to its balance of payments current account. The main competitiveness constraints in Estonia related to the need to upgrade labour productivity to balance the rapid increase in wage rates, possibly by stepping up technological innovation, which is perhaps a more sustainable approach than periodic devaluations of the domestic currency.

Above all, the Estonians view membership of the euro area more in terms of its political dimension than in its economic effects. As Wrobel (2015) has argued, for all Baltic people, keeping their countries independent from Russia was of highest interest and this led to the desire of these countries to incorporate themselves into Western political as well as economic structures, including the euro area.

3.3 Effect of EU membership on competitiveness and innovation

A considerable benefit derived from EU membership relates to competitiveness and innovation. The preparation for the EU membership was clearly the most dominant theme of Estonia's policy agenda in the first half of the 2000s.

Prioritization of the rapid adoption of the *acquis communautaire* was an important part of this process. Although the innovation policy and related objectives were not placed very high on the policy agenda, the harmonization of laws and standards ushered in new investment and led to quality improvement, particularly visible in the food safety and environmental standards which necessitated and continue to necessitate major investments into adoption of new technologies. One could even argue that the adoption of the EU regulations and standards contained an implicit, but very strong innovation policy element, although this was never part of the original intention (Kattel, 2004; Tiits, Kattel and Kalvet, 2005).

In the late 1990s, explicit R&D and innovation policies started to appear, encouraged in part by the looming EU accession. Scientists were, however, almost the only proponents of R&D and innovation policy. This approach was closely related to science-based innovation, assuming a more or less linear correspondence between scientific discovery and innovation performance. Most of Estonia's local industries were simply excluded from these considerations (Polt, Koch and Walters, 2007). Similar approaches were adopted in other CEE countries (Radoševic and Reid, 2006).

In the run-up to EU accession, and following accession, significant resources have been allocated to R&D and innovation from the EU Structural Funds. Foreign financing became of major importance for Estonia and in 2012 accounted for about 19.1% of the total State budget, of which more than three fourths came from various EU funds and programmes (Kalvet, 2013; see also Kattel and Raudla, 2013).

Furthermore, 67% of Estonian R&D and innovation policy measures were co-financed by the EU Structural Funds (INNO-Policy TrendChart, 2009: 17). These funds were to a considerable extent instrumental in the implementation of R&D infrastructural development, the setting up of competence Centres and of Centres of Excellence. Several of these support measures were introduced in the 2002–2006 programming period and were continued more intensively in the 2007–2013 period (Kalvet, 2013).

According to different evaluations carried out by various stakeholders there was a significant positive impact of the EU-funded interventions. In the case of improving enterprise support and R&D, the achievements for 2007–2013 related to better access to the capital required for productivity-enhancing investment, technological modernization of businesses and improved internationalization of Estonian business. For example, private sector R&D investment induced by the EU-supported projects stood at €82 million 2011 which was about 53% of the total private sector R&D investments in that year. The number of firms involved in exporting also increased. With regard to research and development and higher education infrastructure, progress was evident in improving the research and in increasing the international competitiveness and business focus of the R&D that was supported by the EU (Kalvet, 2013).

More concretely, from the early 2000s, the EU started to influence Estonia's economic development policy (Suurna and Kattel, 2010) because innovation became a central concept in politics and policy-making in most EU countries (Soete, 2007), including the less-developed EU member states such as Estonia (Török, 2007). The Estonian innovation policy was further enhanced as a result of the second wave of EU structural funding that started in 2007 (part of the EU Cohesion Policy that represents the single largest source of financial support at EU level for investment in growth and jobs) as a result of which innovation became strongly linked with the private sector, with increased emphasis on addressing innovation system failures.

With the introduction of the EU Lisbon Agenda and prioritizing R&D and innovation in the EU, these topics gained major importance in Estonia. During the 1990s Estonia had a relatively modest number of public support programmes for entrepreneurship and technological development. However, at the turn of the century a full range of business development programmes were initiated. Both the EU Lisbon Strategy and the introduction of the EU Structural Funds were instrumental in bringing about a change in mentality and introducing relatively stable policy programmes that operated on the basis of the multi-annual budget allocation.

Apart from financing direct policy measures, the role of the EU can be considered highly important in advancing institutional reforms and overall development. For instance, EU requests for the preparation of national development (operational) plans and different strategies have been a significant push factor for better planning. Also, strategic planning in a holistic way, including evaluations as part of the policy cycle, have been assigned increased importance following accession to the EU. This led to improvements in policy-making.

The influence of the EU procedures has also ushered in prioritization procedures in the R&D and innovation policies. This is the case with the smart specialization (Foray, David and Hall, 2009) concept that was introduced in the EU R&D, innovation and cohesion policies for the period 2014–2020. This new concept was aimed at preventing European regions seeking to become market leaders in the same R&D-intensive industries, such as ICTs, biotechnology, and others. Instead, the individual EU regions are expected to take their existing economic specialization strongly into account, concentrate knowledge resources and link them to a limited number of priority economic activities. Such prioritization has been missing so far in the Estonian policy-making.

ERDF[5] funds received by Estonia were also used for the co-funding of financial engineering instruments (FEIs), new revolving forms of sustainable finance for investment at long-term, as an alternative instrument to pure grant funding. FEIs for the period 2007–2013 funded by the ERDF in Estonia were mostly utilized to fund innovation and growth capacity of enterprises and to enhance energy efficiency. Extensive assistance had been provided to small and medium enterprises affected by the 2007 credit crunch. The private market in Estonia does not offer adequate capital to entrepreneurs who lack sufficient collateral and/or sufficient levels of self-financing. These issues became much more worrying during the global economic crisis, as credit insurance providers became more conservative. The FEIs addressed these market failures. The highest demand for these FEIs occurred in 2009 and 2010. After 2011, due to the more liberal credit policies of banks, the demand for FEIs decreased. Market failure targeted by the FEI included the excessively high prices of loans for apartment building and renovation.

Also, the use of public purchasing as a deliberate tool to promote technical innovation, a potentially powerful R&D and innovation policy instrument, has been promoted by the EU over the last few years and has obtained more legitimacy locally (Lember and Kalvet, 2014).

In the field of regional development policy, the results were not so impressive. Europeanization (i.e. convergence with EU regulations and values) was most visible in 1994–1998, when an institutional framework was created, in parallel with intensive learning from the West. Overall, in 1999–2004 the application of EU cohesion policy tools took place with significant convergence. After joining the EU in 2004, national regional development programmes were reduced, the institutional framework was frozen and a selective application of EU rules and the use of EU cohesion policy measures for achieving some personal political agendas started, driving Estonian regional development policy away from common European values (Raagmaa, Kalvet and Kasesalu, 2013).

4 Prospects for the Estonian economy

4.1 Macroeconomic forecasts

Recent reports on the economy of Estonia do not paint a bleak picture of its future. The International Monetary Fund (2015) predicts that Estonia's medium-term growth outlook is underpinned by strong economic fundamentals, including macroeconomic stability, sound public finances, and a conducive business environment, supported by effective government services. In addition, there are initiatives to promote innovation and entrepreneurship.

The Estonian real GDP is expected to grow by around 2.6% in 2015–2016 and in the period 2014 to 2020 the economy is forecasted to grow by about 3.4% per annum.[6] Unemployment in Estonia, at about 6.5% in 2015, down from 16.7% in 2010, is expected to continue decreasing.

One of the main risks identified by the IMF is that Estonia is highly dependent on trade, meaning that its economic fortunes are closely tied to external developments. Estonia shares this risk with other small states, due to their high dependence on external trade. A related risk identified by the IMF is that Estonia's banking system is dominated by cross-border banking groups, again exposing the economy to forces beyond its control.

The IMF identifies as a major long-term problem the possibility that external price competitiveness would be undermined if real wage rates continue to increase at their current rate. Wage growth has significantly outstripped productivity growth in recent years, and this tendency has to be reversed if the country's competitiveness is to be enhanced.

The European Commission (2015) report on Estonia also presents a generally optimistic outlook for Estonia, although it also lists a number of macroeconomic weaknesses. The report states that in the coming years, GDP growth is set to gradually increase and to be more balanced due to the expected recovery of external demand. According to the same report, the economy will continue to grow towards the EU average GDP per capita. In 2004, the year of Estonia's accession to the EU, the GDP per capita of Estonia was 55% of the EU average, and reached 75% in 2014.

As was the case in the IMF (2015) report, the European Commission report also sees wage increases as a threat to the sustainability of Estonia's economy, due to their effect on external competitiveness. The report also states that a major problem of the economy of Estonia is its relatively low labour productivity, which is about 70% of the EU, despite some progress in recent years. In addition, despite the fact that Estonia is renowned for its technological and ICT successes, innovation performance is still below the EU average.

The European Commission (2015) report on Estonia states that the business sector is making progress in terms of increasing its research and development investment, but these investments are concentrated in a limited number of companies with insufficient levels of R&D results. Few companies collaborate with research institutions.

With regard to investment in research and development, the European Commission (2015) report further states that capital investment is mostly directed at construction and equipment, and insufficiently at intellectual property products. In addition, despite a tertiary education attainment rate far above the EU average, there is a clear shortage of students in technology and science subjects.

4.2 Prospects for research and innovation

It therefore emerges from the IMF and the European Commission reports that the main challenge that Estonia faces relates to its ability to effectively participate in international markets. This is needed to turn the earlier domestically led growth into export-led growth, and to increase the competitiveness of its enterprises. A major problem is that Estonian industry is still dominated by low and medium-tech industries, which are, by the very nature of these industries, not very R&D intensive.

Considering the high degree of openness of the Estonian economy and the fact that it is closely integrated in the Nordic value chains, it is important that this shortcoming be rectified. This requires the upgrading of the Estonian business enterprises from the status of subsidiaries, affiliates and sub-contractors to actors of innovation. The Estonian attempts and achievements to internationalize its economic system have been, since the early 1990s, mostly associated with the attraction of foreign capital and foreign direct investment. However, the linkages of the largest foreign owned companies with the local innovation system remained limited.

As the Estonian enterprises attempt to enter new markets, their basic production activities need to be complemented by more knowledge intensive activities, such as applied research and product development. Although there are cases of successful internationalization of the Estonian companies (such as Skype), most of the companies lack capacities and capabilities to successfully do this, and the problem partially stems from their small size.

While continued investment into R&D systems remains crucial for Estonian companies to become more strongly incorporated in the cross-border supranational innovation network, it is of utmost importance to maintain and increase the quality of higher education. Research-intensive companies need high-level researchers and marketing specialists, with excellent technical knowledge about research-intensive products, services and processes.

There is currently a trend of policy convergence as a result of policy transfer and the copying of various policy measures from more successful developed innovation economies to other regions in Europe. For example, in the 2000s, the Central and Eastern European countries launched a variety of different policy measures inspired by successful ones adopted in Nordic and other European countries. So far, the results of such policy transfer are a mixed success at best (Karo and Kattel, 2014). Due to the differing policy contexts and available resources, there were various instances where policies that worked well in Nordic countries did not produce similarly successful results elsewhere.

In the case of smaller economies, like Estonia, education policy, capability building, and the acquisition and mastering of foreign-made technology are often more important than indigenous and local R&D efforts. Well-targeted activity for attracting foreign direct investments in technology-intensive industries, apart from creating linkages with local industries, can be highly effective in creating modern industry and/or upgrading existing local industrial enterprises. This can be more effective than indigenous R&D efforts (Tiits, Kalvet and Mürk, 2015).

5 Conclusions

Although Estonia is frequently considered as one of the successful Eastern European countries in its endeavour to catch up with the European front runners, the fast growth that occurred during the immediate years following EU accession did not last long. In fact, Estonia suffered a major contraction in its GDP in 2009 which was among the worst in the World. This was mostly due to the bursting of the bubble formed around major asset and consumption booms in Estonia and to the high exposure of the Estonian economy, which is highly dependent on international trade.

The innovative activities of enterprises and economic growth in Estonia became increasingly decoupled from each other in the 2000s. It was the combination of the relatively high financial inflows and the assets boom in the non-tradable sector that initially led to the remarkable rapid economic growth, which was then followed by the crisis.

The main challenge that Estonia continues to face is how to increase the competitiveness of its enterprises on the global markets and to step up its innovation effort. The role of the EU has been important here. The adoption of the *acquis communautaire* did trigger innovation activities in the Estonian companies. Also, R&D and innovation investments have increased remarkably over the last decade and these have been funded from the EU cohesion funds. Furthermore, considerable changes have followed in the policy landscape as, similar to what happened in the EU, competitiveness and innovation have become central concepts. In addition, policy-making has changed, and evaluations have become an integral part of policy process, as requested by the respective directorates of the Commission.

Still, while there is a trend towards policy convergence in the EU, i.e. policy transfer and the copying of various policy measures from more successful EU economies to other regions, it should be more strongly acknowledged that contexts are different and that policies and instruments should be tailored for specific contexts.

Notes

1 This work was supported by the Estonian Research Council (grants IUT19–13, PUT773, 9395).
2 Available at: http://ec.europa.eu/public_opinion/archives/eb/eb83/eb83_fact_ee_en.pdf.
3 In the Council each country is represented on equal terms, although the voting arrangement (Qualified Majority Voting) does not permit a veto for each member or for all the small states considered in this book acting as a group together. However Estonia's representation in the EU institutions, as is the case with the other small states, is more than proportional to its relative population size. Estonia has six members in the European Parliament, one commissioner (Andrus Ansip who is also Vice President, Digital Single Market), seven members in the Committee of the Regions, and seven members in the Economic and Social Committee. Estonia also has representatives in the European Court of Auditors, the European Court of Justice and in the General Court.
4 Available at: http://ec.europa.eu/public_opinion/flash/fl_309_sum_en.pdf.
5 The European Regional Development Fund (ERDF) is intended to strengthen economic and social cohesion in the European Union by correcting imbalances between the EU regions.
6 See http://www.imf.org/external/pubs/ft/weo/2015/01/weodata/index.aspx.

References

Briguglio, L. (2014) 'A Vulnerability and Resilience Framework for Small States', in D. Bynoe-Lewis, *Building the Resilience of Small States: A Revised Framework*. London: Commonwealth Secretariat.

Christensen, T.A., Freireich, S., Kolar, J. and Nybergh, P. (2012) 'Peer-Review of the Estonian Research and Innovation System Steady Progress towards Knowledge

Society. Expert Group Report prepared for the European Research Area Committee', *Innovation Studies 19/2012*. Tallinn: Ministry of Economic Affairs and Communications. Available at: www.hm.ee/index.php?popup=download&id=11652 (accessed 23 January 2015).

European Commission. (2015) *Country Report: Estonia 2015*. Available at: http://ec.europa.eu/europe2020/pdf/csr2015/cr2015_estonia_en.pdf (accessed 23 January 2015).

Foray, D., David, P. and Hall, B. (2009) 'Smart Specialisation – The Concept', *Knowledge Economists Policy Brief 9*. Available at: http://ec.europa.eu/invest-in-research/pdf/download_en/kfg_policy_brief_no9.pdf (accessed 23 January 2015).

INNO-Policy TrendChart. (2009) *Innovation Policy Progress Report: Estonia*. Available at: http://s3.amazonaws.com/zanran_storage/www.proinno-europe.eu/ContentPages/550748785.pdf (accessed 23 January 2015).

Innovation Union Scoreboard. (2015) Available at: http://ec.europa.eu/growth/industry/innovation/facts-figures/scoreboards/files/ius-2015_en.pdf (accessed 23 January 2015).

International Monetary Fund. (2009) *Republic of Estonia: Staff Report for the 2009 Article IV Consultation*. Available at http://www.imf.org/external/pubs/ft/scr/2010/cr1004.pdf (accessed 23 January 2015).

International Monetary Fund. (2015) *Republic of Estonia: Staff Concluding Statement of the 2015 Article IV Mission*. Available at: http://www.imf.org/external/np/ms/2015/101915.htm (accessed 23 January 2015).

Kalvet, T. (2010) 'Business Models of the Largest Enterprises in a Small Country Context: The Case of Estonia', *Halduskultuur*, 11(1): 128–151.

Kalvet, T. (2012) 'Innovation: A Factor Explaining E-government Success in Estonia', *Electronic Government, an International Journal*, 9(2): 142–157.

Kalvet, T. (2013) *Country Report on Achievements of Cohesion Policy: Estonia*. Expert Evaluation Network Delivering Policy Analysis on the Performance of Cohesion Policy 2007–2013. Brussels: DG Regional Policy.

Kattel, R. (2004) 'Valitsemine innovatsioonipoliitikas: Eesti näide', in V. Pettai and E. Illing, *Valitsemine ja hea valitsemine: konverentsi kogumik*. Tallinn: Poliitikauuringute Keskus Praxis, 53–71.

Kattel, R. and Raudla, R. (2013) 'The Baltic Republics and the Crisis of 2008–2011', *Europe–Asia Studies*, 65(3): 426–449.

Karo, E. and Kattel, R. (2014) 'Public Management, Policy Capacity, Innovation and Development', *Brazilian Journal of Political Economy*, 34(1): 80–102.

Laakso, S., Kostiainen, E., Kalvet, T. and Velström, K. (2013) *Economic Flows between Helsinki-Uusimaa and Tallinn-Harju Regions*. Available at: www.kaupunkitutkimusta.fi/wp-content/uploads/2013/12/Helsinki-Tallinna+talousvirrat.pdf (accessed 23 January 2015).

Laar, M. (2008) 'Leading a Successful Transition: The Estonian Miracle', *European View*, 7(1): 67–74.

Lanzavecchia, A. and Pavarani, E. (2015) 'Democracy or Euro: Who Will Surrender?' *Working Paper EF 02/2015*, Department of Economics, Università degli Studi di Parma: Available at: http://swrwebeco.econ.unipr.it/RePEc/pdf/III_2015-02.pdf (accessed 23 January 2015).

Lember, V. and Kalvet, T. (2014) 'Estonia', in V. Lember, R. Kattel and T. Kalvet (eds), *Public Procurement, Innovation and Policy: International Perspectives*. Heidelberg: Springer, 127–149.

Ministry of Education and Research, Government of Estonia. (2007) *Knowledge Based Estonia – Estonian R&D and Innovation Strategy 2007–2013*. Tartu. Available at: http://cs.ioc.ee/excs/policy/teadm-pohine-eesti2-en.pdf (accessed 23 January 2015).

Ministry of Foreign Affairs, Government of Estonia. (2014) 'Estonia: Ten Years in the European Union. Together we Have Made Estonia Bigger', Available at: http://vm.ee/en/estonia-5-years-european-union (accessed 23 January 2015).

Polt, W., Koch, P. and Wolters, A. (2007) *Evaluation of Estonian RTDI Policy Mix. Results of OMC Peer Review Report 2007. Country Report for Estonia. Innovation Studies 10*. Tallinn: Ministry of Economic Affairs and Communications.

Raagmaa, G., Kalvet, T. and Kasesalu, R. (2013) 'Europeanization and De-Europeanization of Estonian Regional Policy'. *European Planning Studies*, 22(4): 775–795.

Radoševic, S. and Reid, A. (2006) 'Innovation Policy for a Knowledge-based Economy in Central and Eastern Europe: Driver of Growth or New Layer of Bureaucracy?' in K. Piech and S. Radoševic (eds), *The Knowledge-based Economy in Central and Eastern Europe: Countries and Industries in a Process of Change*. Basingstoke: Palgrave Macmillan, 295–311.

Rõõm, T. and Urke, K. (2014) 'The Euro Changeover in Estonia: Implications for Inflation', *Eesti Pank Working Paper Series 6/2014*. Available at: https://www.eestipank.ee/sites/eestipank.ee/files/publication/en/WorkingPapers/2014/wp06_2014.pdf (accessed 23 January 2015).

Schwab, K. (ed.) (2015) *The Global Competitiveness Report 2014–2015*. World Economic Forum. Available at: http://www3.weforum.org/docs/WEF_GlobalCompetitivenessReport_2014-15.pdf (accessed 23 January 2015).

Soete, L. (2007) 'From Industrial to Innovation Policy', *Journal of Industry, Competition and Trade*, 7(3–4): 273–284.

Statistics Estonia. (2015) On-line Statistical Database. Available at: http://www.stat.ee (accessed 23 January 2015).

Suurna, M., Kattel, R. (2010) 'Europeanization of Innovation Policy in Central and Eastern Europe', *Science and Public Policy*, 37(9): 646–664.

Tiits, M., Kattel, R., Kalvet, T. (2005) *Made in Estonia*. Tartu: Institute of Baltic Studies.

Tiits, M., Kattel, R., Kalvet, T. and Tamm, D. (2008) 'Catching up, Forging Ahead or Falling Behind? Central and Eastern European Development in 1990–2005', *Innovation: The European Journal of Social Science Research*, 21(1): 65–85.

Tiits, M., Kalvet, T., and Mürk, I. (2015) 'Smart Specialisation in Cohesion Economies', *Journal of the Knowledge Economy*, 6(2): 296–319.

Tiits, M., Tamm, D. and Tõnnisson, R. (2010) 'Estonia', in *State of the Region Report 2010. The Top of Europe Recovering: Regional Lessons from a Global Crisis*. Copenhagen: Baltic Development Forum, 69–76. Available at: www.bdforum.org/cmsystem/wp-content/uploads/files/state_of_the_region_report_2010.pdf (accessed 23 January 2015).

Török, Á. (2007) 'Industrial Policy in the New Member Countries of the European Union: A Survey of Patterns and Initiatives Since 1990', *Journal of Industry, Competition and Trade*, 7(3–4): 255–271.

Veebel, V. (2014) 'European Union's Institutional Reform Options and Their Impact to a Small Member State: The Case of Estonia', *Journal of Politics and Law*, 7(3): 47–56.

Wrobel, R. (2015) 'From Independence to the Euro Introduction: Varieties of Capitalism in the Baltic States', *Central and Eastern European Journal of Management and Economics*. 3(1): 9–38.

3 Iceland and the challenge of European integration

Is European Union membership feasible?

Hilmar Þór Hilmarsson

1 Introduction

Iceland is a small island state located in the North Atlantic south of the Arctic Circle. It is a resource rich country, highly dependent on foreign trade. According to the World Bank classification, Iceland is a high income economy, but with a population of little more than 300 thousand inhabitants, it is the smallest economy within the Organisation for Economic Co-operation and Development (OECD). The country is closely tied to Europe in its foreign trade, and economic and political integration with the Union is evolving.

The question relating to the most feasible and sustainable level of participation in this integration remains a challenge for the country. Iceland is a member of the European Free Trade Association (EFTA), the European Economic Area (EEA)[1] and Schengen.[2] It was, until recently, a European Union (EU) candidate country, but in 2013 its government decided to withdrew the application for accession to the EU.

Among the sources of evidence used for the analysis in this chapter is secondary data, including analytical reports and scholarly literature. Direct observation also plays a role as the author draws on his experience and observations while living in Iceland following the domestic dialogue on EU accession. The author also draws on his experience as a Special Advisor to the Minister for Foreign Affairs in Iceland from 1995 to 1999 and as a staff member of the World Bank in Latvia from 1999 to 2003, just before Latvia, another small country, became an EU member state.

The author also conducted interviews and collected information at the European Central Bank in June 2015 and at the European Commission and EFTA in July 2015. This information cannot be evaluated on the basis of statistical significance and one should be careful about generalizing or projecting the findings of one case study onto another case or situation. However, some lessons from the study could have wider relevance for other small states with limited institutional capacity and highly exposed to external shocks.

The organization of the chapter is as follows: Section 2 describes the economy of Iceland and also discusses the current stage of integration with the EU. It also assesses Iceland's characteristics as a small state. Section 3 discusses the impact of the 2008 global financial crisis on Iceland, and describes the current performance of the economy. Section 4 deals with the possible benefits and disadvantages of Iceland joining the EU and subsequently the euro area. Section 5 concludes the chapter with an overview of Iceland's future prospects and addresses the question as to whether or not Iceland should continue to rely on the current EEA arrangement or else seek EU membership.

2 The economy of Iceland and its state of integration

2.1 The economy of Iceland

The Icelandic economy is the smallest within the OECD. Its size is about 0.1% of the US economy, 4% of the Danish economy, and 25% of the economy of Luxembourg, while it is more than 50% larger than the economy of Malta (Central Bank of Iceland (CBI), 2014).

Iceland is a high income country with a gross national income (GNI) per capita in 2014 of US$43,930 (World Bank, 2014). In terms of Purchasing Power Parities (PPP), its GNI per capita is the 22nd highest in the world and the 13th highest among the OECD countries (CBI, 2014).

The country has an area of 103,000 km^2 and, with a population of 329,100 (as on 1 January 2015), its population density is very low at 3.2 persons per square kilometre. Politically, Iceland is a constitutional republic, with a president as Head of State and a Prime Minister as Head of Government. Iceland is considered as a Nordic country and has the characteristics of a Nordic welfare state.

Historically, Iceland's prosperity has to a large extent been built on comparative advantage in its marine and energy (hydro and geothermal power) resources with investment and services as the main drivers of growth. Tourism has soared over the past few years and has become one of the main engines of export growth. In fact, tourism has established itself as the third pillar of the Icelandic economy (in addition to the fisheries and energy sectors), and as a result, Iceland's economy has become increasingly diversified. Currently Iceland's largest trading partner countries are the Netherlands, Germany, Norway, the USA, and the UK (CBI, 2014). The euro area constitutes the largest trading partner.

Over the past 10 years, the Icelandic labour market has had a participation rate consistently above 85%, one of the highest among OECD countries. In 2013, female participation was one of the highest in the OECD countries, with women accounting for 48% of the labour force. Participation rates among the young and the elderly have also been quite high (CBI, 2014). Unemployment is also low compared to EU member states and currently is about 4%.

While Iceland participates in European integration via EFTA and the EEA agreement, its history shows that it is sceptical about the benefits derived from participation in international organizations and has not built a strong institutional capacity to cooperate on a multilateral basis. This in not only true with regard to EU-membership scepticism, but also with regard to other multilateral arrangements; in fact Iceland has not sought membership in institutions that other Nordic countries actively participate in, including the regional development banks.[3] Iceland tends to favour more informal multilateral arrangements, bilateralism and sometimes unilateralism during times of crisis (e.g. Hilmarsson, 2014).

2.2 Iceland, the EU and the EEA

The Nordic and Baltic States,[4] all of which are small countries, have chosen different levels of European integration, as shown in Figure 3.1. Norway and Iceland have the lowest level of integration, while the Baltic States and Finland, the highest.

Although Iceland and Norway, which are both EEA members, do not have the right to participate directly in the political decision making within the EU institutions, the EEA Agreement provides their experts with the opportunity to contribute to the shaping of EU legislation at the preparatory stage. This is done via participation in the European Commission's expert groups and committees. These groups advise the European Commission on the drafting

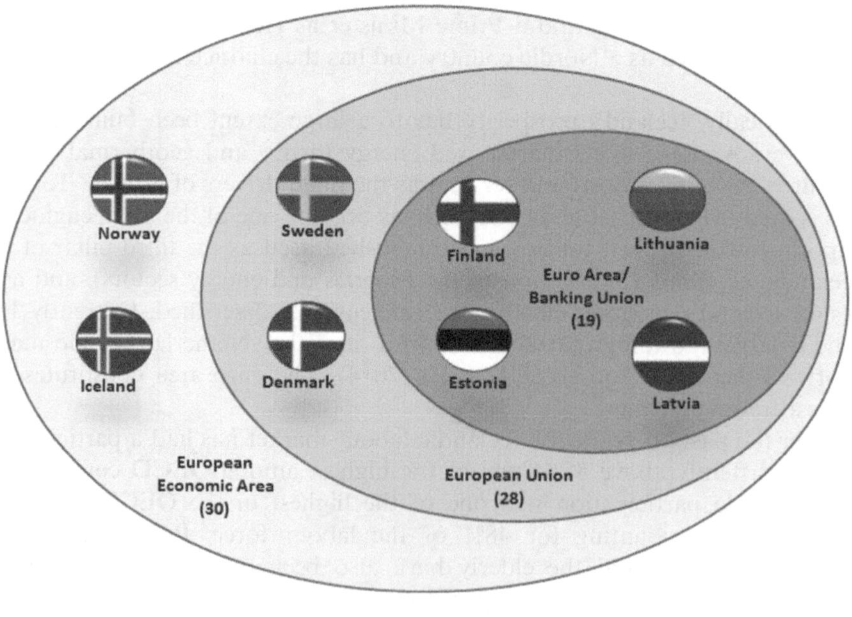

Figure 3.1 Level of integration of Baltic and Nordic States
Source: Constructed by the author.

of new laws, which the EU Council of Ministers and the European Parliament may subsequently adopt.

The participation of EEA experts and representatives in over 500 of these committees and groups is a valuable opportunity to acquire information and contribute to new legislative proposals at the earliest stages of policy formation (EFTA, 2014). This, however, means that the EEA States need to allocate sufficient human resources to take full advantage of this opportunity and this has been a challenge for Iceland (Gunnlaugsson, 2015). The EEA Agreement is supported with its own institutions and a formal cooperative mechanism vis-à-vis the EU institutions. The mechanism for decision shaping (Figure 3.2) has thus been formalized and if used wisely can enable the EEA States to become 'system affecting' in some cases.

2.3 Levels of economic integration

Levels of economic integration range from a free trade area (least integrative) to a customs union, to a common market and finally to an economic union (most integrative). EFTA, of which Iceland has been a member since 1970, is a free trade area and represents the loosest form of economic integration where barriers to trade among member countries are removed, but, unlike the case of a customs union, each country retains its tariff arrangements.

EFTA has three core tasks. The first is the liberalization of intra-EFTA trade. Second, the EFTA States have built networks of preferential trade relations in the world, currently consisting of 25 free trade agreements with 35 partners. Third, three of the four EFTA States – Iceland, Liechtenstein and Norway – are parties to the EEA Agreement,[5] which ensures their participation

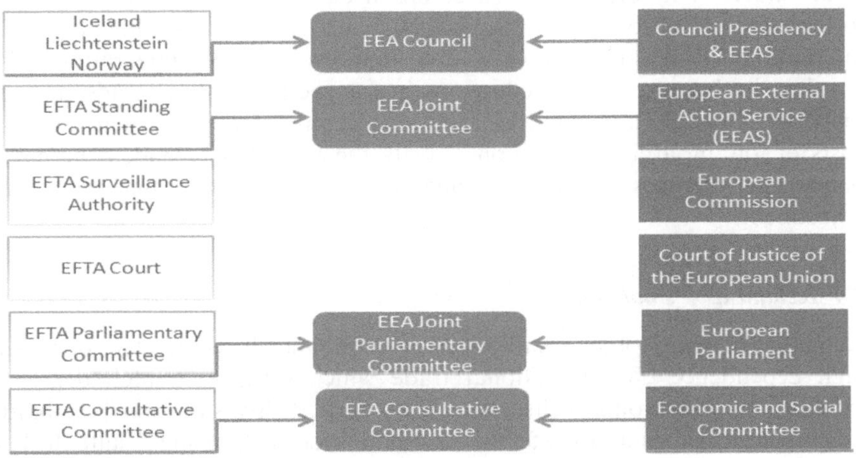

Figure 3.2 Decision shaping under the Two-Pillar Structure of the EEA Agreement
Source: EFTA, 2014.

Table 3.1 European Free Trade Association (EFTA) membership through the years

1960	Austria, Denmark, Norway, Portugal, Sweden, Switzerland and the United Kingdom establish EFTA
1970	Iceland becomes a member of EFTA
1972	Denmark and the United Kingdom leave EFTA to join the European Economic Community (EEC)
1985	Portugal leaves EFTA to become a member of the EEC
1986	Finland becomes a full member of EFTA
1991	Liechtenstein becomes a member of EFTA
1995	Austria, Finland and Sweden leave EFTA to join the EU

Source: EFTA, 2014.

in the internal market of the European Union[6] (EFTA, 2014). Over the years EFTA has lost most of its members, who chose closer economic integration by joining the EU.

The EU is moving towards an economic union. This involves not only abolition of tariffs and quotas among members (like in the case of a tree trade area such as EFTA), but also common tariff and quota systems, abolition of restrictions of factor movements, as well as harmonization and unification of economic policies (including monetary and fiscal policies) and institutions. The formation of an economic union requires nations to surrender a large measure of their national sovereignty to supranational authorities in union-wide institutions.

The level of integration varies among countries within the EU as 19 out of 28 member states have adopted the euro as their common currency and sole legal tender.[7] The formation of a common currency area can bring benefits to the members of the currency union, particularly if there is a high degree of international trade among them (i.e. a high level of trade integration). This is primarily because of the reductions in transaction costs in trade and the reduction in exchange rate risk and uncertainty. However there are also costs of joining a currency union, mostly the loss of independent monetary policy and the loss of the exchange rate as a means of macroeconomic adjustment.

2.4 Iceland as a small state

Iceland, like many other small states, is economically vulnerable, due to its high dependence on international trade which leads to a high degree of exposure to forces outside its control. Its limited diversification possibilities exacerbate its exposure to external economic shocks. As a small state, Iceland also faces constraints associated with its limited ability to reap the benefits of economies of scale, and hence, it cannot compete in certain forms of production which require large runs for efficient production. In addition, it also suffers from the problem of indivisibility, in that certain overhead costs, including those associated with public administration and the infrastructure cannot be downscaled in proportion to the population. There is a large and growing body of literature on the economic aspects of vulnerability (e.g. Briguglio, 1995; Santos Paulino, 2010).

Small states are also politically vulnerable. Iceland, as a small state has limited institutional capacity, which renders it problematic for Iceland to work with large multilateral organizations. In fact Iceland favours small multilateral structures such as EFTA, Nordic cooperation, and bilateralism if possible. It has also resorted to unilateralism, as was the case during the 2008 financial crises (Hilmarsson, 2014).

Iceland is vulnerable when larger nations, including EU and EU member states use strong-arm tactics to resolve disputes. There is a tendency within the EU to exercise authority with unilateral force, sanctions and threats. This was the case with the Icesave dispute[8] as well as when Iceland has had disputes with the EU on the utilization of fisheries sources.

Nordic cooperation is important for Iceland and Iceland cooperates closely with Nordic countries and the Baltic States in multilateral institutions such as the World Bank, International Monetary Fund (IMF) and the European Bank for Reconstruction and Development (EBRD). However, the 2008 crisis showed that Nordic countries are unreliable partners when under pressure from larger EU states.

Small states as well as large states have a choice to engage in bilateral negotiations and/or multilateral arrangements to address issues that cannot be resolved within their borders. Bilateral negotiations are carried out between two nations focusing only on their interests. On the other hand, multilateralism is the international governance of the many, and in the case of the EU, 28 member states, large and small. Multilateral negotiations open up the possibility for small states along with larger states to participate in international decision making. According to Thorhallsson, a leading scholar on small states, the small states literature generally claims that it is beneficial for small states to concentrate on multilateral relations within international organizations (Thorhallsson, 2005).

The views on this issue vary. When discussing multilateralism Kahler (1992: 681) stated that 'Smaller, weaker states were believed to be disadvantaged by bilateralism' and 'In their formal institutional design at least, most post-war multilateral institutions incorporated a larger role in decision making for states that were not great powers and could not aspire to be'. When discussing small states as aid donors, Hoadley (1980: 129) predicted high levels of participation by small states in multilateral agencies. This would apply to the United Nations (UN) as well as multilateral development banks. More recently, Evans and Newnham (1998: 500–501) argued that small states are said to have limited involvement in world affairs, favour intergovernmental organizations, are advocates of international law, shy away from the use of military force and in general have limited, mostly regional, foreign policy priorities.

Finally, Maass (2009: 69) states that 'Membership and participation in international governmental organizations is not only a frequent priority of small states, but it has also been discussed as an indicator of independence, and as such as a secondary definitional requirement for small states in particular'.

A group of small states, acting together, can also be influential as Ingebritsen (2006: 1) contends when discussing Scandinavian countries. This author argues that 'these states exercise collective authority beyond their borders that exceed their military or economic might' and that Scandinavians are likely to be found in groups that seek to strengthen international institutions. Scandinavian countries are indeed active participants in the UN and in multilateral development banks and among them Denmark, Finland and Sweden are EU members and give high priority to active participation within the EU institutional systems.

Keohane (1969: 295–296) suggests that we focus on the systemic role that state leaders see their countries playing. This is critical in understanding the impact that countries can have on the international community. Keohane uses the following categories: 'system-determining' when a state plays a critical role in shaping the international system; 'system-influencing' are states that cannot expect individually to dominate the international system but may be able to influence it through unilateral or multilateral action; 'system-affecting' states are those that cannot affect the international system if acting alone but can exert significant impact on the system if working through small groups or alliances or through universal or regional international organizations; and finally 'system-ineffectual' states are those that can do little to influence the system-wide forces that affect them, except in groups which are so large that each state has minimal influence.

How can this categorization contribute to the behaviour of small states in international organizations? As Keohane (1969: 297) observes, 'a major function of international organizations – perceived by many small and middle powers – is to allow these states acting collectively to help shape developing international attitudes, dogmas and codes of proper behaviour'. For example, Iceland, acting alone or in partnership with a very large number of other countries, would have little impact and would be classified as system-ineffectual. Iceland could do little in most cases to influence system-wide forces. However, situations can exist, including international development cooperation, where small countries that work in partnership such as the Nordic-Baltic group, could become system-affecting (see, for example, Hilmarsson, 2011).

Iceland has in the past cooperated multilaterally with the Nordic countries, and parliamentarians from those countries meet regularly in joint sessions. During the Cold War, Iceland had a strong bilateral relationship with the USA which is a 'system-determining' country. This relationship still includes a bilateral defence agreement. These political ties between the two countries were critical in resolving disputes between Iceland and other countries, most notably the dispute with the UK over fisheries territories. Post-Cold War the relationship between Iceland and the USA is weaker and does not provide the shelter it did in the past. The USA defence force has also left Iceland. Unlike Denmark, Finland and Sweden and the Baltic States, Iceland an EEA EFTA country (with Norway), in not an EU member and is not sheltered by EU institutions (see Figure 3.1). There is a possibility, at least in theory, that the Nordic-Baltic countries could become system-affecting states within the EU if they were to cooperate as a group.

3 The global crisis and recent economic performance

3.1 The collapse of the Icelandic banks

Iceland was among the hardest hit economies during the global economic and financial crisis that erupted in 2008. Prior to the crisis, Iceland had experienced strong economic growth and unprecedented expansion in cross-border investments, especially in the financial sector (Hilmarsson, 2013a; 2013b). According to the IMF (2008), the consolidated assets of the three main Icelandic banks increased from 100% of GDP in 2004 to 923% at the end 2007, reflecting expansion overseas.

By the end of 2007, almost 50% of the three largest banks' assets were held abroad (IMF, 2008: 11). The banks had been privatized several years before the crisis with a light touch regulation and weak supervision in the spirit of *laissez-faire* policies. Before the crisis the government of Iceland publicly announced its ambition to turn Iceland into an international financial centre.

The three largest banks, representing about 85% of the banking system, all collapsed in just a few days in October 2008. The whole economy was severely affected by this economic turbulence. The krona sharply depreciated, GDP fell, inflation and unemployment rose and the government ran large fiscal deficits in the aftermath of the crisis (see Table 3.2). Unlike the fixed exchange rate regime and austerity programmes implemented in some EU member states, the government sought to protect the welfare system resulting in a large fiscal deficit that it hoped would only be temporary. Sharp depreciation of the local currency was expected to boost exports and GDP growth, as had happened, for example, in Finland and Sweden in the early 1990s (e.g. Hilmarsson, 2014).

3.2 Recent economic performance

By 2015, almost seven years after the crisis hit, Iceland had regained a relatively strong macroeconomic position with good growth prospects (Table 3.2). Fiscal and external balances are now in surplus and economic activity will, according to the IMF, surpass its pre-crisis peak in 2015 (IMF, 2015b). According to the Central Bank of Iceland the post-crisis contraction in GDP has reversed in full (CBI, 2015). Public debt is on a downward sustainable path. Unemployment continues to trend down, now at 4%. Growth slowed in 2014 but is expected to pick up to around 3% over 2015–2017, supported by

Table 3.2 Iceland: selected economic indicators 2007 to 2016

	2007	*2008*	*2009*	*2010*	*2011*	*2012*	*2013*	*2014**	*2015#*	*2016#*
Change in real GDP (%)	6.0	1.3	−6.8	−4.0	2.1	1.1	3.5	1.8	3.5	3.2
Unemployment rate (%)	1.0	1.6	8.0	8.1	7.1	6.0	5.4	5.0	4.0	4.0
Consumer price index (average)	5.0	12.4	12.0	5.4	4.0	5.2	3.9	2.0	0.9	2.1
Fiscal balance/GDP (%)	5.4	−0.5	−8.6	−6.4	−5.6	−3.7	−1.7	1.8	0.1	0.1
Current account balance/GDP (%)	−15.7	−28.4	−11.8	−8.4	−5.2	−4.2	5.5	4.7	6.1	4.7

Source: IMF 2010, 2012, 2015a and 2015b.

* estimated; # projected

robust domestic demand and tourism. Consumption expenditure has increased as a result of household debt relief and falling oil prices (IMF, 2015a). The IMF projects GDP growth to be 3.5% in 2015 and 3.2 in 2016.

A source of worry with regard to the Icelandic economy relates to economic stability which may be threatened with the salary increases well beyond the current economic growth rate. Large salary increases could undermine economic recovery and the competitive position of the economy, and lead to a reduction in employment (CBI, 2015). Amid low unemployment, wage pressures are building up. There is a risk that the hard earned macro stability post-crisis may be lost if increases in salaries go out of control, with rising inflation, as has repeatedly happened in Iceland over the decades.

Another issue is the granting of debt relief to homeowners by the government, which has been criticized by the IMF in that its coverage was too wide and should have been 'targeted on distressed households' (IMF 2013: 2). The debt relief effort is also seen as discriminatory against those households who chose to rent their housing and socially vulnerable families who may be in greater need of assistance than homeowners.

3.4 The outlook

According to the IMF:

> the outlook for growth is positive. The economy will grow at around 3% during 2015–2017 under baseline assumptions of large energy-intensive investment projects, robust growth in private consumption boosted by household debt relief, and further expansion of the tourism sector. Terms of trade, consumption, and growth in 2015 will benefit from a sharp decline in oil prices. Investment will be funded by FDI, retained earnings, and, increasingly over time, borrowing. Inflation is expected to stay below 1% this year and rise gradually to target by the end of 2016, as the effects from imported deflation and currency appreciation dissipate and pressures from wages and a closing output gap mount.
>
> (IMF, 2015: 7)

The Central Bank of Iceland projects even stronger GDP growth rate than the IMF, namely 4.5% in 2015 and 3.5% in 2016 (CBI, 2015).

Iceland is highly dependent on international trade mostly due its small domestic market, and has a narrow range of exports rendering it highly exposed to external shocks. This could be reduced by improved diversification, including in sectors generating foreign exchange.

In its discussions with the IMF, the government has expressed deep concerns about the upcoming collective wage bargaining round and implications for stability. Price stability is still within the Central Bank of Iceland target and is helped by disinflation in key trading partners, particularly the euro area, a slump in oil prices, and an appreciating currency in the context of high exchange rate pass-through. If these conditions change, Iceland is likely to be highly impacted.

Iceland has been under capital controls for almost seven years. Strong macroeconomic fundamentals and a healthy financial sector are among the keys for successful capital account liberalization. As the IMF has recently stated:

> Liberalization of the capital account under a revised strategy could pick up pace, boosting confidence and private investment and raising long-term growth – but missteps could lead to a disorderly unwinding or even prolonged controls. Wage demands in the upcoming round of collective bargaining could lead to further strikes, and resulting wage hikes could increase inflation and weaken competitiveness.
>
> (IMF, 2015b: 8)

The question remains whether Icelanders have learned anything from the past – or if the economy will return to the boom and bust scenario yet again as it has for decades and most recently during the 2008 crisis.

4 Advantages and disadvantages of EU membership for Iceland

4.1 Iceland applies to join the EU

Iceland applied for EU membership in July 2009 and began accession negotiations just a year later. The current government that took office in May 2013 decided to put the accession negotiations on a complete hold, dissolved the negotiating structures, and commissioned an assessment of the accession process as well as of developments in the EU (Ministry for Foreign Affairs, 2015). When accession negotiations stopped 27 out of 33 chapters had been opened, out of which 11 have been provisionally closed. Of the six non-opened chapters, negotiating positions were in place for two of them (Institute of Economic Studies, University of Iceland, 2014).

Had negotiations resumed, Iceland would have faced serious and contentious issues relating to the fisheries policy and agriculture, issues that potentially could have derailed an agreement. Since these most difficult chapters were never opened it is hard to say what the outcome of the negotiations between Iceland and the EU on these chapters would have been. Also, if an agreement was reached, the accession treaty would still require ratification by every EU state and be subject to a national referendum in Iceland. Public support for EU accession measured by opinion polls has fluctuated, but at the time of writing this chapter, it is certainly low.[9]

4.2 Benefits of joining the EU

Among the key benefits of joining the EU is access to the common market. Iceland already enjoys this benefit via the EEA agreement, i.e., free flow of goods, services, capital and people across national borders. Iceland was also able to avoid the collapse of the Nordic Passport Union via its membership in Schengen. It thus enjoys many of the benefits (some would say most) of economic integration without EU membership.

In the future there could be questions about the sustainability of the EEA. Will the EU still respect the EEA agreement in the coming decades or is it only a temporary arrangement? Here partnership with Norway in EEA EFTA is critical. Should Norway become a member of the EU, Iceland would hardly have the capacity to engage in negotiations with the EU alone or with Lichtenstein. Being a member of the EU, Iceland could be more confident that the benefits of access to the single market would be in place in the longer term. Membership would also ensure regular consultations and participation in EU decision making instead of continuing to receive instructions via email from Brussels. Regular consultations could help a small country with limited institutional capacity to increase administrative professionalism.

EU membership could also possibly shield Iceland during times of crisis, both economically and in terms of security. There is a greater need for outside support/shield given weaker ties with the USA in the post-Cold War era. Closer cooperation with EU member states and support from EU institutions could contribute to stability for Iceland, given its history of economic boom and bust.

The risks associated with small population, including close ties between individuals that can result in corruption and rent seeking, could be reduced with EU membership. During the 2008 crisis there was loss of confidence in the Icelandic political and institutional system. General elections took place in the spring of 2009 and an EU application followed three months later. This is hardly a coincidence.

EU membership would mean that Iceland could possibly, after two years of membership, join the euro area. Currently Iceland does not participate in the EU's monetary system and cannot adopt the euro and remain in good standing with the EU at the same time. The adoption of the euro unilaterally does not seem to be a viable option (e.g. Buiter, 2000; European Central Bank (ECB), 2008). The exchange rate of the local currency has fluctuated greatly in the past, and during the 2008 capital controls were introduced as a temporary measure, although they are still in place almost seven years after the crisis. The government has recently announced plans to abolish these controls.[10]

4.3 Disadvantages of joining the EU

The main bones of contention, as far as Iceland is concerned, relate to the EU's Common Fisheries Policy (CFP) and Common Agriculture Policy (CAP). As already mentioned, these potentially most difficult chapters were not opened during accession negotiations so it is impossible to say if a compromise could have been reached and at what cost to Iceland. By staying out of the EU, Iceland avoids implementing the CFP and CAP of the EU. The nation is divided with regard to support for EU membership. Membership of the EU has stronger support by employers outside the fishing industry and agriculture. The political importance of the agriculture sector in Iceland is much greater than its economic contribution would suggest.

If Iceland becomes a member of the EU, its influence within such a large institutional structure would be minimal. In fact, given its small size, influence via membership would be a token benefit only. Of course one could argue that Iceland would have more influence in this matter than its size would suggest as a result of degressive proportionality in the EU parliament and representation in the European Commission. Nevertheless Iceland's influence within the EU would remain small.

Iceland would also have a very limited influence in the euro area economy should it adopt the euro. A common currency would have limited Iceland's possibilities to respond to the 2008 crisis when depreciation of the króna played an important role in bringing about adjustment of Iceland's trade deficit. Of course Iceland could join the EU but not adopt the euro like Denmark and Sweden have done and then at least in theory go for depreciation if deemed necessary.

Small states have experienced difficulties in dealing with the larger EU states and EU institutions and this became very clear during the 2008 crisis. Large EU states, supported by the EU institutions, did not hesitate to use strong-arm tactics against small states. An example of this was the EU's handling of the crisis in Ireland and Latvia. The UK and the Netherlands, supported by the EU also used strong-arm tactics against Iceland during the so-called Icesave dispute. This dispute had negative effects on popular sentiment in Iceland towards the EU and European nations, including the Nordic countries, as the latter countries supported the Netherlands and UK in the dispute with Iceland during the crisis.

When discussing Iceland's response to the crisis, the European Central Bank commented as follows:

> When Iceland's policy response in the wake of the crisis is compared with that of other affected countries, there are two measures that stand out most. First, Iceland introduced capital controls to protect itself from the worst repercussions of the sudden reversal of capital flows that it faced at the end of 2008, a strategy that has possibly aided its subsequent recovery. However, as time goes by, evidence is mounting regarding the distortive and often detrimental effects that these restrictions are having on the decision-making of economic agents and the difficulties that Iceland's authorities face in decisively reducing the substantial stock of krónur that continues to be held offshore and returning to a fully liberalized capital account in the near future. Second, Iceland decided not to nationalise the debts of its oversized banking sector, instead opting to inflict losses on its financial institutions' creditors and foreign depositors. Although this

> saved the government from assuming liabilities that would potentially have been beyond its debt-servicing capacity, it also opened the door to a series of legal challenges (with final decisions still pending in some instances), thereby introducing a significant degree of uncertainty for authorities, businesses, foreign investors and the general public.
>
> (ECB 2012: 97)

This comment could be viewed as some sort of advice from the EU to the Icelandic authorities. But one could also view it as a warning, implying that a small nation that does not yield to the EU and its larger member states will sooner or later suffer the consequences, as happened in the cases of Latvia and Ireland. Such comments may not have increased the confidence Icelanders have in the EU.

Eventually the Icesave dispute went to the EFTA Court[11] which ruled in Iceland's favour. After receiving the court ruling the Icelandic Ministry for Foreign Affairs commented as follows:

> The EFTA Court ruling on Icesave rejected all claims by the EFTA Surveillance Authority that Iceland should be declared in breach of the EEA Agreement. The Court rejected the claim that Iceland has breached the Deposit Guarantee Directive or has discriminated against depositors contrary to EEA law. It is a considerable satisfaction that Iceland's defence has won the day in the Icesave case; the EFTA Court ruling brings to a close an important stage in a long saga.
>
> (Ministry for Foreign Affairs, 2013)

Had Iceland yielded to EU demands this could have brought its debts to an unsustainable level.

Several scholars have commented on the damaging effect the Icesave dispute had on Iceland's sentiments towards the EU. Thorhallsson and Rebhan (2011) contend that while Iceland struggled to obtain assistance from the International Monetary Fund, Britain and the Netherlands allegedly blocked such assistance on a number of occasions, with the formal and informal approval of other European states. Professor Gylfi Magnússon, who served as a Minister for Economic Affairs in the government coalition after the crisis hit Iceland, commented that the attitudes of Britain and the Netherlands were very hard for Icelanders to accept and they undermined support for EU membership in Iceland (Magnusson, 2010).

The EU's handling of the euro crisis may also have dissuaded Icelanders from seeking EU accession. Currently one can say that the EU is faced with three crises: (i) a financial crisis, including a banking and a debt crisis, (ii) an economic policy crisis, including austerity programmes, cutting welfare programmes and increasing taxes, and (iii) a political crisis, where market forces compete against democracy. Post crisis economic performance in the EU is characterized by slow economic growth, long term unemployment (especially among the youth) and increasing income inequality. It is unlikely that Iceland will want to join during this current period of uncertainty.

5 Conclusions

The Icelandic economy is recovering from the 2008 global economic and financial crisis and is, according to the IMF (2015b), expected to surpass pre-crisis GDP levels in 2015. According to the Central Bank of Iceland this has already happened. Current economic growth is healthy and unemployment is low compared with high income EU countries. The economy is now better diversified than it was a decade ago. In terms of foreign exchange revenues it is based mainly on three main pillars, (i) the traditional fisheries sector, (ii) aluminium production using domestic clean energy sources, and (iii) a flourishing tourism sector. However, challenges remain, including the removal of capital controls imposed during the crisis and salary increases that could result in inflation above the CBI inflation target.

When the 2008 crisis hit the country, there was a certain loss in confidence in the Icelandic institutional systems, leading to the EU application submitted by the government in July 2009. One can argue that this included the recognition that Iceland needs to be shielded by stronger, more competent and less corrupt institutions and that EU membership could provide that shield and increased professionalism.

Iceland clearly benefits from the access to the EU common market via the EEA agreement, enjoying gains from trade and economies of scale. This is possible as long as the EU is willing to respect the EEA agreement and as long as Norway is part of the EEA agreement. Without Norway, Iceland would not have the institutional capacity to cooperate with the EU under the agreement and given the small size of Iceland and Lichtenstein it is doubtful if the EU would be interested in such cooperation.

Should Iceland become a member of the EU it is clear that the union would only give a small weight to Iceland in its decision-making arrangements relative to its small population and economic size. This would also apply to the ECB, should Iceland eventually become a member of the euro area. According to Keohane's theory, Iceland as an EU member would fall under the 'system-ineffectual states' category, i.e. those states that can do little to influence the system-wide forces that affect them, except in groups which are so large that each state has minimal influence. Iceland could strive to become a 'system-affecting state', i.e. among those states that cannot affect the international system if acting alone, but can exert some impact on the system by working through small groups or alliances.

Cooperation with like-minded nations, especially the Scandinavian countries, and to some extent the Baltic States, could be an option for strengthening the voice of Iceland within the EU. These countries cooperate within the World Bank, the IMF and the EBRD (Hilmarsson, 2011). However, during times of crisis, experience shows that Iceland cannot rely on support from these small states, which are more likely to follow their own interests or those of larger more powerful EU member states. This became clear during the 2008 crisis and also when the Nordic countries failed to strongly support Iceland during its fisheries disputes with the UK.

As stated, Iceland has always been reluctant to participate actively in international organizations unless the benefits from such participation are clear, such as in the North Atlantic Treaty Organization (NATO), where membership of this organization involves a bilateral defence agreement with the USA, with both security and economic benefits attached.

History shows that Iceland has preferred to use bilateral relations in solving its problems in the past – and during crises it also has made unilateral moves. Iceland has not hesitated to take action on its own against larger nations or groups of nations including during the so-called Cod Wars[12] and during the 2008 global crisis. These unilateral actions have been successful. This contradicts the small states literature that generally claims that it is beneficial for small states to concentrate on multilateral relations within international organizations. The Icesave dispute also shows that protection that can be extended by the EU could come at a high price, as has been the case of Latvia and Ireland during the euro crisis.

The question remains as to what is the most feasible arrangement for Iceland's long-term prosperity. This depends in part on whether access to the common market remains via the EEA agreement. The slow growth, high unemployment and ongoing crisis in some EU member states do not make EU membership attractive at least in the short term.

EFTA membership and the EEA agreement appear to have been the best arrangement for Iceland, and may still be so at present. The EEA agreement, shaped under the two-pillar structure of EEA and EFTA bodies, that in many ways match those of the EU free movement arrangements in the internal market, has so far served Iceland well.

However, this can change in the medium or long-term and the decision made by the government of Iceland that the country should not be considered a candidate or potential EU candidate country may have been unwise. Iceland should not take any decisions that cannot be reversed in the future given how quickly the global environment can change.

Notes

1 The EFTA consists of four members, namely Iceland, Liechtenstein, Norway, and Switzerland. The first three are also members of the EEA, excluding Switzerland, which has separate agreements with the EU.

2 The Schengen Area comprises most European Union member states as well as the four EFTA members who agreed to abolish passport and other types of border control at their respective borders, and apply a common visa arrangement called Schengen Visa.

3 These are the African Development Bank, the Asian Development Bank and the Inter-American Development Bank.

4 The Nordic States are Denmark, Finland, Iceland, Norway, and Sweden. The Baltic States are Estonia, Latvia and Lithuania.

5 The EEA Agreement does not include the following EU policies: Common Agriculture and Fisheries Policies; Customs Union; Common Trade Policy; Common Foreign and Security Policy; Justice and Home Affairs (the EFTA States are part of the Schengen area); Economic and Monetary Union.

6 The EEA EFTA States do not have the right to participate in the political decision making within the EU institutions. The EEA Agreement does, however, provide the EEA EFTA State experts with the opportunity to contribute to the shaping of EU legislation (EFTA, 2014).

7 The members of the euro area are Austria, Belgium, Cyprus, Estonia, Finland, France, Germany, Greece, Ireland, Italy, Latvia, Lithuania, Luxembourg, Malta, the Netherlands, Portugal, Slovakia, Slovenia and Spain.

8 The Icesave dispute related to the demand by Britain and the Netherlands that the government of Iceland provided sovereign guarantee for the obligations of the privately owned Icelandic bank Landsbanki when it went bankrupt in October 2008.

9 A public opinion poll conducted in Iceland by Capacent Gallup in March 2014 showed that 37% of those asked were in favour of EU membership, 47% were against and 16% did not express an opinion. http://www.visir.is/assets/pdf/XZ1509313.PDF. An overview of opinion polls conducted by Capacent Gallup in Iceland between 2006 and 2013 clearly show a deteriorating support for EU membership in Iceland post crisis. This overview was prepared by Samtök Iðnaðarins, see http://web.archive.org/web/20130601051702/http://www.si.is/malaflokkar/althjodlegt-samstarf/evropumal/skodanakannanir/.

10 See, for example, a recent government report: 'Progress of the Plan for Removal of Capital Controls'. A report as provided for in Act No. 16/2013 of the Althingi, available at: http://www.ministryoffinance.is/media/frettatengt2015/Progress-of-the-Plan-for-Removal-of-Capital-Controls-September-2015.pdf.

11 The EFTA Court, based in Luxembourg, corresponds to the Court of Justice of the European Union in matters relating to the EEA EFTA States. The Court deals with infringement actions brought by the EFTA Surveillance Authority (ESA) against an EEA EFTA State with regard to the implementation, application or interpretation of an EEA rule. The Court also handles the settlement of disputes between two or more EEA EFTA States. It hears appeals against decisions taken by the ESA and gives advisory opinions to courts in the EEA EFTA States on the interpretation of EEA rules (EFTA, 2014).

12 These 'wars' were a series of confrontations and disputes between the United Kingdom and Iceland related to claims by both countries to territorial waters and fishing rights in the North Atlantic. The disputes were concluded in Iceland's favour.

References

Briguglio, L. (1995) 'Small Island Developing States and Their Economic Vulnerabilities', *World Development*, 23(9): 1615–1632.

Buiter, W.H. (2000) 'Is Iceland an Optimal Currency Area? Central Bank of Iceland'. Working Paper, No. 10. Available at: http://www.sedlabanki.is/uploads/files/wp_10.pdf (accessed on 28 April 2015).

Central Bank of Iceland (CBI). (2014) *Economy of Iceland.* Available at: www.cb.is/publications-news-and-speeches/news-and-speeches/news/2014/09/19/Economy-of-Iceland-2014/ (accessed on 26 July 2015).

Central Bank of Iceland (CBI). (2015) *Monetary Bulletin*, 17(2). 13 May 2015. Available at: www.cb.is/default.aspx?pageid=399ea528-f88f-11e4-93fa-005056bc0bdb (accessed on 26 May 2015).

European Central Bank (ECB). (2012) 'Recent Economic and Financial Developments in EU Candidate Countries', *ECB Monthly Bulletin November 2012*. Available at: https://www.ecb.europa.eu/pub/pdf/other/art2_mb201211en_pp87-104en.pdf (accessed on 26 May 2015).

European Central Bank (ECB). (2008) 'The Adoption of the Euro: Principles, Procedures and Criteria', Speech by Jürgen Stark, Member of the Executive Board of the ECB delivered at the Icelandic Chamber of Commerce Reykjavik, 13 February 2008. Available at: https://www.ecb.europa.eu/press/key/date/2008/html/sp080213.en.html (accessed on 26 May 2015).

EFTA. (2014) *This is EFTA*. Available at: http://www.efta.int/sites/default/files/publications/this-is-efta/this-is-efta-2014.pdf (accessed on 20 May 2015).

Evans, G. and Newnham, J. (1998) *The Penguin Dictionary of International Relations.* London: Penguin Books.

Gunnlaugsson, S.H. (2015) 'Auka ber pólitískan forgang í þágu EES-samningsins' (The EEA Agreement should be given more political priority), *Þjóðmál, Tímarit um stjórnmál og menningu* (Thjodmal: Journal on Politics and Culture), Year 11, 2nd edn, Summer: 26–30.

Hilmarsson, H. (2011) 'How Can the Baltic States as Non-DAC Donors Best Contribute to International Development Cooperation?' *Baltic Journal of Economics*, 11(2): 27–40.

Hilmarsson, H.Þ. (2013a). 'The Banking Crisis in Iceland: Did the Government Pretend that Facts from Reality were Other than they Were?' in Tiia Vissak, Maaja Vadi (eds), *(Dis)Honesty in Management: Manifestations and Consequences*, Advanced Series in Management, Vol. 10, Bingley: Emerald Group Publishing Limited: 61–84.

Hilmarsson, H.Þ. (2013b). 'Small states and big banks – the case of Iceland,' *Baltic Journal of Economics*, 13(1): 31–48.

Hilmarsson, H.Þ. (2014) *Small States in a Global Economy – Crisis, Cooperation and Contributions.* Series on Economic Issues, Problems and Perspectives. Nova Science Publishers, Inc.

Hoadley, J.S. (1980) 'Small States as Aid Donors', *International Organizations*, 31(1): 121–137. Available at: www.jstor.org/stable/2706619 (accessed on 20 May 2015).

IMF. (2008) *Iceland: Financial System Stability Assessment – Update.* Available at: http://www.imf.org/external/pubs/ft/scr/2008/cr08368.pdf (accessed on 16 May 2015).

IMF. (2010) *Iceland: 2010 Article IV Consultation and Third Review under Stand-By Arrangement and Request for Modification of Performance Criteria-Staff Report* (Staff Supplement). Available at: http://www.imf.org/external/pubs/cat/longres.aspx?sk=24256.0 (accessed on 16 May 2015).

IMF. (2012) *Iceland: Staff Report for the 2012 Article IV Consultation and First Post-Program Monitoring Discussion.* Available at: http://www.imf.org/external/pubs/cat/longres.aspx?sk=25853.0 (accessed on 26 May 2015).

IMF. (2013) *Iceland 2013 – Article IV Consultations and Third Post-Program Monitoring Discussions.* Available at: http://www.imf.org/external/pubs/cat/longres.aspx?sk=40863.0 (accessed on 6 September 2015).

IMF. (2015a). *IMF Executive Board Concludes 2014 Article IV Consultation and Fifth Post-Program Monitoring Discussion with Iceland.* Available at: http://www.imf.org/external/np/sec/pr/2015/pr15114.htm (accessed on 6 May 2015).

IMF. (2015b). *Iceland: 2014 Article IV Consultation and Fifth Post-Program Monitoring Discussions-Staff Report.* Press Release and Statement by the Executive Director for Iceland. Available at: http://www.imf.org/external/pubs/cat/longres.aspx?sk=42782.0 (accessed on 2 May 2015).

Ingebritsen, C. (2006) *Scandinavia in World Politics*, Lanham, MD and Oxford: Rowman & Littlefield Publishers.

Institute of Economic Studies at the University of Iceland. (2014) *Status of the Accession Negotiation between Iceland and the EU.* Available at: www.mfa.is/status-of-the-accession-negotiations-between-iceland-and-the-eu/ (accessed on 12 May 2015).

Kahler, M. (1992) 'Multilateralism with Small and Large Numbers', *International Organizations*, 46(3): 681–708. Available at: http://www.jstor.org/stable/2706992 (accessed on 26 April 2015).

Keohane, R.O. (1969) 'Lilliputians' Dilemmas: Small States in International Politics', *International Organizations*, 23(2): 291–310.

Maass, M. (2009) 'The Elusive Definition of the Small State', *International Politics*, 46 (1): 65–83. Available at: http://www.palgrave-journals.com/ip/journal/v46/n1/abs/ip200837a.html (accessed on 26 April 2015).

Magnusson, G. (2010) *Iceland and the Importance of Becoming a Member of the EU Family.* Available at: http://www.atvinnuvegaraduneyti.is/radherra/raedurGM/nr/2826 (accessed on 26 April 2015).

Ministry for Foreign Affairs. (2013) 'Iceland Welcomes Acquittal in Icesave Case'. Available at: http://www.mfa.is/news-and-publications/nr/7515 (accessed on 26 April 2015).

Ministry for Foreign Affairs. (2015) Letter from the Minister for Foreign Affairs to the European Commission. Available at: http://www.mfa.is/media/gunnar-bragi/Bref-ESB-ENS-pdf.pdf (accessed on 26 July 2015).

Santos-Paulino, A. (2010) 'Terms of Trade Shocks and the Current Account in Small Island Developing States', *Journal of Development Studies*, 46(5): 855–887.

Thorhallsson, B. (2005) 'What Features Determine Small States' Activities in the International Arena? Iceland's Approach to Foreign Relations until the mid-1990s', *Stjórnmál og stjórnsýsla – Veftímarit, Stofnun stjórnmála og stjórnsýslu* (*Icelandic Review of Politics and Administration*), 1(1): 107–140. Available at: http://www.irpa.is/article/view/861/pdf_4 (accessed on 6 May 2015).

Thorhallsson, B. and Rebhan, C. (2011) 'Iceland's Crash and Integration Takeoff: An End to European Union Scepticism?' *Scandinavian Political Studies*, 34(1): 53–73. Available at: http://onlinelibrary.wiley.com/doi/10.1111/j.1467-9477.2010.00261.x/abstract (accessed on 6 April 2015).

World Bank. (2014) *Doing Business 2015 – Going Beyond Efficiency.* Available at: http://www.doingbusiness.org/reports/global-reports/doing-business-2015 (accessed on 26 May 2015).

4 Latvia after European Union accession

Weathering the storm?[1]

Aleksandrs Cepilovs and Lauma Muižniece

1 Introduction

Latvia is located in the North-Eastern part of Europe, on the eastern shore of the Baltic Sea, sharing its borders with Estonia, Lithuania, Russia and Belarus. The population of Latvia in 2015, according to Eurostat, amounted to approximately two million persons – it has been declining during the first two decades of Latvia's independence from its maximum of approximately 2.7 million in 1991. Latvia is relatively sparsely populated with a density of 31 inhabitants per square kilometre, spread across 64,589 square kilometres. Latvian, an Indo-European, and more specifically a Baltic language, is the official language of Latvia and one of the official languages of the European Union (EU).

Due to its strategic location and a relatively large and prosperous trading hub Riga, Latvia has over the centuries been conquered by various powers. First by the Teutonic order, then by the Polish-Lithuanian Commonwealth, by Sweden, and more recently by the Russian Empire. During the Second World War, Latvia was first briefly occupied by the Soviet Union in 1940, and invaded and occupied by Nazi Germany less than a year later, in July 1941. At the end of the war in 1944–1945 Latvia was yet again occupied by the Soviet Union, remaining a part of the Soviet Union for almost five decades, until the dissolution of the Soviet Union.

Latvia is one of the smaller economies in the European Union. With the gross domestic product (GDP) of €24,059 million (current prices, 2014), as shown in Table 4.1, Latvia is the fourth smallest EU member state, after Malta, Cyprus and Estonia.

Also in terms of per capita income, Latvia is one of the weakest performers in the EU, ranking 24th out of 28 countries, with GDP per capita of roughly €12 thousand (current prices, 2014). Latvia has a relatively high level of human development, with a rank 48th out of 187 countries in the 2014 UNDP Human Development Index.[2] According to the World Bank's income classification,[3] Latvia was classified as a upper-middle-income country up to 2012, but according to the new classification, it has joined the club of the rich, being ranked as a high-income country. As we argue below, one needs

Table 4.1 Latvia: some economic indicators

Parameter	*Value*
Population (2015)	1.986 m.
Area	64 589 km^2
GDP (2014)	€24,059 million
GDP per capita (2014)	€12100
Government debt/GDP (2014)	40%
Government budget balance/GDP (2014)	−1.4%
Balance of trade/GDP (2014)	−0.8%
Unemployment (2014)	10.2%
Employed persons/Working age population (16–64 years)	66.3%

Source: Eurostat (http://ec.europa.eu/eurostat/data/database) and Central Statistical Bureau of Latvia (http://www.csb.gov.lv/en).

only scratch the surface to see that Latvia is far from being part of the high-income club.

Latvia has not thus far attracted much attention in the literature on small states.[4] Most published studies on Latvia cover three periods, with the first relating to the collapse of the Soviet Union (e.g. Lejiņš and Ozoliņa, 1997), the second to Latvia's EU accession (e.g. Mikkel and Pridham, 2004; Schimmelfennig, Engert and Knobel, 2003), and the third and most important to the recent financial crisis and the resulting economic and fiscal crises (e.g. Aslund and Dombrovskis, 2011; Blanchard, Griffiths and Gruss, 2013; Kattel and Raudla, 2013; McCollum et al., 2013; Sommers and Woolfson, 2014). The post-crises literature covered different aspects from fiscal policy to migration to neoliberalism and economic policy more generally. Only a few studies have, implicitly or explicitly, used small country size as an explanatory variable (e.g. Cepilovs, 2014; Panke, 2010).

This chapter attempts to look at Latvia's EU accession in the wider context, by referring to the economic structure and performance of Latvian economy, covering three broad periods, starting from the country's independence (1918–1940), the Soviet period, and the pre-EU-accession years. The chapter also refers to Latvia's specific opportunities and constraints as a small country.

The chapter is organized into six sections. Section 2, which follows this introduction, deals with the structure and performance of the Latvian economy between 1918 and 1991, the year when Latvia gained its independence from the Soviet Union. Section 3 discusses the pre-accession period (1992–2004), while Section 4 deals with the consequences of Latvia's EU membership, culminating in the most recent financial and resulting economic and fiscal crises. Section 5 considers the positive and negative aspects of Latvia as a small state. Section 6 concludes this chapter with some remarks on future prospects of the Latvian economy.

2 The Latvian economy before 1991

2.1 Before the Soviet annexation

Before the Second World War, the level of economic development in Latvia, as well as its productive structure were comparable to that of Finland. The agrarian reform implemented in the early years of the first period of independence, which lasted from 1918 until 1940, helped develop a relatively productive agricultural sector. Between 1933 and 1935 Latvia had the third highest per capita level of grain production in Europe (Shteinbuka, 1993). By the end of the 1930s Latvia was running a trade surplus, to which exports of agricultural products to Western Europe contributed substantially. Thus, in 1938 exports of agricultural products reached 46.7% of total exports, of which exports of butter alone contributed 23.9%. Exports of timber as well as plywood accounted for a high share of non-agricultural exports, and these products still constitute a significant share of Latvia's exports today. At the same time imports were to a significant extent dominated by manufacturing equipment and machinery, fuel as well as artificial fertilisers (State Bureau of Statistics, 1939).

While agricultural commodities constituted the bulk of exports, Latvia did produce some sophisticated equipment relying mostly on German technology. Thus in the 1930s a radio and telephone equipment manufacturer VEF[5] was established and produced the smallest film camera in the world at the time – VEF Minox – designed by an Estonian engineer. The very same factory produced telephone exchanges that quickly substituted imported switches, and were also exported. In the mid-1930s Latvia began producing automobiles and trucks. While important on the domestic market, those goods did not constitute a significant share of exports at the time. As we argue below, the Latvian economy has gone full circle and after the collapse of the Soviet Union – it has returned to a productive structure very similar to that of the first Republic, namely one based on the export of commodities and products with relatively low value added.

Looking at the composition of the external trade of Latvia in the late 1930s, it is clear that Latvia depended to a great extent on its two main trade partners, Germany and the United Kingdom, that were jointly responsible for roughly 67% of Latvian exports and 64% of imports. The UK – the main trade partner at the time – was alone responsible for 39% of imported goods and consumed close to 40% of Latvian exports. Therefore, one can argue, the Latvian economy was already deeply integrated with the core European economies in the early twentieth century. This also made Latvia potentially vulnerable to external shocks, given its export structure, which was concentrated on very few commodities as well as on very few key trade partners.

2.2 The annexation by the Soviet Union

With the annexation by the Soviet Union, as the then existing trade relations were cut, the Latvian economy went through a gradual process of restructuring and integration into the Soviet economy. As specialization patterns across the Soviet Union were to a certain degree based on comparative advantage, Latvia retained some of the manufacturing capabilities that were developed earlier (e.g. telecommunication and radio equipment, manufacturing machinery).

After the Second World War, with Latvia forming part of the Soviet Union, the country went through a process of rapid industrialization, transforming itself from a predominantly agricultural into a predominantly industrial economy. A number of large enterprises were created, some of which developed and supplied parts for the soviet military industry that was spread throughout the entire Soviet Union. Most of the companies located in Latvia depended on the rest of the Soviet Union for both supplies of raw materials as well as markets. The structure of the economy changed substantially during the 1950s through 1960s, and went through a period of relatively rapid industrialization, retaining a more or less stable economic structure in the decades before the collapse of the Soviet Union.

The total share of industry in the Latvian economy by 1980 was estimated at 56%, which subsequently declined to roughly 50% in 1990. By 1990, Latvia was still ahead of every other Soviet republic but one – Estonia – in terms of industrial production per capita. Table 4.2 shows the sectoral composition of industrial production in that year.

Table 4.2 Sectoral composition of industrial production (1990)

	Share in industrial output (%)	*Number of firms*	*Employment (% of industrial employment)*
Total	**100**	**407**	**100**
Heavy industry	**56**	**240**	**70**
Electric power	1.6	1	1.8
Fuel	0.4	10	0.7
Steel and other metal manufacturing	1.6	4	0.9
Chemicals	7.4	15	5.7
Machinery	27.9	87	38.9
Wood processing, pulp and paper	5.4	55	9.6
Construction materials	3.1	30	4.6
Glass and porcelain	0.6	6	1.5
Light industry	**18.6**	**74**	**17**
Food	**24.7**	**89**	**12.7**
Others	**0.7**	**4**	**0.3**

Source: Central Statistical Bureau of Latvia (1990) and Eurostat (http://ec.europa.eu/eurostat/data/database).

In some sectors Latvia held monopolistic or dominant positions in the entire Soviet Union. This was the case, for example, in railway passenger cars (100% of the total production in the Soviet Union), telephone sets (53%), motorcycles (57%), but also in electric devices for the automotive industry, agricultural machinery, pharmaceutical products, small construction machinery and instruments.

In some industrial branches most of the goods produced were exported to other Soviet republics. For example, 98% of automatic telephone exchanges, 93% of motorcycles, 89% of washing machines, 79% of radio sets and other consumer audio equipment, as well as diesel engines and diesel electric power generators produced in Latvia in the late 1980s were exported to the other members of the Soviet Union. On the one hand it meant stability of demand as long as the Soviet Union existed, on the other it yet again made Latvia dependent on a very few markets and thus vulnerable should there be problems in the core markets.

Given a relatively high share of industrial activities in the economy, many of which were with relatively high value added, and also given the availability of mass education, Latvia had a well-educated and skilled workforce, especially when compared to other Soviet republics. Another two distinctive features of the Latvian labour market were a high participation rate of women in the labour market, as well as ethnical segmentation, which meant that the majority of Russian speakers were employed in industry, whereas the majority of Latvians were employed in agricultural activities (Shteinbuka, 1993).

The production system of the Soviet Union was well adapted to the dominating techno-economic paradigm of mass production. Production specialization patterns were driven to a large extent by considerations of both existing manufacturing capabilities and economies of scale, as well as agglomeration effects, given that integration into large scale vertically and horizontally integrated conglomerates was a fundamental principle of the Fordist paradigm (Perez, 2002). It was not, however, well-suited to the requirements of the contemporary paradigm of information and communication technologies, where five-year plans and vertical integration lose their relative importance due to much faster pace of technical change as well as possibilities for distributed manufacturing provided by all-pervasive information and communication technologies.

By the end of the 1980s a significant share of Latvian exports consisted of consumer goods, where Latvia's trade was in significant surplus. However, most of the goods produced were exported to other Soviet republics. Therefore, when the Soviet Union finally collapsed, Latvia, similarly to other Soviet Republics, found itself outside the existing supply chains and with no markets to sell to. While one can only speculate, whether it was the shift of techno-economic paradigms that provided the basis for dissolution of the Soviet Union, it is clear that the economies that broke away in the early 1990s, found themselves in an environment where they had to transform themselves almost entirely in order to remain afloat, or else be submerged by the wave of competition from both East and West.

3 The post-Soviet period

3.1 Latvia regains independence

Latvia followed a liberal trade regime from the very first years after regaining independence in 1991. By submitting a Trade Memorandum in preparation for accession to the World Trade Organization (WTO) and engaging in negotiations with WTO members, Latvia clearly signalled its willingness to abandon any remaining restrictions on trade and to participate in international markets on equal terms. In early 1995, a free trade agreement with the EU became effective, eliminating tariffs on the majority of industrial goods, as well as defining a schedule for reduction of tariffs on a range of agricultural products over the next five years. Liberalization of trade reached its climax in 2004 when Latvia together with nine other countries joined the EU, in which Latvia has since been an equal partner. The question, however, is whether this has led to convergence towards European levels of productivity and welfare, or whether, conversely, this has led to increasing divergence and long-term unsustainability of the Latvian economy.

3.2 The restructuring of the economy

Latvia and its northern neighbour Estonia were perhaps the most ardent proponents of shock therapy[6] as a means of restructuring the economy away from a rigid system of Soviet planning and towards a free market economy. It was, however, a shock without the subsequent therapy. Most of the Central and Eastern European (CEE) countries set off on a reform path in the early 1990s, focusing on a standard set of reforms often propagated by the Western institutions including the International Monetary Fund (IMF) and the World Bank, complemented by a range of reforms of institutional nature – the so-called 'Augmented' Washington Consensus (Rodrik, 2006). The primary emphasis of the reforms was on the liberalization of the economy. There was a clear and widely shared understanding that a move away from the past public ownership strategy towards a market economy was necessary. The reforms thus primarily focused on handing over the allocation of resources to the private sector, which was met with increasing enthusiasm both among the elites and population more generally.

The other side of the reforms was focused on containing inflation and ensuring wage and price stability, reducing the tax burden and in general strengthening the workings of the market. Following a spurt of inflation in 1991, after 1992 the Government of Latvia focused on anti-inflationary policy as part of the programme supported by the IMF. The programme, widely advocated in countries across the post-soviet space, emphasized price liberalization as well as strict fiscal, monetary and incomes policies, as a basis for economic development. These policies were effective in reaching the objectives posed. Thus, by late 1992 the consumer price index was stabilized, with the Bank of Latvia strengthening the Latvian rouble (temporary currency introduced as a passage from the Soviet rouble to Latvian lats), as well as gradually reducing interest rates for commercial lending. These policies also helped to turn both the current account and the trade balance positive, as well as keep the state budget balanced. However, while the financial conditions were showing signs of stabilization, the real economy was facing a steep cliff. At the time not many realized that rapid and deep liberalization of prices, trade barriers and elimination of state intervention would ultimately result in the collapse of output, a spike in unemployment, poverty and subsequent depopulation. Between 1990 and 1993, following the collapse of the Soviet Union, Latvia experienced a GDP per capita drop of 40% in real terms and since then lost more than 20% of the population along the way.

While many analysts ascribed the decline of output to a typical Keynesian recession, fuelled by decline in consumption (e.g. Berg et al., 1992), Calvo and Coricelli (1993) argued that it was not a normal Keynesian recession, but an effective 'trade implosion', as a result of the break from the old system of economic coordination and production. This argument served as grounds for development of the theory of optimal transition speed (e.g. Aghion and Blanchard, 1994; Tiits et al., 2008).

3.3 Trade in the aftermath of the Soviet period

Before the break-up of the Soviet Union, Latvia depended on a few Soviet republics for its exports. With the break-up of the Union, demand for goods produced in Latvia in the post-Soviet space collapsed almost instantly. The shift to world market prices for energy, oil and other raw materials resulted in adverse terms of trade with the former Soviet Union countries – the main suppliers of raw materials as well as consumers of products produced in Latvia. Sharp increases of prices on energy and raw materials resulted in rapid increases in production costs, which further exacerbated the fall of output. The volume of industrial production fell sharply, in 1992 it represented only 65% of the level of output in 1991. A similar situation could be observed in agriculture, where in 1992 output constituted just 70% of that in 1991, while at the same time prices continued to grow faster than expected. By 1993 GDP was 40% lower than the 1990 GDP (see Figure 4.1) with the largest decline in the construction industry (-65.4%).

Due to their small domestic markets, small countries are significantly more dependent on exports than larger ones. With the increasing liberalization of trade regimes across the world, larger countries have also been increasing their share in international trade, especially during the 1980s and in the following decades. This resulted in increasing competition on international markets and, as a result, a much more difficult environment for a small state like Latvia.

As Reinert and Kattel (2007, 2004) argue, the earlier wave of European integration that brought the southern countries of Greece, Italy, Spain and Portugal into the union, allowed these countries to go through a gradual

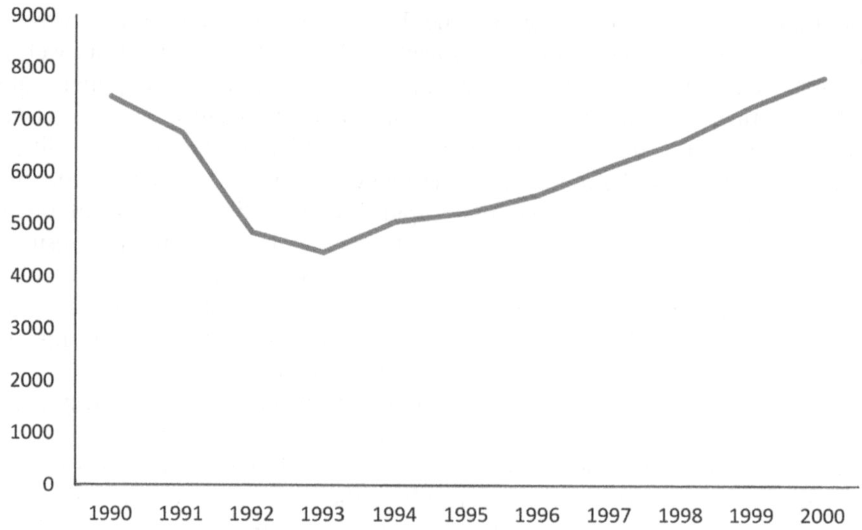

Figure 4.1 GDP at current US$ (millions)
Source: United Nations (UN) DATA and World Development Indicators (http://data.un.org/Data.aspx?d=WDI&f=Indicator_Code%3ANY.GDP.MKTP.CD), the World Bank.

adjustment process. The above-mentioned Southern European states (perhaps with the exception of Greece) were able to develop productive structures similar to those of the core countries through a period of gradual and relatively slow liberalization of their trade regimes. The integration of the Southern-European states was not however an absolute success, particularly given the effects of the recent financial crisis. They do, however, still exhibit higher levels of GDP per capita, value added and productivity than Latvia. Integration of the Southern-European states was similar to the upgrading of the East Asian countries, which went through a process of sequential technological upgrading – the so called flying geese pattern of development (see e.g. Ozawa, 2003). In the case of the Nordic countries, to use a taxonomy of integration devised by Reinert and Kattel (2004), integration was symmetrical, as all countries were at a relatively similar level of technological development, and their economies were largely built upon increasing returns activities. In the case of the Baltic States, including Latvia, and more generally across the rest of the former Socialist countries, integration was of a rather different nature.

In contrast to the previous wave of integration, Latvia opened its markets almost instantly, which did not allow for a gradual transition and restructuring of the economy. Neither did it allow Latvia to maintain and further develop the manufacturing capabilities it had in place at the time of the disintegration of the Soviet Union. By the late 1990s the proportion of GDP contributed by manufacturing declined from above 50% to around 30%.

Latvia along with other CEE countries, was integrating into a union made up of countries with substantially higher productivity levels, and thus the Latvian companies that operated in the same markets as companies from Germany or Denmark were not competing on a level playing field. This led to a so-called Vanek–Reinert effect, meaning that in the case of rapid liberalization of trade and markets between countries (or regions, as in the case of integration of East Germany with the West) with significantly different levels of development, the first to suffer will be the most advanced industries in the least advanced country (or region) (Reinert, 2004). This is what effectively happened in Latvia during the 1990s. As Figure 4.2 suggests, over the last decade, productivity in all Baltic States, including Latvia, has improved only marginally and has remained at significantly lower levels than in the more advanced European countries, but also below the EU average. Therefore, convergence of the Baltic States with the rest of Europe in terms of productivity remains a long-term objective.

While one could argue that this was an effect of the tertiarization of economy, similar to what has happened across the developed world since the 1970s, data suggest this was not the case. For high quality knowledge-intensive services to develop, manufacturing is absolutely essential, as it ensures the domestic demand necessary for development of such services (Reinert and Kattel, 2007). The deindustrialization of the 1990s did not lead to the development of knowledge-intensive services, with the exception of consumer banking, which was driven in part by the influx of non-resident finance from the East as well as the entry of several Scandinavian banks onto the market. Value added data suggest that Latvia did not develop any significant knowledge-intensive services with export potential.

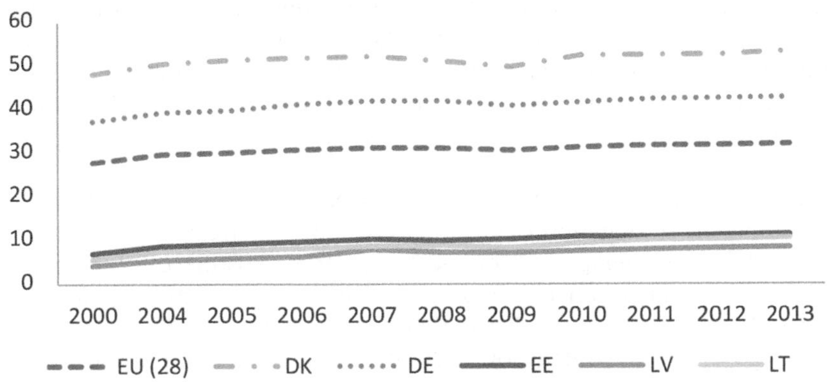

Figure 4.2 Labour productivity per hour worked (in euros)
Note: DK – Denmark; DE – Germany; EE – Estonia; LV – Latvia; LT – Lithuania.
Source: Eurostat (available at: http://ec.europa.eu/eurostat/en/web/products-datasets/-/TSDEC310).

During the 1990s the share of industrial employment and value added declined, whereas the share of services in both employment and value added increased. This structural change led to significant trade imbalances, which was, however, offset by inflow of foreign direct investment, which gradually picked up from the mid-1990s onwards.

3.4 FDI as a development strategy: promises not fulfilled

As from the early 1990s Latvian policy makers focused their attention on the attraction of foreign direct investment (FDI) as the single most important policy instrument for economic development. Many believed at the time, as many still do, that by creating an environment favourable to FDI primarily through lowering taxation and weakening regulation of business activities, FDI would instantly flow in and transform the economy, ultimately leading to prosperity. The common view was that FDI would not only bring the financial resources necessary to restructure the newly liberalizing economies, but would also provide the necessary managerial and accounting skills, technology and knowledge, as well as access to new markets that would not be accessible otherwise. It was thus argued that FDI would inevitably lead to faster economic development in countries that opened their borders to it (Porter, 1990).

Latvia was not alone in favouring such a strategy. A number of countries relied on FDI to a lesser or greater extent in order to drive the structural transformation of their economies. FDI can serve both as a source of finance to balance the current account, as well as a source of technology and knowledge necessary for economic transformation. One such mechanism for technological upgrading through foreign direct investments is integration in global value chains. However, as Tiits et al. (2008) suggest, this strategy does not necessarily and always lead to success. Unlike larger countries that are able to pool capital to achieve the minimum necessary scale, smaller countries face greater challenges as they cannot rely solely on domestic savings in order to finance development and industrialization and therefore often have to depend on foreign investment as the core source of funds.

Some countries, such as Singapore and Ireland, managed to utilize FDI as a development strategy more or less successfully (for Ireland see Buckley and Ruane, 2006; for Singapore, Lim and Pang, 1991). History offers examples of both positive and negative effects of FDI on economic development. What historical examples also suggest is that FDI operating within a broader context of government strategy or a development plan is more effective as a means to industrialization than an approach that relies on private sector driven FDI choices only.

The Latvian government did not opt for a strategic approach to FDI, but rather allowed the market actors to decide on this matter. The specific policy measures to attract FDI focused on a relatively standard set of instruments, such as tax incentives. An important factor during the early 1990s was privatization of state-owned enterprises, which, however, was not as successful as in Estonia, given the powerful domestic interests that often created obstacles for strategic foreign investors willing to invest in Latvia. Relatively low taxation was accompanied by low levels of regulation of business activity – two important FDI attractions. Other attractions offered by Latvia in this regard were the possibility of a new market and the relatively inexpensive production inputs, including labour, energy and some raw materials (Johansen, 2000).

The Nordic countries from early on perceived the Baltics as part of their home markets, resulting, since the mid-1990s, in an increasing presence of Nordic financial companies, as well as wholesale and retail operations in Latvia and the other Baltic States. Some of the companies entered Latvia directly, for others Estonia became a platform for entering the other Baltic markets, as well as Russia (Tiits, 2006). As Figure 4.3 suggests, throughout the two decades after re-independence, FDI in manufacturing remained relatively low in Latvia, staying at around 20% until 2003 and then declining steadily, as FDI flowed in the FIRE (finance, insurance and real estate)

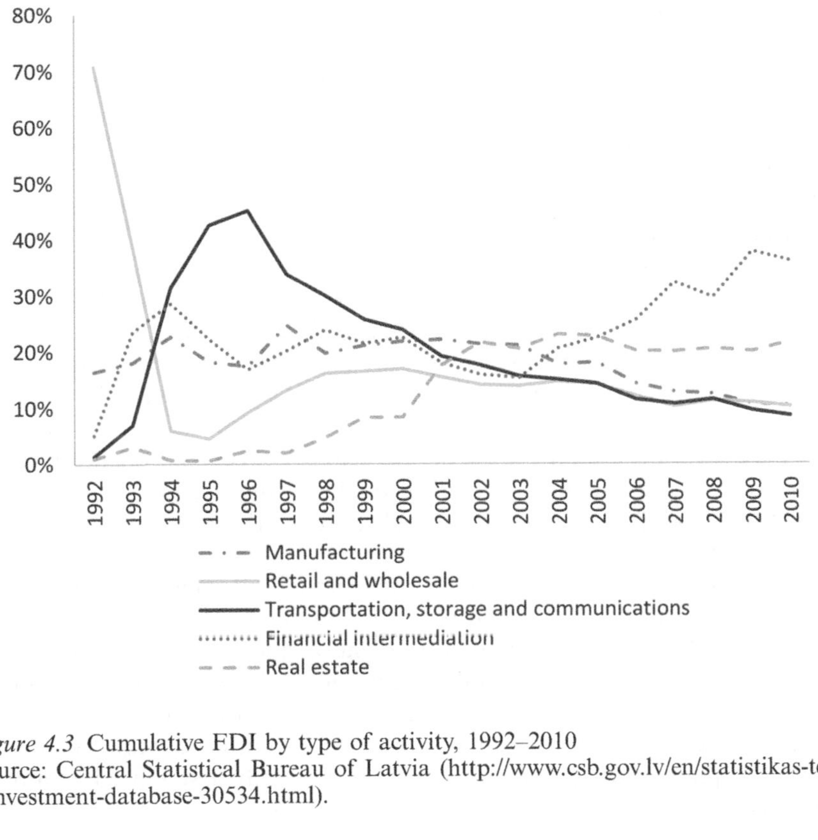

Figure 4.3 Cumulative FDI by type of activity, 1992–2010
Source: Central Statistical Bureau of Latvia (http://www.csb.gov.lv/en/statistikas-tema s/investment-database-30534.html).

sector. In manufacturing, most of foreign direct investment in Latvia went into relatively resource-intensive low-tech industries, such as wood processing, food processing, as well as textiles and clothing, and to a much lesser extent into mid-tech or high-tech manufacturing, such as electronics (Tiits, 2006). Similarly to other countries that liberalized their markets, Latvia had quickly developed substantial current account deficits and FDI played an important role in balancing both trade and current account deficits, which Latvia would not have been able to balance through exports alone.

By focusing on low taxation and low cost of inputs as the main advantage for attracting FDI, Latvia was competing on the market with a number of developing countries around the world. While Latvia did have a relatively well-educated workforce, it did not focus enough on upgrading skills and human capital more generally. It is, however, difficult to sustain a low-cost strategy in the long term, whilst at the same time trying to increase the standard of living, given that at some point the costs of inputs will eventually increase. Most of the CEE countries, including Latvia, had experienced difficulties in providing the skills necessary for enterprises operating in global production networks. The earlier experience of East and South East Asian economies suggests that focusing on the development of specific skills that are considered important for future industries is crucial to both sustaining the inflow of FDI as well as developing local industries. This also, to a degree, explains the pattern of FDI in Latvia, where most of the FDI inflow was in finance, insurance and real estate sectors, as well as retail and transportation, with a relatively small share going into low- and medium-tech manufacturing.

The inflow of FDI fuelled consumption expenditure and construction, at a time when the Latvian labour force was contracting, and this therefore led to rapid wage increases. The major European industrial countries relying on the mechanisms of a coordinated market economy,[7] managed to contain growth of labour costs at relatively low levels. This, together with growing productivity, led to divergence and not convergence of competitiveness between the 'old' and the 'new' EU member states (Hancké, 2013). As Figure 4.4 suggests, while labour costs in the 'core' countries of the EU kept stagnating, in Latvia they were growing steadily most of the years between the break-up of the Soviet Union and the financial crisis of 2008, thus severely affecting the competitiveness of local industry as well as Latvia's attractiveness as a low cost destination for FDI.

The approach adopted initially – welcoming all kinds of FDI in all industries – failed to take into account the aspects discussed above, thus failing to utilize FDI for domestic industrialization and therefore also creating a system relying on foreign capital inflows in order to balance the current account. The massive inflow of foreign investment that began in the years leading to accession to the EU, and subsequently continued until 2008 driving the consumption and real estate boom, had effectively destabilized an already fragile system.

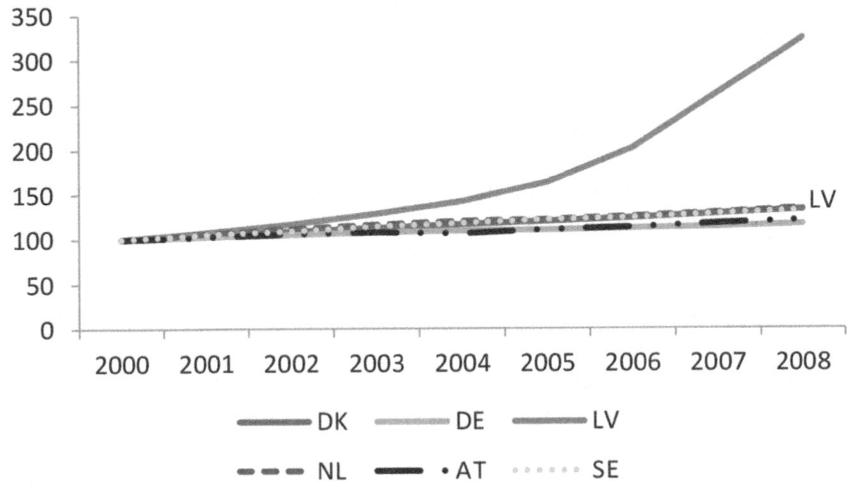

Figure 4.4 Labour cost index in Latvia compared to selected market economies (2000=100%)

Note: DK – Denmark; DE – Germany; LV – Latvia; NL – Netherlands; AT – Austria; SE – Sweden.

Source: Eurostat (available at: http://ec.europa.eu/eurostat/web/labour-market/labour-costs/main-tables).

4 Latvia as an EU member

4.1 The prelude

With the benefit of hindsight it can be said that Latvia entered the EU from a policy environment that determined the subsequent outcomes. Certain policy decisions made over the first decade of independence created a path which it was politically difficult to leave. First, it was a conscious choice to rely on liberal economic policies without creating an institutional environment necessary for the normal functioning of a market economy. Second, the decision to maintain the currency peg did not allow Latvia to develop internal capacity for effective monetary policy. Third, the choice to have a relatively low tax burden effectively limited the power of government when dealing with financial and economic crises.

During the first decade after re-gaining independence, Latvia had to re-create a market economy from scratch. However, given the already mentioned lack of resources – both financial and human – Latvia faced severe difficulties in creating an institutional environment to support the effective and efficient functioning of a market economy. The insolvency and bankruptcy law was underdeveloped, and the court system lacked, and arguably still lacks, the necessary resources in order to effectively carry out its duties. Regulations of financial markets and institutions were lax, and the capacity and capabilities of regulators were weak, resulting in a number of banking crises in the 1990s, 2008, and 2011. This, in turn, led to a very unstable economy. In contrast to its northern neighbour, Estonia, from the early 1990s Latvia developed its own oligarchy, which affected the process of privatization, the functioning of state-owned enterprises, as well as the political system. Latvia also had relatively high levels of tax evasion, which had a negative effect on both public service provision and the efficiency of the Latvian economy more generally. Therefore, EU membership offered an opportunity to strengthen the institutional environment and thus improve the efficiency of the economy.

Since the very early years of the new republic, there had been a commitment to maintain the currency peg, first to the currency basket, and later to the euro. The exchange rate at which the lats was pegged to the SDR[8] in 1994 was relatively high, which in turn had two effects on the Latvian economy: first, to the benefit of consumers, imports became relatively cheap; second, to the disadvantage of the exporting producers, their exports became more expensive, making them less competitive in their export markets. The conditions under which Latvia was integrating into the wider Europe therefore strongly resembled the conditions under which Eastern Germany integrated with Western Germany with somewhat similar consequences (see e.g. Pohl, 1991).

There was also the commitment of centre-right governments to maintain low tax burden over the last two decades, with the average tax burden fluctuating somewhere close to 30%, substantially limiting the scope of instruments at the government's disposal in case of a major economic crisis.

4.2 Latvia accedes to the EU

Latvia acceded to the EU in 2004, together with nine other countries, seven of which were Central and Eastern European countries and two Mediterranean island states. Following accession, the average annual growth rate between 2004 and 2007 was 10.3% – a growth rate Latvia had never experienced before. Growth, however, has not been organic or sustainable, as it was to a large extent based on foreign lending which fuelled the real estate market. It was also accompanied by a double-digit inflation, a housing boom with housing prices tripling in just five years between 2003 and 2007 (European Commission, 2010), and an appreciating real exchange rate (see Figure 4.5), all which signalled an overheated economy.

Throughout the boom years, unemployment went down from 14% in 2000 to 6% in late 2007. Labour market imperfections[9] in Latvia led to unprecedented wage increases throughout the pre-crisis years, in the whole economy, and particularly in sectors related to real estate.

The rapid wage rate increases could also have been caused by the relatively high emigration rates as surplus labour left the country (for a detailed account see Woolfson, Sommers and Juska, 2015). According to the most recent census of 2011, Latvia lost close to 15% of its population over the prior decade and this trend has continued since (see Figure 4.6).

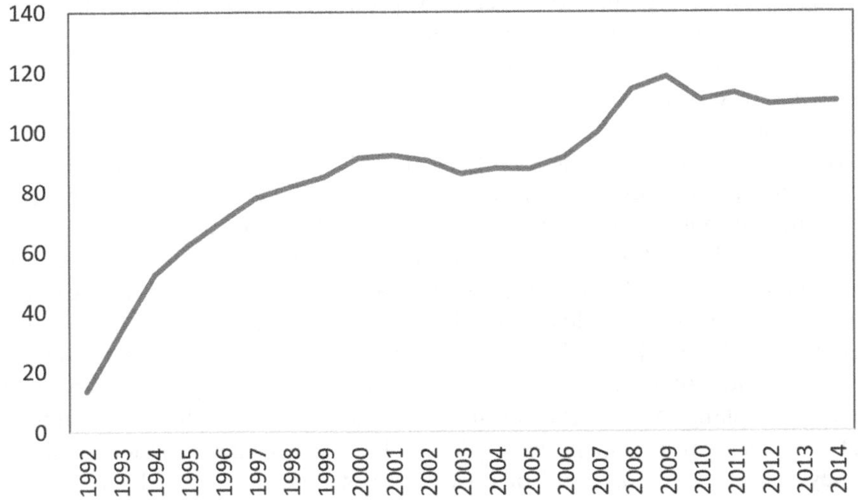

Figure 4.5 Real effective exchange rate (CPI-based) 67 trade partners
Source: Bruegel database (available at: http://bruegel.org/publications/datasets/real-effective-exchange-rates-for-178-countries-a-new-database/).

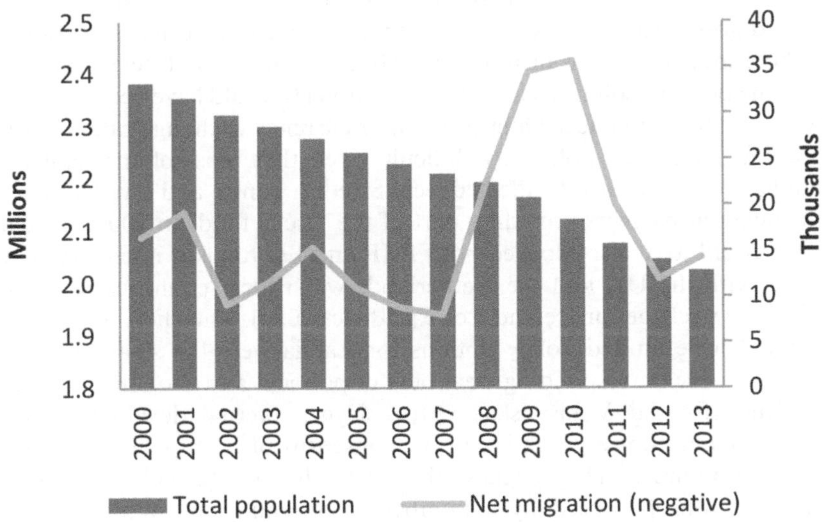

Figure 4.6 Population dynamics
Source: Eurostat – Population change – Demographic balance and crude rates at regional level, NUTS 3 (available at: http://ec.europa.eu/eurostat/en/web/products-datasets/-/DEMO_R_GIND3).

Wage growth significantly exceeded productivity growth and led to a deterioration of the competitiveness of domestic exporting industries and of those producing for the local market. This in turn led to growing trade deficits in the balance of payments.

There are different strategies available for adjustment to the balance of payments imbalances. Some countries, including Latvia, tightened monetary policy through interest rates (foreign lending was already very limited at the time) and cut public spending. These measures, in combination, led to a severe recession, with substantial losses of output (over 20% of GDP over three years from 2008–2010).[10] Other countries, such as Poland or Iceland used external devaluation in order to deal with the crisis. (Iceland is a special case here, being a member of the EEA, but not a member of the EU.) Hungary went for a combination of both – currency depreciation and budget cuts. There are different explanations for the variation in choices between different countries, but what is clear is that policy makers' choices in terms of macroeconomic policy responses to this kind of crises are not determined solely by rational economic considerations, but also by path dependencies, existing commitments, political considerations and certain ideas dominating policy discourse. This was the case in Latvia with regard to the policy decision as to whether internal devaluation, by adjusting unit labour costs, was to be preferred over external devaluation, by adjusting the exchange rate of the domestic currency.

While in theory currency devaluation could have helped exporting industries, it would not have helped those industries where the import content of produced goods was high. At the same time currency depreciation would have hurt those individuals and firms owing debt denominated in foreign currencies. One of the possible solutions to avoid bankruptcies would have been to legislate debt re-denomination according to the new currency exchange rate. However, this would have been politically difficult given that most of the banks that would have been negatively affected were Swedish banks, and Sweden was one of the bilateral partners providing part of the rescue funds in 2009. Arguably, Sweden could have also blocked both IMF and EC funds if necessary, as was the case with the UK and the Netherlands when these countries blocked an IMF rescue package for Iceland (see e.g. Boyes 2009). Thus here again factors that could have limited policy options for Latvia were the small size of the country and the corresponding weakness in political and economic clout.

As Kuokštis and Vilpišauskas (2010) argue, internal devaluation was a preferred policy choice grounded in the consensus of both policy makers and expert communities. They suggest that even though the policy of external devaluation was proposed by a number of prominent economists, such as Krugman (2008) and Roubini (2009), this policy option was not given any substantial thought. As Raudla and Kattel (2013) further argue, adoption of the euro was viewed as an exit strategy by governments of all Baltic states, hence giving up the peg would have meant giving up – at least for the time being – the adoption of the euro, and therefore also losing a real, almost tangible objective of policy action. In addition, given the history of monetary policy in Latvia, the Central Bank had no experience with managing a free-floating currency, and thus no competences to manage a non-automatic currency system (Raudla and Kattel, 2011).

5 Latvia as a small state

5.1 Integration – not simply an economic problem

While it is clear that integration into the wider Europe was essential for Latvia for purely economic reasons, there was certainly more to it than just economics. Small countries have been seeking for some kind of economic, political or military protection for centuries (Alesina and Spalaore, 2005), mostly through bilateral arrangements, in order to compensate for their weakness (Handel, 1990). In the twentieth century with the establishment of a number of international organizations in the aftermath of the Second World War, small states turned to multilateral arrangements to provide them shelter. These states, some of which had gained their independence from colonial powers in the 1960s, sought economic protection in such multilateral organizations as the International Monetary Fund, the World Bank, and the World Trade Organization.

The small Western European countries also utilized multilateral organizations in order to compensate for their weaknesses – the Organisation for Economic Co-operation and Development, the Organization for Security Co-operation in Europe (OSCE), as well as NATO and the EU. Nordic countries formed their own alliance – the Nordic Council – in order to increase economic well-being through cooperation and enhance their political power.

As Thorhallsson (2011) argues, small states can adopt different approaches to dealing with the effects of the globalized economy coming in the form of financial or economic crises, or both. Some small states, following Katzenstein (1987, 1985), rely on a domestic buffer in order to deal with the effects of economic openness. This domestic buffer comes in the form of domestic corporatist arrangements and development of a comprehensive welfare state and active labour market policies, as was the case in the Nordic countries facing economic uncertainty in the mid-1980s.

Given that small countries can be hit by a crisis swiftly and particularly hard due to their high degree of trade openness, especially when their most important exporting industry suffers a blow, this kind of corporatist and welfare arrangement can help soften the shock and manage the crisis, thus containing the potential long-term damages. These arrangements, Thorhallsson (2011) argues, worked well at the time of the Bretton Woods system, which regulated capital flows, thus effectively limiting the effects of the crisis to the level of an economic sector or, at worst, a national currency. With the liberalization of international financial flows that ensued after the break-up of the Bretton Woods system, these internal arrangements have become increasingly less effective as a mechanism for containing financial or economic shocks.

A major challenge in the case of countries with small open economies is managing an independent currency. In spite of limitations relating to policy capacity and currency reserves necessary, even a relatively small country can successfully manage its own currency, as the examples of Norway and Sweden suggest. However, for some countries, having their own currency can at times be more of a disadvantage. One such example is Iceland, which suffered a substantial currency depreciation after its recent financial crisis (see e.g. Boyes, 2009; Thorhallsson and Kattel, 2012). This was also the case with larger countries such as the UK in 1992 and a number of Asian countries in 1997 (for an account of such financial crises see Eichengreen, 2004).

On the economic front, as Latvia was transferring to a free market economy and restructuring its industry, there were many unknowns with regard to the policies most suitable for the creation of a sustainable economy that would be capable of weathering both internal and external shocks. The new system required both new political leadership, capable of steering a nascent market economy, as well as a new bureaucracy, capable of implementing the policies. As domestic capacity to effectively manage change was very limited, Latvia had no other option but to seek external support in both carrying out the reforms, and in ensuring external security.

5.2 National security considerations

Latvia also found itself in a system with too many unknowns on both economic and political fronts. Until 1994 Latvia still had a Russian military presence on its territory, posing an immediate threat from within. However, Latvia was successful in exploiting its membership in international organizations such as the UN and the OSCE in order to put pressure on Russia to move its military forces out of Latvian territory.

National security was at the core of the process of integration. Latvia, being itself a small state, was surrounded by other small states – most of them sharing a similar post-Communist background. At the same time Latvia, along with Estonia and Finland was (and still is) sharing a border with Russia – a rather unpredictable neighbour, especially in the light of the war in the Chechen Republic (see e.g. Baumanis, 1996). Latvia's expenditure on defence remained around 1%, rising up to 1.4 in the post-accession and pre-crisis years of 2004–2007. Both its Southern neighbour Lithuania and Northern neighbour Estonia spent substantially more, at around 3% and 2% respectively. However, given the size of the countries, their independent military spending in absolute terms is so minuscule that without an external partner they can hardly protect themselves in case of military aggression from the East. Thus, for Latvia, joining international organizations such as the EU and NATO was a question of national security and therefore of paramount priority (see e.g. Apinis and Lejiņš, 1995, 1996; Baumanis, 1996; Lejiņš and Bleiere, 1996).

Thus in addition to the neoliberal economic ideology dominating within the political elite, which was the main force driving economic integration, it was also the uncertain security situation that served as an additional stimulus for faster integration into the wider union.

5.3 Latvia's small size and EU accession

In large part, it was the size of Latvia that limited the scope of available policy options. Thus, lack of local capacity and capabilities within the public sector, often found in small countries (see e.g. Randma-Liiv, 2002), affected the quality of policy making in all areas. Here, integration in the EU had a positive effect, improving policy-making at least in some areas. Weak regulation of the financial sector, with regulators unwilling or unable to take an active stance, resulted in a fragile system, which, in turn exacerbated the effects of the recent global financial crisis. A passive approach to economic policy-making, marked by unwillingness to engage in strategic steering of the economy, resulted in a productive system that is still relying on cost of inputs as the main competitive advantage – hardly a sustainable strategy for a small open economy.

The same unwillingness to prioritize and focus resources in certain strategically important areas of science and research, resulted in a fragmented science and research system, with too few resources available in order to reach the critical mass. Even the process of implementation of the concept of smart specialization (see e.g. McCann and Ortega-Argilés, 2013), which has specialization at its core, resulted in the selection of areas of specialization defined so broadly as to include all industrial and scientific branches. Smart specialization is a regional concept and is used as such in large countries, however, in smaller countries, such as Latvia, it is used on a national level. Yet again, one can see that smallness affects policy choices – policy makers fear specializing in certain sectors or industries as there is the possibility that the wrong one might be chosen.

6 Conclusions

The objective of this chapter was to point out the challenges faced by Latvia during the pre-accession period, the impact of EU integration on the Latvian economy, and to define the context within which the changes took place. Covering all aspects of European integration within the confines of a single chapter is something we did not intend to do; instead we focused on economic challenges. Of course, addressing economic challenges should also have included a discussion of the Latvian research and innovation system and the challenges pertinent to it. The idea that innovation is essential for sustainable economic growth and development is no longer on the margins of economic thought and policy-makers across the world, and especially in the EU, place strong emphasis on innovation as one of the main drivers of the economy. Science and research thus become essential, as they are the main sources of inputs into both the knowledge and human resources necessary for innovation in the public and private sectors. However, due to space limitations, we decided to avoid this discussion altogether. The chapter also discussed some implications associated with Latvia's small size.

We argued that some policy choices made before accession to the EU to a great extent predetermined the policy landscape within which new policies were and are being designed and implemented. We also argued that, to a large extent, it was the size of Latvia that limited the scope of available policy options.

As to the advantages and disadvantages of Latvia's accession to the EU there are, as always, two sides to the argument. One can only speculate, what would have happened to Latvia had the country not chosen to join the EU – it is after all impossible to run experiments on such a scale. Integration in the EU provided a sense of security. It also provided a source of investment in infrastructure, which Latvia most likely would not have been able to secure on its own. It also improved policy making in no small way, especially when it comes to fiscal and financial policy making in the post-crisis years. But it also had its negative effects, leading to deindustrialization and the resulting substantial emigration – mostly of those most needed in the economy, and also contributing to the severe economic crisis that Latvia went through following the global financial crisis. It therefore remains to be seen whether Latvia will find its own path for sustainable development or remain dependent on the rest of Europe in future.

Notes

1 Acknowledgement: the authors thank Riaz K. Tayob for comments on the earlier draft of the chapter. All remaining mistakes and omissions remain the authors' responsibility. Research leading to these results has received funding from the Estonian Science Foundation grant No. 9395, Estonian Research Council grant No. PUT1142, and the Norwegian Financial Mechanism 2009–2014 under project No. EMP264.
2 Available here: http://hdr.undp.org/en/composite/HDI.
3 Information about the World Bank classification of countries into income-group categories is available at: http://data.worldbank.org/about/country-and-lending-groups. The World Bank periodically revises the income per capita thresholds.
4 Some studies on Latvia as a small state were published by the Latvian Institute of International Affairs and the Bank of Finland Institute for Economies in Transition.
5 Valsts elektrotehniskā fabrika is the Latvian State Electro-technical Factory.
6 This refers to the rapid implementation of a comprehensive set of reforms aimed at transforming a post-socialist into a normal market economy (see also e.g. Sachs, 1995).
7 Varieties of capitalism typology are suggested by Hall and Soskice, 2001.
8 Special Drawing Rights – a reserve asset, created by the IMF on the basis of four international currencies.
9 On the role of labour market institutions in explaining the outcomes of the crisis for the members of the euro zone see Hancké (2013).
10 For dissenting views see Blanchard, Griffiths and Gruss (2013) and Walter (2013).

References

Aghion, P. and Blanchard, O.J. (1994) 'On the speed of transition in Central Europe', in S. Fischer and J.J. Rotemberg (eds), *NBER Macroeconomics Annual 1994*, 9: 283–330. Cambridge, MA: MIT Press.

Alesina, A. and Spalaore, E. (2005) *The Size of Nations*. Cambridge, MA: MIT Press.

Apinis, P., Lejiņš, A. (eds) (1995) 'The Baltic States on their Way to the EU (Security Aspects)', Conference Proceedings. Riga: Latvian Institute of International Affairs.

Apinis, P., and Lejiņš, A. (eds) (1996) 'NATO and EU Enlargement: The Case of the Baltic States', Conference Proceedings. Riga: Latvian Institute of International Affairs.

Aslund, A. and Dombrovskis, V. (2011) *How Latvia Came through the Financial Crisis*. Washington, DC: Peterson Institute.

Baumanis, T. (1996) *Latvijas integrācija Eiropas struktūrās – drošības politikas risinājums* (Latvian integration in the European structures: The security politics solution). Riga: Latvian Institute of International Affairs.

Berg, A., Sachs, J., Baldwin, R.E. and Flemming, J. (1992) 'Structural Adjustment and International Trade in Eastern Europe: The Case of Poland', *Economic Policy*, 7(14): 118–173. Available at: http://www.earth.columbia.edu/sitefiles/file/about/director/documents/EconomicPolicyApr1992withBergStructuralAdjustmentandInternationalTradeinEasternEuropetheCase.pdf (accessed 23 January 2016).

Blanchard, O.J., Griffiths, M. and Gruss, B. (2013) 'Boom, bust, recovery: forensics of the Latvia Crisis', *Brookings Papers on Economic Activity*: 325–388. Available at: http://muse.jhu.edu/login?auth=0&type=summary&url=/journals/brookings_papers_on_economic_activity/v2013/2013.2.blanchard.html (accessed 23 January 2016).

Boyes, R. (2009). *Meltdown Iceland: Lessons on the World Financial Crisis from a Small Bankrupt Island*. Pittsburgh: Bloomsbury. Retrieved from: http://media.economist.com/media/pdf/meltdown-iceland-boyes-e.pdf (accessed 23 January 2016).

Buckley, P.J. and Ruane, F. (2006) 'Foreign Direct Investment in Ireland: Policy Implications for Emerging Economies', *The World Economy*, 29: 1611–1628.

Calvo, G.A. and Coricelli, F. (1993) 'Output Collapse in Eastern Europe: The Role of credit', *Staff Papers – International Monetary Fund*, 40 (1): 32–52.

Central Statistical Bureau of Latvia. (1990) *Statistical Yearbook of Latvia*, State Committee for Statistics of the Republic of Latvia.

Cepilovs, A. (2014) 'Public Procurement for Innovation in Small States. The Case of Latvia', in F. Decarolis and M. Frey (eds), *Public Procurement's Place in the World: The Charge Towards Sustainability and Innovation*, Basingstoke: Palgrave Macmillan, 93–130. Available at: https://www.researchgate.net/profile/Aleksandrs_Cepilovs2/publication/265417495_Public_Procurement_for_Innovation_in_Small_States._The_Case_of_Latvia/links/550fbb520cf21287416bf10c.pdf (accessed 23 January 2016).

Eichengreen, B.J. (2004) *Capital Flows and Crises*. Cambridge, MA: MIT Press.

European Commission (2010) 'Cross Country Study: Economic Policy Challenges in the Baltics', *Occasional Papers No. 50*. Brussels: European Commission.

Hall, P. and Soskice, D. (2001) *Varieties of Capitalism: The Institutional Foundations of Comparative Advantage*. Oxford: Oxford University Press.

Hancké, B. (2013) *Unions, Central Banks, and EMU: Labour Market Institutions and Monetary Integration in Europe*. Oxford: Oxford University Press.

Handel, M. (1990) *Weak States in the International System*. London: Frank Cass.

Johansen, H. (2000) 'Nordic Investments in the Former Soviet Baltic Frontier: A Survey of Firms and Selected Case Studies', *Geografiska Annaler* (Human Geography), 82: 207–219.

Kattel, R. and Raudla, R. (2013) 'The Baltic Republics and the Crisis of 2008–2011', *Europe-Asia Studies*, 65: 426–449.

Katzenstein, P. (1985) *Small States in World Markets*, Ithaca: Cornell University Press.

Katzenstein, P. (1987) *Corporatism and Change: Austria, Switzerland, and the Politics of Industry*. Ithaca: Cornell University Press.

Krugman, P. (2008) 'Latvia is the New Argentina (Slightly Wonkish)', *New York Times Blog*, 23 December. Available at: http://www.forbes.com/2009/06/10/latvia-sweden-imf-swedbank-danske-devaluation-opinions-columnists-roubini.html (accessed 23 January 2016).

Kuokštis, V. and Vilpišauskas, R. (2010) 'Economic Adjustment to the Crisis in the Baltic States in Comparative Perspective', Presented at the 7th Pan-European International Relations Conference, Stockholm. Available at: http://eisa-net.org/be-bruga/eisa/files/events/stockholm/Economic%20Adjustment%20to%20the%20Crisis%20in%20the%20Baltic%20States%20in%20Comparative%20Perspective.pdf (accessed 23 January 2016).

Lejiņš, A. and Bleiere, D. (eds) (1996) *The Baltic States: Search for Security*. Riga: Latvian Institute of International Affairs.

Lejiņš, A. and Ozoliņa, Ž., (1997) *Small States in a Turbulent Environment: The Baltic Perspective*. Riga: Latvian Institute of International Affairs.

Lim, L.Y.C. and Pang, E.F. (1991) *Foreign Direct Investment and Industrialisation in Malaysia, Singapore, Taiwan, and Thailand*, Singapore: Research Collection Lee Kong Chian School of Business.

McCann, P. and Ortega-Argilés, R. (2013) 'Smart Specialization, Regional Growth and Applications to European Union Cohesion Policy', *Regional Studies*, 49(8): 1–12.

McCollum, D. and Shubin, S., Apsite, E., Krisjane, Z. (2013) 'Rethinking Labour Migration Channels: The Experience of Latvia from EU Accession to Economic Recession', *Population, Space and Place*, 19: 688–702.

Mikkel, E. and Pridham, G. (2004) 'Clinching the "Return to Europe": The Referendums on EU Accession in Estonia and Latvia', *West European Politics*, 27: 716–748.

Ozawa, T. (2003) 'Pax Americana-led Macro-clustering and Flying-geese-style catch-up in East Asia: Mechanisms of Regionalized Endogenous Growth', *Journal of Asian Economics*, 13: 699–713.

Panke, D. (2010) 'Good Instructions in No Time? Domestic Coordination of EU Policies in 19 Small States', *West European Politics*, 33: 770–790.

Perez, C. (2002) *Technological Revolutions and Financial Capital: The Dynamics of Bubbles and Golden Ages*. Cheltenham: Edward Elgar.

Pohl, G. (1991) 'Economic Consequences of German Reunification', Working Paper, Policy Research. Socialist Economies Reform. Geneva: The World Bank.

Porter, M.E. (1990) *The Competitive Advantage of Nations*. New York: Free Press.

Randma-Liiv, T. (2002) 'Small States and Bureaucracy: Challenges for Public Administration', *Trames*, 6: 374–389.

Raudla, R. and Kattel, R. (2011) 'Why did Estonia choose fiscal retrenchment after the 2008 crisis?' *Journal of Public Policy*, 31: 163–186.

Raudla, R. and Kattel, R. (2013) 'Fiscal Stress Management during the Financial and Economic Crisis: The Case of the Baltic Countries', *International Journal of Public Administration*, 36: 732–742.

Reinert, E.S. (2004) *Globalization, Economic Development and Inequality: An Alternative Perspective*. Cheltenham: Edward Elgar.

Reinert, E.S. and Kattel, R. (2004) 'The Qualitative Shift in European Integration: Towards Permanent Wage Pressures and a "Latin-Americanization" of Europe?' MPRA Paper 47909, Germany: University Library of Munich. Available at: https://ideas.repec.org/p/pra/mprapa/47909.html (accessed 23 January 2016).

Reinert, E.S. and Kattel, R. (2007) 'European Eastern Enlargement as Europe's Attempted Economic Suicide?' *The Other Canon and Tallinn University of Technology Working Papers in Technology Governance and Economic Dynamics*, No. 14. Available at: http://technologygovernance.eu/files/main/2007070309122525.pdf (accessed 23 January 2016).

Rodrik, D. (2006) 'Goodbye Washington Consensus, Hello Washington Confusion? A Review of the World Bank's Economic Growth in the 1990s: Learning from a Decade of Reform', *Journal of Economic Literature*, 44: 973–987.

Roubini, N. (2009) 'Is Eastern Europe on the Brink of an Asia-Style Crisis?', Weekly Column in *Forbes*, 6 November. Retrieved from: http://krugman.blogs.nytimes.com/2008/12/23/latvia-is-the-new-argentina-slightly-wonkish (accessed 23 January 2016).

Sachs, J.D. (1995) 'Shock Therapy in Poland: Perspectives of Five Years', *Tanner Lectures on Human Values*, 16: 265–290. Available at: http://tannerlectures.utah.edu/_documents/a-to-z/s/sachs95.pdf (accessed 23 January 2016).

Schimmelfennig, F., Engert, S. and Knobel, H. (2003) 'Costs, Commitment and Compliance: The Impact of EU Democratic Conditionality on Latvia, Slovakia and Turkey', *Journal of Common Market Studies*, 41: 495–518. Retrieved from: https://www.researchgate.net/profile/Frank_Schimmelfennig/publication/4764048_Costs_Commitment_and_Compliance_The_Impact_of_EU_Democratic_Conditionality_on_Latvia_Slovakia_and_Turkey/links/00b49520cd66514c7a000000.pdf (accessed 23 January 2016).

Shteinbuka, I. (1993) 'Latvia in Transition: First Challenges and First Results', *Review of Economies in Transition*. Institute for Economies in Transition, No. 8, 61–94, Helsinki: Bank of Finland. Available at: http://www.suomenpankki.fi/pdf/0893IS2.PDF (accessed 23 January 2016).

Sommers, J. and Woolfson, C. (2014) *The Contradictions of Austerity: The Socio-economic Costs of the Neoliberal Baltic Model*. London and New York: Routledge.

State Bureau of Statistics. (1939) *The Achievements of Latvia in Statistics* (in Latvian).

Thorhallsson, B. (2011) 'Domestic Buffer Versus External Shelter: Viability of Small States in the New Globalised Economy', *European Political Science*, 10: 324–336.

Thorhallsson, B. and Kattel, R. (2012) 'Neo-Liberal Small States and Economic Crisis: Lessons for Democratic Corporatism', *Journal of Baltic Studies*, 2011: 1–21. Available at: http://uni.hi.is/baldurt/files/2012/10/Neo-liberal-small-states-Estonia-Iceland-by-Thorhallsson-Kattel.pdf (accessed 23 January 2016).

Tiits, M. (2006) 'Industrial and Trade Dynamics in the Baltic Sea Region Since 1990s', in *Creative Destruction Management: Meeting the Challenges of the Techno-Economic Paradigm Shift*. Tallinn: PRAXIS Center fof Policy Studies, 101–118. Available at: http://www.praxis.ee/wp-content/uploads/2014/03/2006-Industrial-and-trade-dynamics-in-baltic-sea-region.pdf (accessed 23 January 2016).

Tiits, M., Kattel, R., Kalvet, T. and Tamm, D. (2008) 'Catching Up, Forging Ahead or Falling Behind? Central and Eastern European Development in 1990–2005', *Innovation: The European Journal of Social Science Research*, 21(1): 65–85. Available at: http://www.cesruc.org/uploads/soft/130221/1-130221125213.pdf (accessed 23 January 2016).

Walter, S. (2013) *The Fiscal Policy Implications of Balance of Payments Imbalances, in: Governance Challenges and Innovations: Financial and Fiscal Governance*. Oxford: Oxford University Press, pp. 89–113. Available at: http://www.stefaniewalter.de/resources/Walter.2013.GovReport.Hertie.pdf (accessed 23 January 2016).

Woolfson, C., Sommers, J. and Juska, A. (2015) 'Migration and the New Austeriat: The Baltic Model and the Socioeconomic Costs of Neoliberal Austerity', Presented at the W.I.R.E. Workshop on Immigration, Race, Ethnicity, Ash Center for Democratic Governance and Innovation at the Harvard Kennedy School. Available at: http://ash.harvard.edu/files/woolfsonsommersmigrationausterity.pdf (accessed 23 January 2016).

5 The Lithuanian economy as a European Union member state

Structure, performance and prospects

Algirdas Miskinis and Aušytė Rastenienė

1 Introduction

Lithuania is the largest of the three Baltic States,[1] with a population of three million people. The country regained its independence in 1991, joined the European Union (EU) in 2004 and adopted the euro in 2015. Although Lithuania started the transition to a market economy later than some other new member states, its business environment is one of most liberal not only in the EU but also in the world. The free market created favourable conditions for economic growth and today the Lithuanian economy is far ahead in comparison to most other states of the former Soviet Union. Since 1995, the Lithuanian gross national income (GNI) per capita in purchasing power parity (PPP) terms has more than doubled, from US$7,368 (in 2005) to US$16,858 in 2012 (UNDP, 2014).

Lithuania ranked 35th out of 187 countries on the 2013 Human Development Index and is thus one of the countries with 'very high human development'. For Lithuania this is the best result since its first rankings. Among the member states that joined the EU in 2004, only few countries are above Lithuania in this ranking, namely Slovenia (25th), Czech Republic (28th), Cyprus (32nd) and Estonia (33rd).

This chapter is organized into seven sections. Section 2 presents information about the structure of the Lithuanian economy, while Section 3 discusses the performance of the economy. Section 4 deals with the characteristics of a small country like Lithuania. Matters related to Lithuania's accession to the EU are analysed in Section 5. Section 6 presents a discussion on the major challenges faced by the economy and that need to be addressed to improve the sustainability of the economy. Section 7 concludes the chapter with a summary of the main findings.

2 Structure of the Lithuanian economy

2.1 The Lithuanian economy after independence

After the restoration of independence, the economic situation in Lithuania could be defined as one of economic turmoil. The Banks and the monetary system had to be re-created, the national currency, the litas, was introduced and new governance institutions were established.

The new government of independent Lithuania had to decide how to stabilize the economy and foster confidence in the market participants. The government of the country, together with the Bank of Lithuania, and Lithuanian as well as foreign experts, decided that the best means to reach this goal was to fix the exchange rate of the domestic currency. For this purpose, a currency board arrangement was introduced in April 1994, taking into consideration the fact that Lithuania was a small open economy, and that, at that time, there was a shortage of specialists capable of carrying out monetary policy properly. In addition there was the need to further build confidence in the financial market and in governmental institutions.

The setting up of a currency board, and the support this received from politicians, accompanied by a sound fiscal policy, ensured the successful control of inflation and fostered trust in the Lithuanian state and the country's financial market. The most serious challenge to the currency board arrangement was in 1996, with a bankruptcy crisis among Lithuanian banks, and the following year during the Russian financial crisis.

The introduction of the currency board arrangement sent a clear signal to business that the exchange rate policy would not be used to stimulate exports and that the competitiveness of business enterprise in Lithuania had to depend on the ability of entrepreneurs to find foreign markets, forecast market trends, be flexible and innovative, adopt modern technology and upgrade management structures.

2.2 Liberal economic governance

Following independence, the Lithuanian government chose an economic system which may be called liberal capitalism (Girdėnas, Giedraitis and Rasteniene, 2003; Kuokštis, 2014). The most important feature of economic governance during this period was flexibility. This made Lithuanian business and labour market actors adaptable to change. As a result, Lithuania received relatively high scores in the world competitiveness ranking (IMD, 2015), and in some cases Lithuania outperformed its neighbours.

The independence period demonstrated that the Lithuanian business community understood the signals transmitted by the state very well. The capacity of business to adjust to drastic economic and political changes was manifested in the reaction of the business community to the Russian financial crisis of 1997 and the global financial crisis in 2008.

2.3 The sectoral composition of the Lithuanian GDP

The structure of the Lithuanian economy has changed considerably between 1995 and 2013, as shown in Table 5.1.

Table 5.1 Sectoral composition of GDP (%)

Sector	*1995*	*2004*	*2013*
Agriculture, forestry and fisheries	9.3	4.8	3.8
Mining and quarrying	0.4	0.5	0.4
Manufacturing and construction	25.9	24.2	24.5
Market services	10.4	35.0	40.3
Of which			
- Transport and distribution	8.4	9.5	12.9
- Financial services	2.0	2.2	2.2
Public sector	15.2	15.5	13.5

Source: Lithuanian Department of Statistics and Eurostat.

Table 5.1 shows that in 2013 distribution and transport industries accounted for 12.9% of gross domestic product (GDP), a share which has increased since 1995. Such a high share reflects the fact that Lithuania acts as a bridge for transportation of goods between Western and Eastern parts of Europe and that this sector is very important for the Lithuanian economy. This sector thrives in a situation of free trade.

The table shows that the manufacturing sector is also of major importance for the Lithuanian economy. In 2013 this sector produced 24.5% of gross value added when the EU average was only 19.1%. The strongest sector in manufacturing is the chemical industry inherited from the Soviet era, led by petrochemical and fertilisers' subsectors.

With regard to the services sector, it can be seen from Table 5.1 that Lithuania has a small financial sector, the smallest in the EU (2.2% in comparison to 5.4% EU average).

The public sector is also relatively small in Lithuania, and second smallest within the EU, after Latvia (13.5% in Lithuania when EU average is 19.4%).

The share of traditional agriculture in 2013 accounted only 3.8% of gross value added indicating that the agriculture sector does not play a crucial role in the economy.

In 2014, the fastest-growing sector after five years of post-crisis stagnation was construction. In the first quarter of 2014, home sales jumped by 44% year-on-year. Most purchases of houses and apartments were made without mortgages indicating that borrowing from banks remains weak despite very low interest rates, demonstrating that banks are not eager to undertake risks.

2.4 Final expenditures

Table 5.2 shows the final expenditures in Lithuania. It can be seen that the Lithuanian economy has become increasingly dependent on foreign trade. The share of exports to the GDP is constantly growing and in 2013 reached

Table 5.2 Final expenditures (in current prices, million euro)

Final expenditures	*1995*		*2004*		*2013*	
	€m	*%*	*€m*	*%*	*€m*	*%*
Private consumption expenditure	4952.7	63.5	11888.9	65.2	21947.7	62.8
Public consumption expenditure	1909.5	24.5	3457.3	19.0	5861.6	16.8
Gross fixed capital formation	1581.2	20.3	4176.1	22.9	6457.2	18.5
Exports of goods and services	3700.5	47.5	8643.7	47.4	29387.9	84.1
Total final expenditure	6862.2	88.0	15346.2	84.1	28950.6	82.8
Less imports of goods and services	4530.5	58.1	9924.8	54.4	28950.6	82.8
Gross Domestic Product at market prices	7797.9	100	18237.4	100	34962.2	100

Source: Eurostat National accounts and Lithuanian Statistics Department.

84.0%. A large part of exports is simply re-export of goods and services, showing that Lithuania is making use of its geographical position and increasing entrepot trade. This in turn indicates that the country serves as a bridge for markets in other countries. Most of re-exported goods are transported by Lithuanian freight carriers making the logistics sector important in creating value added and services export.

The low share of gross fixed capital formation in 2013 indicates that investments did not recover to a full extent after the economic crisis. Public consumption expenditure is decreasing in relative terms demonstrating that the redistribution of incomes is diminishing and the role of the public sector is shrinking.

According to data issued by the Lithuanian department of statistics, the main Lithuanian export partners in 2014 were Russia (20.8% of export), Latvia (9.2%), Poland (8.3%) and Germany (7.2%), while import partners were the same – Russia (21.6% of import), Germany (10.9%), Poland (9.4%) and Latvia (6.9%). In 2007 the share of the Russian market was lower in both exports (15%) and imports (18.2%) indicating that the importance of Russian trade after the economic crisis increased. In 2013 re-exports from Lithuania to Russia was around nearly six times larger than export of goods of Lithuanian origin and that export of services exceeded export of goods by 75%.

The main traded goods in 2014 were mineral products (17.8% of exports and 25.3% of imports), machinery and electrical equipment (correspondingly 15.4% and 17%) and chemical products (correspondingly 92% and 10.4%). In Lithuania, traditionally, a very important export sector was textiles, accounting for more than 15% of export, but currently its share is negligible.

The composition of foreign trade partners has changed considerably over time: the change started even before Lithuanian accession to the EU, when it was envisaged that Lithuania would become an EU member state. In 1998 the share of the Commonwealth of Independent States (CIS) countries, the main former trade partner, dramatically decreased from 46.6% in 1997 to 18.2% in 1998, as the share of the EU states and other European countries increased. Such a change of trade partners was speeded up by the 1997 Russian financial crisis, but preconditions for it were created by the trade liberalization arrangement between the EU and Lithuania, through the implementation of Free Trade Agreement for industrial goods in 1995. Decreased trade with the CIS countries was replaced also by growing trade with European Free Trade Association (EFTA) countries. In recent years the EU market share has made up more than half of the export markets. The CIS countries' share in the export markets currently accounts for about a quarter, but fluctuates due to the unilateral decisions of Russian foreign trade policy. In their search for stable markets, Lithuanian producers have increased exports to the USA, Turkey and Asian countries.

Imports to Lithuania almost tripled between 2004 and 2014, and the cost of imported products, contrary to economic expectations, increased, possibly because cheaper and frequently lower quality products from the CIS were replaced by higher quality and more expensive products from the EU (Miskinis, 2013).

3 Recent economic performance

Since 2002, Lithuania has enjoyed relatively stable economic growth interrupted by the global financial and economic crisis in 2009, when GDP fell by 14.8%, but recovered in the following years. Table 5.3 presents some relevant indicators in this regard.

Table 5.3 Main socio-economic indicators

Indicator	*2002*	*2004*	*2006*	*2008*	*2010*	*2012*	*2013*
Annual GDP growth (%)	6.9	7.4	7.8	2.9	1.6	3.7	3.3
Inflation (%)	0.3	1.2	4.5	8.5	1.6	3.2	1.2
Unemployment rate (%)	13.8	11.4	5.6	5.8	17.8	13.4	11.8
GDP per capita PPS/EU average (%)	43	50	56	63	60	69	73
Current account/GDP (%)	−5.3	−7.6	−10.6	−12.9	−0.3	−1.2	1.6
Fiscal balance/GDP (%)	−1.9	−1.5	0.4	−3.3	−7.1	−3.2	−2.1
Public sector debt/GDP (%)	22.3	19.3	17.9	15.5	37.4	41.2	39.4
Export growth (%)	10.5	16.2	15.8	28.5	32.7	14.4	6.5
Net migration per 1000 population	−3.4	−9.5	−7.5	−5.2	−25.2	−7.1	−5.7

Source: Lithuanian Department of Statistics and Eurostat.

As can be seen from Table 5.3, economic growth in Lithuania before the global economic crisis was impressive, averaging about 7% per annum. Such fast growth can partially be explained by the fact that Lithuania started from a very low level after the system transformation in 1990–1995. However it was also due to the huge potential of Lithuania in terms of production capacity.

According to Eurostat, the Lithuanian GDP per capita in purchasing parity standard (PPS) in 2002 accounted only for 43% of the EU average while in 2013 it reached 73.0%, catching up with Greece. Such a leap forward was possible due to the fast productivity growth in the Lithuanian economy and to an extent also as a consequence of a decrease in the EU average due to the membership of Bulgaria and Romania. There was also the effect of extensive emigration of unemployed persons and of low paid Lithuanian persons.[2] In 2014 GDP per capita in Lithuania reached €12,381 and was very close to Latvia's (€12,052) and Estonia's (€14,860).

The main driving force in the Lithuanian economy between 2008 and 2012 was export performance. During this period, export growth reached around 30% per annum. However, mostly due to the deterioration of the trade terms with Russia, the growth in exports of goods and services slowed down in 2013 to 6.5% per annum.

In Lithuania, as in many emerging countries, the major expenditure in total final expenditure is consumption expenditure. In 2014, Lithuania's consumption expenditure amounted to 63.7% as a percentage of GDP, while the EU average in the same year was 56.9%, with the lowest being that of Luxembourg at 29.6%. When in 2013 Lithuanian exports faced severe trade barriers in Russia and harsh competition in other countries, the economic growth to a large extent was the result of increases in private consumption expenditure.

Eurostat's indicator of Actual Individual Consumption (AIC) measured in PPS, which refers to all goods and services actually consumed by households indicating the welfare of households, reached a level of 78% of the EU average, increasing from 70% in 2011. This shows that there was a very swift recovery from the economic crisis. The current AIC in Lithuania is higher, in relation to the EU average, than that of all new EU member states, with the exception of Cyprus and Malta.

3.1 An overheated economy

Fast economic growth before the global economic crisis resulted in an overheated economy that gave rise to inflationary pressures leading to an inflation rate of 8.5% in 2008, accompanied by a relatively high current account deficit, which reached 12.9% in the same year. Before the 2008/09 crisis, the Lithuanian economic growth was partially fuelled by external debt and financial resources from foreign banks, as well as extensive investments in real estate. With the slowing down of capital inflows, there was a sharp decline of domestic demand, leading to a sharp fall in GDP in 2009.

The basic three economic flaws before the great recession were that economic growth was too much based on real estate rather than on the tradable sector, investments relied too much on direct or indirect foreign loans instead of on domestic savings, and the government did not adequately manage foreign capital inflows, all of which created an economic bubble. At that time, the pegged exchange rate of the domestic currency restricted the manoeuvrability of the government's ability to control external trade and capital flows by the means of monetary policy.

After the economic crisis, the current account balance substantially improved, from -12.9% to GDP in 2008 to -0.3% in 2010 and turned positive in 2014. However the fiscal deficit increased to 7.1% of GDP in 2010 and public debt reached 37.4% of GDP in that year, continuing to increase to about 39% in 2014. The recovery of the economy after economic crisis had a positive impact on the labour market as unemployment declined from 17.8% of the labour forces in 2010 to 11.8% in 2014.

3.2 Public finances

Total general government revenue in 2014 in Lithuania accounted for 34.3% of GDP, compared to the EU average of 45.2%. The only country with a lower ratio was Romania (33.4% of GDP). In Lithuania the rate of redistribution of income is relatively low, one reason being that successive Lithuanian governments were reluctant to introduce universal real estate taxes or taxes on passenger cars, and the country is currently one of few EU member states to apply a flat rate personal income tax. Lithuania tax revenue is largely dependent on indirect and labour taxation, while the revenue from environmental and wealth taxation remains very low.[3] While redistribution of income was low, wages in the public sector and pensions tended to be relatively low also. At the end of 2014, the average old-age pension in Lithuania was only €241 whereas in Estonia it was €350.

When government revenues are low, public spending also tends to be low. Public expenditure as a percentage of GDP in 2013 was one of the lowest in the EU, accounting only for 35% of GDP, while the EU average was 47.6%. Before the fiscal consolidation that followed the economic crisis, the share of expenditure in Lithuania was much higher – around 45%. The expenditure cuts that accompanied the fiscal consolidation were rather drastic, including the freezing or cancellation of projects, cuts in wages and pensions, and reduction of other social benefits. Low public spending indicates low input by the government into final consumption and low impact on economic growth. The government so far has not used public spending as an expansionary tool to stimulate growth to the same extent as other EU countries.

A low rate of income redistribution may be expected to lead to income inequality. According to Eurostat,[4] the average Gini coefficient in the EU in 2013 was 30.5 whereas that for Lithuania was higher at 34.6. Inequality in Lithuania is much higher than that existing in egalitarian countries such as Slovakia

(Gini coefficient 24.2), Slovenia (24.4) and Czech Republic (24.6). As inequality is high, the risk of poverty is also high. According to Eurostat, the at-risk-of-poverty rate or social transfers in Lithuania in 2013 was 27.3% when the EU average was 24.4%.[5]

3.3 The 2009 global crisis

A major challenge faced by the Lithuanian economy after the reestablishment of independence in 1990 was the economic and financial crisis of 2009. The crisis not only had a devastating impact on economic growth and welfare but also damaged the prestige of Lithuania among foreign investors as political risks increased and the long-term economic potential looked uncertain. As already explained, in 2009 GDP fell by 14.8%, however, the recovery was also rather fast and already in 2010 the country's economy experienced 1.6% GDP growth. To a large extent, such fast recovery was due to austerity measures undertaken by the Lithuanian government and, to an extent, it was achieved at the expense of the population's wellbeing. The major tool to combat recession was the so-called internal devaluation, encompassing cuts in public spending including to social programmes and such budget expenditures as pensions, social benefits and others.

The policy of cutting budget expenditure, though not popular in some countries like Greece, worked very well in Lithuania and by 2014 Lithuania was again one of the fastest growing countries in the EU. Austerity-based recovery permitted the revival of the economy, although there may yet be long-term negative social consequences associated with unemployment and emigration.

During the economic crisis there were two government decisions that could have long-term detrimental economic consequences. One of these was to borrow funds from the market at very high interest rates rather than borrow from the International Monetary Fund (IMF), as was done by Latvia; this substantially increased Lithuanian public debt from 15.5% of GDP in 2008 to 40% of GDP in 2009. The other government decision was to invest in the construction of a liquefied natural gas (LNG) terminal, with the aim of diversifying the gas supply, so as not to rely excessively on Russian gas. However, LNG supplied domestically was much more expensive than that supplied by Gazprom. Lithuanian companies were forced to purchase expensive gas from the Lithuanian LNG terminal and to bear a share of the cost of the terminal maintenance.

3.4 The current economic environment in Lithuania

Economic growth very much depends on the business environment where economic activity is undertaken. This section will present the scores assigned to Lithuania on some global indicators, which suggest that Lithuania in many ways can be considered as a country with a business environment conducive to the attraction of investment, although the role of incentives remains a major consideration in this regard.

According to the 2015 IMD World Competitiveness rankings (IMD, 2015), Lithuania improved its position from 34th to 28th place with a score above that of other Baltic States Estonia (31st) and Latvia (43rd). IMD ranking measures the effectiveness of the application of the country's physical, financial and human resources to enhance economic growth. The ranking takes into account more than 300 criteria, part of which are based on statistical indicators and others on a survey of international executives. Lithuania reached the best place among new member states and only a few EU member states are ahead, including Denmark, Sweden and Germany.

The scores in the Global Competitiveness Index (GCI) were also relatively high for Lithuania. In the GCI rankings for 2014–2015 (Schwab, 2014), Lithuania was placed 41st, with only Estonia and Czech Republic from new member states being ahead. Lithuania holds the best positions in higher education and technological readiness and the worst in market size and financial market development.

The most problematic area for business in Lithuania is inefficient government bureaucracy. In the area of corruption Lithuania still has a problem as according to Amnesty International the perceived corruption level in Lithuania in 2014 was rather high – Lithuania ranked 39th out of 179 countries, far behind neighbouring Estonia which was ranked 26th.

In 2015, in World Bank's 'Ease of Doing Business Index' ranked Lithuania 24th out of 189 countries.[6] On this index, Lithuania did well in registering a property and starting a business, and not so well in getting electricity. The ranking demonstrates that conditions for developing business in Lithuania are very good.

The Heritage Foundation's 2015 Index of Economic Freedom (IEF)[7] assigned a score of 74.7 to Lithuania, which indicates that Lithuania's economy was the 15th freest in the world and 6th freest in the European Union. The IEF has ten separate components, most of which focus on policies within a country, assessing the liberty of individuals to use their labour or finances without undue restraint and government interference. Since 2010 Lithuania was especially successful in the implementation of sound fiscal and monetary policies and combating corruption. Lithuania and Estonia were ahead of the other new member states in terms of the IEF.

Labour costs are very important for a country's competitiveness in the world market and for that country's economic success in general. Although since joining the EU in 2014, total hourly labour costs in Lithuania have doubled, wage rates remain relatively low. In 2014, hourly labour cost in the private sector was €6.5 (lower only in Bulgaria and Romania) while EU average was €24.6 and in Denmark €40.3. Even in Greece, a country facing a huge debt problem, hourly labour cost is more than twice that in Lithuania (€14.6). Low labour cost makes the Lithuanian economy and especially labour intensive industries competitive, but is associated with other problems, including increased emigration and slow convergence with the EU average labour cost.

A major Lithuanian advantage is that it has one of most educated labour forces in the EU. In 2012, according to Eurostat, the share of the population aged 30–34 with completed tertiary education in Lithuania accounted for 48.7%, a rate much higher than EU target for 2020, which is set at 40%. A higher level of education in 2012 was reached only by Ireland (51.1%), Cyprus (49.9%) and Luxembourg (49.6%). Lithuania, however, faces a problem with such a high level of education in that the education and training offered is not always relevant to the labour market needs. This is leading to a shortage of workers ready to take blue-collar jobs. Over-education and the shortage of blue-collar workers are two reasons why some foreign industrial companies are reluctant to invest in Lithuania.

3.5 Research and development and foreign direct investment flows

High productivity and new technologies, accompanied by research and innovation, are crucial to securing sustainable growth. In the EU gross domestic expenditure on research and development (R&D) as a percentage of GDP in 2013 accounted for 2.01% and a target is set for 3% for 2020. In Denmark, Finland and Sweden R&D expenditure exceeds 3% of GDP, creating a solid basis for the modernization of their economies. In Lithuania, expenditure on R&D is half as much (0.95%) as the European average. This low level of expenditure on R&D can stifle the development of new products and technologies in the private sector and does not allow Lithuania to satisfactorily move up the value chain. In 2014, high-tech export in Lithuania accounted for only 6.4% of total exports of goods, much less than the EU average of 15.6%. Only in five EU countries does high-tech export have a lower share, while on other hand the case of Malta, with a share of 28.9%, indicates that even a small country can be very successful in high-tech exports.

Another important driver of economic development is external finance, especially foreign direct investment (FDI), which is over and above domestic savings and does not create external debt. According to the United Nations Conference on Trade and Development (UNCTAD),[8] in 2013 FDI stock in Lithuania was US$17.5 billion, or about 36% of GDP, indicating that Lithuania was not very successful in attracting FDI despite the attractive business environment just described. In comparison, another Baltic State, Estonia, managed to attract US$21.5 billion FDI, or about 88% of GDP.

Miskinis and Reinbold (2010) argue that the main motive for FDI is a search of new markets, and that cost reduction is not as important. The reasons for cost-reducing vertically integrated investment are high labour cost, lack of skilled labour and restrictive labour market regulations in the home country. The determining factors that encourage FDI include investment incentives and favourable policies in the recipient country. The location of the recipient country is also an important determinant. The Czech Republic,

Estonia, Slovakia and Hungary, may be better locations than Lithuania for attracting FDI in terms of distance from major markets, and this could possibly be one reason why they tend to attract relatively more FDI than Lithuania. Another factor that is likely to influence FDI flows is the size of the country. Large countries with a large domestic market, an abundant workforce and natural resource endowments tend to attract FDI more than small countries like Lithuania. Miskinis and Juozenaite (2015) further argue that government striving to attract FDI has to create favourable conditions for business, fight against corruption, and control budget and public debt effectively, all factors that render a country attractive for foreign investors.

3.6 Labour productivity

The fast recovery of the Lithuanian economy after the economic crisis, already referred to, was partially achieved as a result of the rapid growth of productivity. According to Eurostat,[9] real labour productivity per hour worked in Lithuania grew by 14% between 2009 and 2010, when in the EU on average the figure was only 2.4%. Labour productivity in Lithuania is still growing at a fast rate despite the relatively low level of investment, which is still however lower than the pre-crisis level. Although capital formation as a ratio of GDP in Lithuania is at par with the EU average (19.3%), it is still significantly below that of some other new member states – for example in Estonia it is 25.8%, and in the Czech Republic 25.3%.

In spite of its rapid growth rate, labour productivity per hour worked in Lithuania is still relatively low within the EU, indicating that the Lithuanian industries are producing predominantly low value added products and services. By way of example, in 2013 one hour worked in Lithuania on average produced a value of €10.6, when the EU average was €32.1 euro. The highest labour productivity in the EU in 2012 was in Luxembourg (€58.2), Denmark (€53.4) and Ireland (€48.8).

Innovation is also an important determinant of economic development. Lithuania ranks 39th out of 143 in the Global Innovation Index (2014), lagging behind the other EU new member states of Estonia, Malta, Slovenia and Latvia, but ahead of Croatia and Bulgaria.[10] Lithuania has a high rank in ISO 14001 environment certificates (ranking 8th among 143 states), pupil teacher ratio (10th), school life expectance (12th), tertiary enrolment (13th), Gross domestic expenditure on R&D (13th). However Lithuania registered low ranking in the following indicators: cost of redundancy dismissal (111th), gross capital formation (108th), high-tech imports (107th) and cluster development (105th).

According to the EC's Summary Innovation Index,[11] aggregating 25 indicators, Lithuania is included in the group of moderate innovators and is ahead of only four countries – Bulgaria, Romania, Latvia and Poland. The innovation leaders in the EU are Sweden, Denmark, Germany and Finland, with a score more than double that of Lithuania, and this in spite of the fact that Lithuania has a developed tertiary and youth education system. In terms of the potential of human resources, Lithuania is sixth among all EU countries, and close to the EU average in innovation finance and support, outperforming the other 18 EU countries.

The weakest aspect of Lithuania's innovation performance relates to the linkages with entrepreneurship. Another weak point in financing innovations in Lithuania is a low input by business sector. In 2012, in the EU, average annual business spending on innovations was €338 euro per capita, which is relatively low, compared to Sweden (€993 euro), Finland (€869), and Germany (€657), however relatively high when compared to Estonia (€165 euro).

Yet another weakness in this regard is the lack of cooperation of business companies and research institutions in Lithuania, due to long and complex bureaucratic procedures, especially in public procurement.

4 Lithuania as a small country

Lithuania is one of the smallest states of Europe, and it is characterized by certain tendencies generally found in other small states, including a high degree of economic openness and a limited ability to reap the benefits of economies of scale.

4.1 Trade openness in Lithuania

Trade openness is often measured by the average of exports and imports of goods and services as a percentage of GDP. Figure 5.1 presents data on trade openness in the seven small EU member states. It can be seen that Lithuania is highly dependent on imports and exports (75% of GDP), although Estonia, Malta and Luxembourg have a much higher trade dependence. Larger states usually have a smaller openness ratio and the five largest countries (France, Germany, Poland, Spain and the UK) have an openness ratio at about 38%.

Such exposure renders a country highly vulnerable to external shocks. The reason for such high dependency on international trade is that generally these states have a small domestic market and therefore have to rely on exports to produce a critical mass in order to compete. These states also tend to have limited natural resource endowments and therefore rely heavily on imports.

Lithuania, as many other small states (Briguglio, 2014), have a relatively high dependence on fuel which is considered a strategic import and therefore highly income and price inelastic. In 2013, 31% of Lithuanian imports were accounted for by mineral products.[12]

4.2 Limited ability to reap economies of scale

Small states face problems associated with small scale production, and this leads to limitations in their ability to reap the benefits of economies of scale with also the related problem of indivisibility, meaning that overhead costs cannot be downscaled in proportion to the population.

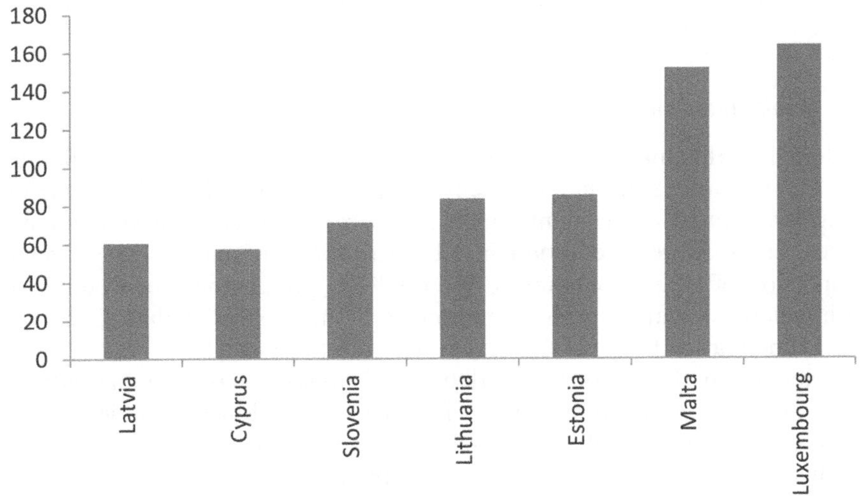

Figure 5.1 Trade openness of the seven small EU member states
Source: UNCTAD Statistics: Trade Indicators (see http://unctadstat.unctad.org/wds/ReportFolders/reportFolders.aspx?sRF_ActivePath=p,15912&sRF_Expanded=,p,15912).

Smaller countries are associated with a relatively larger and less efficient public sector. Alesina and Wacziarg (1998) document that the share of government spending over GDP tends to decrease as GDP increases – that is, smaller countries have larger governments, even after controlling for several other determinants of government size.

The per capita cost of many public goods in smaller countries tend to be relatively high due to the already mentioned indivisibility problem because fewer taxpayers pay for them and fewer people use them. These include roads, libraries, hospitals, and national parks.

Small states are also characterized by a relatively larger number of smaller firms in the private sector. According to data by the Lithuanian Department of Statistics, in 2014 small and medium sized enterprises (SMEs) in Lithuania accounted for 99.8% of private sector firms, with micro companies with fewer than ten employees accounting for 80%, while in Germany the corresponding figure is 35%. In Lithuania SMEs employ 76% of private sector employees and create around 63% of value added.

One advantage enjoyed by small states in participating in economic integration is that this can expand their export market, thereby enabling these states to benefit from economies of scale in the private sector. In addition, such integration renders small countries like Lithuania more attractive for foreign investors. In the case of Lithuania, after this country joined the EU, the export of Lithuanian companies became an engine for economic growth, while public spending contracted in relative terms. As a result of its integration into the Common Market, Lithuania gained access to the vast European market and was able to find niches for its unique products, which in turn led to improved usage of technology.

4.3 Small states and EU institutions

Although Lithuania is a small country, its interests can be defended within the EU institutions through a system of representation. Through the qualified majority voting arrangement, small states cannot exercise a veto on most issues, but their representation in EU institutions is much higher than the proportion of their population to the total EU population. For example, the Lithuanian population is three million or 27 times smaller than Germany's, but Lithuania's vote in the Council is only ten times smaller.

Likewise, in the European Parliament, Lithuania has 11 representatives, and in the European Commission it has one commissioner, again leading to a representation much higher than the proportion of the population.

This so-called degressive proportionality works in favour of small states, although it has to be admitted that the voice of the larger states remains very influential in EU decision-making processes.

5 Lithuania's accession to the European Union

5.1 The road to EU accession

Official relations and co-operation between Lithuania and the European Community started on 27 August 1991 when the European Community recognized the independence of Lithuania and included it into its technical assistance programme PHARE. On 11 May 1992, Lithuania and the European Community signed the Agreement on Trade and Commercial and Economic Co-operation, which was followed, on 18 July 1994, by the signing of a Free Trade Agreement between the EU and Lithuania, which came into force in 1995.

Lithuania's road towards EU membership may be said to have started in a concrete manner through the signing of the Association Agreement in 1995 with the EU, and in 1999 Lithuania was invited to enter into negotiations with the European Commission on membership. This process was completed in December 2002. The support of the Lithuanians regarding accession was expressed in a referendum held in 2002.

As in other EU candidate countries, there was a very lively debate on the advantages and disadvantages of EU membership. The most important economic benefit from integration was identified as the availability of a large market, without import controls, for the exports originating from Lithuania. Other advantages that were identified included incentives for efficient use of resources, lower costs due to market competition, improved variety of the products and EU funds for projects (Vilpišauskas, 2002). Economic integration was also expected to provide opportunities for Lithuania, as a small country, to use the advantage of a large European market and share risks.

Apart from the economic benefits, social advantages were also identified, such as a lower probability of conflicts between member states, internal political stability, and external security. The EU Commission was also seen as an authority that can make independent decisions (Vilpišauskas, 2002).

A number of possible disadvantages were identified. These included increases in the cost of living, higher cost of imports from the third countries, higher tax rates, losing part of the nation's sovereignty, emigration growth and health care problems (Vilpišauskas, 2002).

There are only a few quantitative estimations of the integration impact on the Lithuanian economy. An ex-post research carried out in 2006 (UAB, 2007) indicated that as a result of EU membership, increased export affected GDP growth by an average of 1.8 percentage points per annum between 2004 and 2006. The total impact of integration on GDP was estimated at 2.7 percentage points growth per annum. This ex-post evaluation indicated that the gains were higher than those forecasted in ex-ante research in 2002. According to the same authors, the influence of integration on FDI inflows was insignificant.

5.2 Trade diversion and trade creation associated with EU membership

In the context of EU accession it is useful to assess the trade creation or trade diversion effects resulting from Lithuania's integration into the EU. Table 5.4 shows the structure of domestic consumption of goods and its change since 2000. As can be seen from the data presented in the table, consumption of locally manufactured goods decreased consistently, while the consumption of imported goods increased, except for a temporary increase during the global economic crisis. This may be due to Lithuania's growing openness and demonstrates the existence of trade creation.

Table 5.4 also shows that imports from EU countries grew constantly until 2009, and decreased slightly after that year. Such a share of the EU countries' products in the consumption of Lithuania demonstrates that even though CIS products' were cheaper, they were replaced by EU products and this could be due to a trade diversion effect.

Given these changes, it appears that, in the case of Lithuania, the trade creation effect prevailed, as expected, leading to a growth of export volume since the beginning of the integration into the EU.

5.3 High value-added sector

An interesting aspect of EU membership relates to whether or not this has speeded up the growth of sectors with high value added. Between 1996 and 2014 the share of traditional Lithuanian industries, namely, food, textiles and furniture, in total exports of goods decreased gradually, while the share of high value-added sectors grew consistently. As a matter of fact, during the 1996–2003 period, the share of high-technology exports accounted for an

Table 5.4 Structure of Lithuanian domestic consumption

	2002	*2003*	*2004*	*2005*	*2006*	*2007*	*2008*	*2009*	*2010*	*2011*
Domestic production as share of consumption expenditure	42.1	45.5	45.2	40.3	37.1	39	36.4	39.1	35.9	34.7
Imported products apparent consumption expenditure	57.9	54.4	54.8	59.7	62.9	61	63.6	60.9	64.1	65.3
Products imported from the EU in consumption expenditure	31.5	29.6	31.0	33.3	39.8	36.2	39.8	41.4	36.7	38.3
Non-EU products imported in consumption expenditure	26.3	24.8	23.8	26.4	23.1	24.8	23.8	19.4	27.4	27.0

Source: Author's calculation based on EUROSTAT data.

average of 3.8% in manufactured exports, while in 2008 it reached 11.4% (Miskinis, 2013). This tendency is collaborated by IOC, Lithuania (2014), which calculates that in 2012 the export share of high-tech products amounted to 10.2% of total exports of goods.

Lithuania's integration into the EU therefore had major trade effects, one of which was that EU products replaced CIS products, and that exports with high value added increased their share of total exports. Product variety also improved, but the prices of imported goods went up due to the fact that EU products carry a higher price than similar CIS products.

Membership in the EU has also created conditions for more efficient utilization of the labour force due to the fact that employment increased in the expanding high-tech sector (biochemistry, nanotechnology, medical products), and in the branches of foreign companies which often employ well-educated Lithuanian workers.

5.4 Other effects of EU membership

The EU's financial support from structural funds is intended to contribute to the economic well-being of the recipient country, particularly in a small country like Lithuania. The support that Lithuania received significantly improved its infrastructure and was mostly used in public sector programmes.

EU accession may also have helped to generate competitiveness in Lithuania, as the free movement of goods within the EU has forced Lithuanian firms to compete with foreign firms, leading the former to seek niches with higher value added.

Some disadvantages that were expected as a result of integration into the EU proved to be true. The increased dependence of Lithuanian export on the EU makes Lithuania dangerously contingent on the EU economic cycles that are beyond the control of the Lithuanian government.

Another important downside in this context relates to emigration. After joining the EU, emigration from Lithuania was much higher than expected. It was forecasted that about 120,000 inhabitants would emigrate from Lithuania between 2004 and 2010 (Kuokštis, 2014: 111). However, during this period, more than 200,000 inhabitants left Lithuania (Kuokštis, 2014). The rate of emigration per 1,000 population from Lithuania was the highest among new member states. This partly solved the unemployment problem, however, in the long term it generated problems associated with pensions, education and health care systems, as well as public finance sustainability.

With regard to the funds received from the EU, there is some debate regarding their disadvantages, including that such support may give rise to inflation, that it may not be spent according to market needs, as there are set priorities for its use, and that it may give rise to corruption.

5.5 Lithuania's adoption of the euro

Lithuania was the seventh in the group of countries that joined the EU in 2004 to adopt the euro. Although the original target, set in 2005, was January 2007, the date of adoption had to be postponed due to Lithuania not meeting some of the thresholds set by the Maastricht criteria. In 2006, the government of Lithuania approved a convergence plan, which pushed the expected adoption date to post-2010. In February 2013, the government of Lithuania approved a plan, endorsed by Parliament in April 2014, setting 2015 as the year of euro adoption.[13]

On 23 July 2014, the European Council decided that Lithuania had fulfilled the necessary conditions for the adoption of the euro, and as a result the country adopted the euro on 1 January 2015. The banks and their automatic teller machines were available for withdrawals of euro cash on that date. During the two weeks that followed, there was a dual circulation of the euro and the litas. The changeover required considerable preparation, involving the banking sector, post offices, and credit unions.

A European Commission survey carried out between 16 and 19 January 2015 found that 91% of the respondents did not experience problems when exchanging litas or withdrawing cash during the first week of January.[14]

A major source of concern associated with the changeover was that this would generate inflation. Therefore steps were taken to avert abuse in retailing: prices were monitored by the authorities and retailers were required to display dual prices (litas and euro) as from August 2014, where the rounding of prices was set. In addition business people were invited to commit themselves not to take advantage of the changeover for their own profit, and about 90% of all retailers in Lithuania adhered to this scheme.

It is too early to assess the actual impact of the euro on the Lithuanian economy. However studies which were conducted before the introduction of the euro were generally in favour of this changeover. The conclusions of a study on the impact of the introduction of the euro carried out by the Bank of Lithuania in 2013 (Lietuvos bankas, 2013: 35–36) stated that due to the impact of euro introduction in 2015 real exports, excluding mineral products, were expected to increase by 5% annually over a seven-year period (2015–2021). The study also predicted that real GDP in the medium as well as in the long term would be higher with the introduction of the euro.

As member of the eurozone – an elite economic club – Lithuania should reduce its interest rates and improve its fiscal policy in line with the Stability and Growth Pact. This should in turn lead to higher credit ratings for the Lithuanian economy.

6 Challenges and prospects

The major challenges currently facing the Lithuanian economy are: (a) the trade restrictions imposed by Russia on EU imports, (b) the need to modernize the production methods, and (c) the large emigration flows.

6.1 The Russian embargo

The trade restrictions imposed by Russia on EU imports[15] are having negative direct and indirect effects on Lithuania's international trade. The restrictions of food imports by Russia in August 2014, and later the restrictions on transport services in November 2014 negatively affected Lithuania's merchandise exports (a reduction of about 4% from 2013) a large proportion of which were re-exports. Most of the decline was connected with oil products (24.4%) which used to account for about a quarter of Lithuanian merchandise exports, and to the re-export of vehicles (20%). The failure of major Lithuanian exporter Orlen Oil Refinery was the result of increasing world competition in the sector which was exacerbated by the Russian situation.

Export of food and agricultural products of Lithuanian origin to Russia in 2014 decreased by 28.3%, including export of meat by 44.8% and dairy products by 35.3%. The contraction of food export to Russia to some extent was offset by an increase in export to the EU and other markets.

Lithuanian exports were affected not only by the embargo on food but also by a sharp deceleration of private consumption and investments in Russia. The Russian demand for imports is also being hampered by the devaluation of the rouble.

The loss of exports to Russia has ancillary effects on transport services. Currently, nearly 90% of Lithuanian exports to Russia are re-exports, the shrinkage of which will have a relatively high negative effect on transportation companies.

The fall in exports to Russia is compelling Lithuanian businesses to seek new markets for their products. These efforts should be supported by the Lithuanian government and would transform a challenge into an opportunity as the exercise may result in the diversification of export markets and as a result of the economy.

6.2 Modernization of the economy

The second major challenge facing Lithuania is the need to modernize its economic institutions and structures. So far, the Lithuanian economy has been to a large extent based on traditional low or medium value-added industries. Competitiveness in the production of goods and services was mainly attributable to low costs, including wages and salaries. It is unlikely, and not desirable, that in the future companies will secure growth with low salaries, one reason being that there are pressures to increase them, including those brought about by economic growth. In addition, as members of the labour force improve their skills they expect to receive salaries commensurate with their skills and qualifications. However, in order for firms to pay higher salaries, without losing competitiveness, it is necessary for them to produce higher value added per unit of labour, so as to ensure that unit labour costs do not increase.

There are calls for the further modernization of the economy through investment in technological advance. This is the only way for Lithuanian companies to compete sustainably in the export market, so that they can create well-remunerated jobs for highly skilled labour, without necessarily increasing unit labour costs. Low wage rates do not offer a sustainable economic future for Lithuania, and the solution is to improve labour productivity, which would permit the increases in returns to labour. This would also improve living standards and usher in further convergence with the EU. This was identified by the IMF (2015) as the main policy challenge.

One problem that could work against the modernization of the economy is the economic uncertainty in the eurozone. Another is the huge capital outlays that are required for this purpose. Although investment during 2014 increased, it is still lower than the pre-crisis level. In 2008 gross fixed capital formation accounted for 26% of GDP, a ratio which fell to 18.2% in 2013.

6.3 Emigration

The third major challenge facing Lithuania relates to demographic changes mostly caused by emigration, which is leading to a decrease in the working-age population. Emigration, coupled with an aging population, are and will adversely affect the sustainability of the pension system.

According to the EU Country Report on Lithuania (European Commission, 2015), the government has not taken any decisive action to put in place a pension system reform, which would ensure the long-term sustainability of the system. Some steps have already been taken, such as that related to the statutory retirement age, which has been and is being gradually increased. Overall, the challenges for Lithuania's pension system remain, and may be intensified by continuing emigration unless a drastic reform is implemented.

Emigration is also affecting the sustainability of the education system, which is being adversely affected by the decreasing number of students. This calls for the merging of educational institutions in order to optimize the number of students per school. The Lithuanian education system needs further reforms to make teaching more applicable to the needs of the labour market.

One possible solution to reduce the negative effects of emigration is to step up labour productivity, which could result in higher labour earnings and this would render domestic employment more attractive. Another possibility is to attract workers from other countries. However, taking into consideration the fact that the majority of European countries offer higher wages than in Lithuania, this possibility can hardly be expected to be realized. In addition, the import of foreign workers may create social problems.

According to IMF (2015), it is important for the government of Lithuania that put in place policies that maximize the utilization of the demographically shrinking labour resources through the modernization of the labour law, and improvements in the labour-market relevance of education.

7 Conclusion

In this chapter it has been argued that the decision of the Lithuanian government to establish and maintain a fixed exchange rate using a currency board arrangement during the country's transformation period stabilized the Lithuanian economy and built up confidence in the state and in the financial markets.

It has been shown also that integration into the EU substantially contributed to the development of the Lithuanian economy, opening new markets for Lithuanian producers, providing financial support and creating conditions that make use of the country's geographic advantage. However EU accession may have also brought about some stresses such as the dependence on economic cycles of external markets and large migration flows.

Three major challenges facing the economy of Lithuania that need to be addressed to foster growth and stability in the country have been identified. These are (a) the trade restrictions imposed by Russia calling for diversification of exports, (b) the need to modernize the production methods and economic structures to increase labour productivity, and (c) the need to address the emigration problem, which calls for improving employment attractiveness in the country and for urgent pension reform.

However there is room for optimism with regard to Lithuania's economic prospects. As IMF (2015) put it, the Lithuanian past resilience augurs well for future growth. The improved prospects of stability within the euro area, and Lithuania's drive to continue diversifying exports, to modernize the economy and to usher in a pension reform, could possibly offset the negative effects mentioned in this chapter, including those associated with the Russian embargo and recession.

Notes

1 The other two are Estonia and Latvia.
2 Net migration in 1990–2012 was 617.5 thousand or around 17% of the population. Since 2010 emigration has remained high but immigration has started to increase, thus reducing net migration flow.
3 See Council Recommendation on the 2015 National Reform Programme of Lithuania. Available at: http://ec.europa.eu/europe2020/pdf/csr2015/csr2015_lithuania_en.pdf.
4 Available at: http://ec.europa.eu/eurostat/tgm/table.do?tab=table&init=1&plugin=1&pcode=tessi190&language=en.
5 Available at: http://ec.europa.eu/eurostat/statistics-explained/index.php/People_at_risk_of_poverty_or_social_exclusion.
6 Available at: www.doingbusiness.org/~/media/GIAWB/Doing%20Business/Documents/Annual-Reports/English/DB15-Chapters/DB15-Report-Overview.pdf.
7 Available at: http://www.heritage.org/index/pdf/2015/book/Index_2015.pdf.
8 Available at: http://unctad.org/en/Pages/DIAE/World%20Investment%20Report/Annex-Tables.aspx.
9 Available at: http://ec.europa.eu/eurostat/tgm/refreshTableAction.do?tab=table&plugin=1&pcode=tsdec310&language=en.
10 Available at: www.globalinnovationindex.org/userfiles/file/reportpdf/gii-2014-v5.pdf.

11 Available at: www.innovationdata.be/a/EC_IUS2014/Innovation_Union_Scoreboard_2014.
12 Statistical Yearbook of Lithuania (2014) is available at: http://osp.stat.gov.lt/services-portlet/pub-edition-file?id=2910.
13 An account of the process of Lithuania's adoption of the euro is given in the European Commission report entitled 'The introduction of the euro in Lithuania', available at: http://ec.europa.eu/economy_finance/euro/countries/documents/lithuania_the_introduction_en.pdf.
14 http://ec.europa.eu/public_opinion/flash/fl_412_sum_en.pdf.
15 For more information about the Russian embargo on EU products see 'Information note on the Russian ban on agri-food products from the EU', available at: http://ec.europa.eu/agriculture/russian-import-ban/pdf/info-note-03-09_en.pdf.

References

Alesina, A. and Wacziarg, R. (1998) 'Openness, Country Size and Government', *Journal of Public Economics*, 69: 305–321. Available at: www.anderson.ucla.edu/faculty_pages/romain.wacziarg/downloads/openness.pdf (accessed 23 January 2016).

Briguglio, L. (2014) 'A Vulnerability and Resilience Framework for Small State', in D. Bynoe (ed.) *Building the Resilience of Small States: A Revised Framework*. London: Commonwealth Secretariat.

European Commission (2015). *Country Report for Lithuania, 2015*. Available at: http://ec.europa.eu/europe2020/pdf/csr2015/cr2015_lithuania_en.pdf (accessed 23 January 2016).

Girdenas, S., Giedraitis, V.R. and Rasteniene, A. (2013) *Development of States and Forms of Capitalism: An Empirical Examination of their Relationship*. Academic Publishing Platforms, Business and Academic Horizons. Available at http://academicpublishingplatforms.com/volume.php?journal=BEH&id=3&number=9 (accessed 23 January 2016).

Global Innovation Index (2014) *The Human Factor in Innovation*. Fontainebleau, Ithaca, and Geneva: Cornell University, INSEAD, and WIPO. Retrieved from https://www.globalinnovationindex.org/userfiles/file/reportpdf/gii-2014-v5.pdf (accessed 23 January 2016).

IMD (2015) *World Competitiveness Yearbook*. Lausanne: Word Competitiveness Centre. Available at: http://www.imd.org/uupload/imd.website/wcc/scoreboard.pdf (accessed 23 January 2016).

IMF (2015) *Republic of Lithuania 2015 Article IV Consultation*. Available at: https://www.imf.org/external/pubs/ft/scr/2015/cr15138.pdf (accessed 23 January 2016).

IOC, Lithuania (2014) *Technologijų sričių didţiausio potencialo ţinių, inovacijų ir mokslo rezultatų eksporto galimybių studija* (Feasibility study on potential areas of technology, knowledge and innovation in exports). Available at: www.lvk.lt/uploads/File/Asistentas1GS/32Nauju_technologiju_eksportas.pdf (accessed 23 January 2016).

Kuokštis, V. (2014) *Lietuvos narystė Europos sąjungoje: ekonominė raida* (Lithuania's economic development during European Union membership), *Politologija*, 4(76): 92–123.

Lietuvosbankas (2013) 'Euro įvedimo Lietuvoje 2015 m. kiekybinio poveikio šalies ekonomikai vertinimas' (The adoption of the Euro in Lithuania in 2015: Quantitative impact assessment on the country's economy). *Teminių straipsnių* serija, 2013(1). Available at: http://www.lb.lt/kiekybinis_euro_tyrimas (accessed 23 January 2016).

Miskinis, A. (2013) 'Overview of Lithuanian Experience in Free Trade Zone', in Зёни вільнёїтёргівлі на *пёчаткуXXI стёліття* (*Free Trade Areas at the beginning of the 21st century*). Kiev: Publishing Center, Kyiv University: 314–335.

Miskinis, A. and Reinbold, B. (2010) 'Investments of German MNS into Production Networks in Central European and Baltic States', *Technological and Economic Development of Economy*, 16(4).

Miskinis, I. and Juozenaite, A. (2015) 'Comparative Analysis of Foreign Direct Investment (FDI) Factors', *Ekonomika*, 94(2): 7–28.

Schwab, K. (2014) *The Global Competitiveness Report 2014–2015*. World Economic Forum. Available at: http://www3.weforum.org/docs/WEF_GlobalCompetitivenessReport_2014-15.pdf (accessed 23 January 2016).

UAB (2007) 'Lietuvos integracijos į es poveikio Lietuvos ekonomikai 2002–2006 metais (ex-post) vertinimas' (The economic impact of Lithuania's integration with the EU 2002–2006: ex-post evaluation). Lithuania: UAB. Available at https://www.urm.lt/uploads/default/documents/uzienio_politika/ES/ES_tyrimai/7_%20Ex_post_ataskaita.pdf (accessed 23 January 2016).

UNDP (2014) *The Human Development Reports*. Available at: http://hdr.undp.org/en/content/table-1-human-development-index-and-its-components (accessed 23 January 2016).

Vilpišauskas, R. (2002) 'Lietuvos integracijos į Europos Sąjungą pasekmių analizė' (Analysisis of the effects of Lithuania's integration into the European Union). Paper commissioned by the Government of the Republic of Lithuania.

6 The economy of Luxembourg

Serge Allegrezza

1 Introduction

Luxembourg, officially the Grand Duchy of Luxembourg, is a landlocked country located in Western Europe and bordered by France, Belgium and Germany. With a population of just over half a million, Luxembourg is the second smallest EU member state, with only Malta being smaller. Currently, Luxembourg registers the highest GDP per capita in the European Union (EU).

Although the recorded history of Luxembourg can be traced back to Roman times, the history of the country is considered to begin in 963 as Lucilinburhuc.[1] Over the following five centuries, the powerful House of Luxembourg emerged, but its extinction put an end to Luxembourg's independence. After a brief period of Burgundian rule, Luxembourg passed to the Habsburgs in 1477 who defended their possessions against the French kings. Revolutionary France annexed Luxembourg, which became the 'département des forêts'. After the Napoleonic wars, the Treaty of Vienna of 1815 transformed Luxembourg into a Grand Duchy in personal union with the king of the Netherlands. Following the revolution in Belgium of 1830, Luxembourg became a province of the new Belgian state. The territory was partitioned in 1839, with the French-speaking part being incorporated into Belgium while the German-speaking part remained as a Grand Duchy, but with a reduced territory, belonging to the king of the Netherlands and part of the German confederation. In 1842 Luxembourg was integrated into the Zollverein, a customs union with Germany, which offered a large market to the nascent steel industry. After the Franco-German war of 1870–1871, the German empire finally respected Luxembourg's formal independence while tying the economy closely to German business interests.

After the First World War, Luxembourg passed through a period of political crises, economic turmoil and social unrest, and it had to struggle for its survival once again. It joined into a customs and monetary union with Belgium (union belgo-luxembourgeoise) to open markets for its products, and at that time also joined the League of Nations. After the Second World War, the foundation of European institutions, including the European Coal and Steel Community (ECSC) and the European Community, in the establishment of which Luxembourg was involved, led step by step to the unification of Europe. From that time on, Luxembourg became a member of the European Community (now European Union). The treaty of Rome of 1957 laid the foundation for a true internal market and the Maastricht Treaty paved the way for a true economic union and a common currency. European integration turned out to be the launching pad of Luxembourg's economic success.

This chapter is organized into six sections. Following this brief historical introduction, Section 2 outlines economic development in Luxembourg since the 1960s, referring to the transition from steel to finance. Section 3 discusses characteristics of Luxembourg as a small open economy, while the section that follows assesses the benefits of the economy derived from EU membership. Section 5 identifies a number of challenges faced by the economy. Section 6 concludes the chapter.

2 The economy of Luxembourg since 1960

2.1 From steel to finance

For a very long time, the economy of Luxembourg was associated with the steel industry, and during the nineteenth century, starting in the 1870s, Luxembourg's steel production became one of the most important in Europe. The steel industry still occupies an important place in the economy of Luxembourg, even after the restructuring of the economy since the 1960s.

During the 1970s, the old economic model based on steel came to an end with the process of globalization, the oil crisis and the industrial recession. Luxembourg had a hard time to manage the looming social crisis so as to avoid mass layoffs with the closing of the steel mills, erstwhile symbols of the success of the country. During the 1960s, and to a lesser degree the 1970s, economic growth in Luxembourg fell below the average growth rate of its neighbouring countries (Figure 6.1).

From the beginning of the 1980s, the nascent financial sector took off, propelled by worldwide deregulation and the globalization of financial services. This was an economic revolution for Luxembourg in terms of its consequences: it ushered in high growth figures for the country's gross domestic product (GDP) and created employment whilst stimulating a swift transformation of the economic structure from one based mainly on iron and steel to one highly based on financial services (Figure 6.2).

As a result of the great recession of 2008/2009, triggered by the international financial and banking crisis, the vulnerabilities associated with a high degree of economic specialization in financial services became increasingly recognized.

The economy recovered well after the great recession of 2008/2009, although it is unlikely that the growth rates will reach the levels of the period before the crisis, when output growth averaged 4.75% over the period 2000–2007. According to the latest (October 2015) data by STATEC, growth has risen in

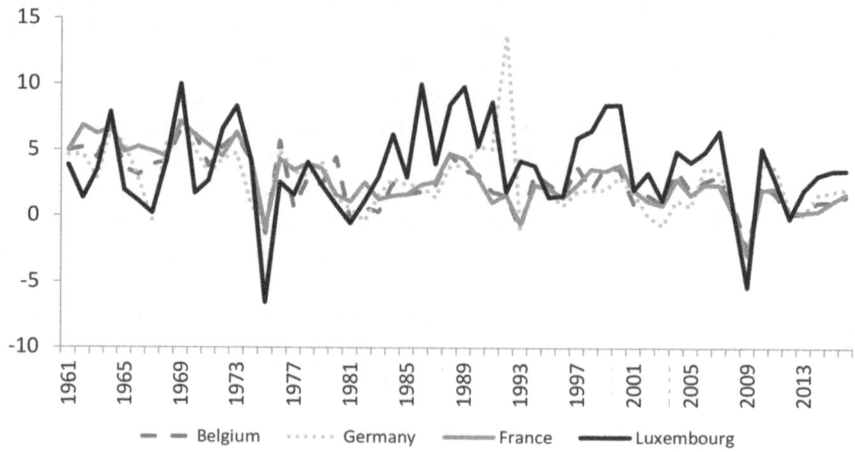

Figure 6.1 Luxembourg's economic growth compared to its neighbours (percentage change)

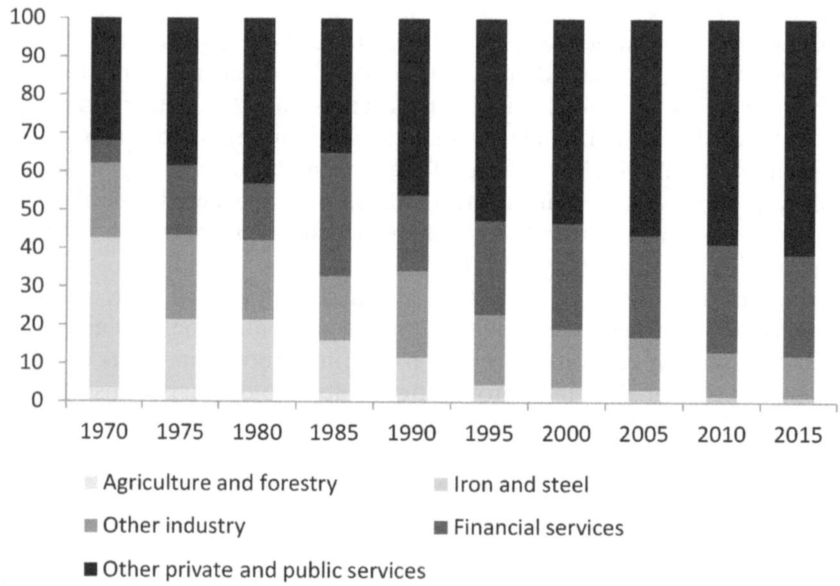

Figure 6.2 The percentage composition of gross value added (1970–2014)

2014, mostly due to the good performance of the services sector. Despite significant uncertainties related to the international economic and political context, real GDP growth in 2014 was 4.1%. For 2015, in line with economic indicators known at this stage – that reflect an overall strengthening of economic dynamics – STATEC expects growth to remain at about 3.5%. For 2016, growth should remain above 3%, mainly due to the strengthening economic momentum in the euro area and the direction of activity in the financial sector of Luxembourg.

Regarding inflation, the recent fall in oil prices has largely contributed to a sharp downward revision to the inflation outlook for 2015, with a rate of 0.8%, although there was a VAT hike of 2%. This slowdown of inflation alleviated pressure on wage rates, and this is expected to be felt in the next wage rate changes, which should take place in the last quarter of 2016, in line with the automatic wage indexation mechanism. Assuming the stabilization of oil prices and economic activity gaining momentum inflation should rise to 1.5% in 2016.

Public finance has remained quite healthy during the last 10 years, with relatively small deficits of less than 1% in 2004 and in 2009 and 2010. The government announced that it would stick to the target of a structural surplus of 0.5% so that gross public debt should stay below 30%. The public debt has increased significantly since the great recession from 7% in 2007 to 23.6% in 2014.

When taking account of the rebalancing of the budgetary policy called 'Zukunftspak' ('package for the future' increasing taxes and reducing public expenditures), the nominal budget balance (revenue minus expenditure) is expected to remain positive over the projection horizon, between 0 and 0.5% of GDP. The structural balance should deteriorate by contrast, while respecting – until 2017 – the target of a surplus of + 0.5% (STATEC, 2015).

The labour market has shown remarkable resilience throughout the crisis. Although the growth rate recorded before the crisis is not likely to be matched, the pace of job creation remained sustained at 2% in 2013 and accelerated in 2014. Apart from the industrial sector, where overall employment continues to contract, all sectors recorded positive growth in 2013, including the financial sector as a whole, where employment grew by 0.9%. The outlook for employment growth over the coming years remains positive, though a slow-down in the pace of job creation is expected, in line with GDP projections.

Unemployment is expected to remain close to 7% in 2015, relatively low when compared to other euro area members[2] but historically high for Luxembourg. As from 2016, due to the anticipated slowdown in economic activity, the net job creation is expected to slow down to 2%.

Thus employment as well as unemployment increased in recent years (STATEC, 2014a). This decoupling of employment and unemployment may be explained by the fact that about half of the jobs in Luxembourg are taken by cross-border workers coming from France, Belgium and Germany, as well as by difficulties in the transition from school to work for the resident population. Recent evidence shows that the employment growth has to reach 4% per year in order to keep the unemployment rate constant, ceteris paribus.

Labour productivity levels remain among the highest in the euro area, though their growth rate has stagnated in recent years. This can be partly explained by labour hoarding practices, encouraged by public support schemes like short-time work (*chômage partiel*) and the difficulty to recruit highly qualified personnel. A specific feature of the country is the sizeable divergence of labour productivity across economic sectors, with the financial sector registering by far the highest level. The stagnation in labour productivity and the steady increase in nominal wages have led to an increase in nominal unit labour costs over the last decade. Unit labour costs rose by 56.8% in Luxembourg between 2000 and 2013, more than twice as fast as the euro area average of 26.0% and compared to 12.5% in Germany over the same period (European Commission, 2015). This is a major source of concern in Luxembourg, and has led to disputes the between the social partners and the government.

Luxembourg is dependent on imports for almost all its energy needs, but nonetheless the government set a very ambitious goal of 20% reduction of greenhouse gas (GHG) emissions. This target will probably be missed by a wide margin, possibly the highest projected gap among all EU member states. Luxembourg's energy intensity remains moderate, even though Luxembourg has substantial 'heavy industry' and a sizeable amount of transport fuel sales, as well as a high rate of fuel exports at its borders. Luxembourg is the best performer in the EU in terms of resource productivity, in terms of the degree of the efficient use of material resources to produce wealth. Government efforts to promote energy efficiency focus in particular on buildings.

In 2011, transport accounted for 57% of all GHG emissions in Luxembourg and transport-related emissions increased by 40% between 2000 and 2014. Around 70% of these emissions are connected to fuel exports, in part a result of comparatively low excise duties on fuels.

3 Luxembourg as a small state

3.1 The special characteristics of small states

Are the patterns relating to economic performance or the well-being of the population in small states different from those in large states? This matter is important because often Luxembourg is compared to its larger neighbours, particularly Germany and France, and occasionally to Belgium, without taking into account the intrinsic features of a small open economy. Neglecting this peculiar feature may introduce a potential bias in benchmarking.

Both theoretical and empirical research shed light on this issue. For example Alesina and Spolaore (2005) have formulated a theoretical framework and laid the ground for empirical work on the link between openness, size and specificities of small countries. Large countries have many advantages over small countries. There are economies of scale in the production of public goods, and as a result the per capita cost of many public goods is lower in larger states, when compared to smaller ones. This is mainly due to the problem of overhead costs indivisibility, as such costs do not decrease in proportion to population size.

Some studies (see for example Doyle and O'Connor, 2013; Favaro, 2008) suggest that those small states that assign importance to small solutions to strengthen the innovation capacities, would, as a result, enhance their competitiveness and reap further benefits from their trade openness.

A recent paper produced by the International Monetary Fund (IMF, 2013), based on an analysis of a sample of small mainly developing countries as well as fuel exporting countries, compared the growth experienced by the small states relative to their larger peers, covering the period 1980–2010. The IMF study found that small states grew slightly slower than their larger peers after controlling for standard growth determinants. However, this difference is only marginally significant statistically. In addition, the average per capita gross national income (GNI) of small states was broadly comparable to that of larger states in 2011. Indeed, regression analysis, controlling for regional effects, indicated that small states had somewhat higher income levels than larger peers.

A working paper posted by Alouini and Hubert (2010) using a composite dimension to measure country size (population, GDP and arable land), employed panel-data regressions on 163 countries, and showed that there is clear negative relation between country size and the growth rate of GDP. However, they concluded that trade openness has a clear positive effect on growth.

The findings that resulted from different studies indicate that it is useful to consider the specificities in small states. However, a study by the present author shows that size, measured by population size, has no significant impact on GNI per capita in the EU, confirming that small country size, in an open and fair context, may not matter.[3]

3.2 The advantages and disadvantages of trade openness

One common conclusion that emerges is that small and very open economies seem to be advantaged as a result of trade openness, with the main downside being that their high exposure to external economic forces can lead to relatively high economic volatility.

Small states tend to have a high degree of trade openness, principally because they need foreign buyers for their products in view of their small domestic market. In addition, due to the limited resources endowments of such states, they need to import most of their industrial supplies.

Openness can be advantageous for small states, mainly because it trade spurs competiveness. Various authors (Easterly and Kraay, 2000) have argued that the trade openness is a key element in the economic success of small economies like Luxembourg.

However, there are costs associated with a small domestic market. One such cost relates to the fact that international trade implies crossing state borders. To quote Alesina and Spolorare (2005: 1504):

> a vast literature has convincingly shown that even in the absence of explicit trade policy barriers, crossing borders is indeed costly, so that economic interactions within a country are much easier and denser than across borders. This is true both for trade in goods and financial assets. What explains this border effect, even in the absence of explicit policy barriers is unclear. Whatever the source of the border effect, however, the correlation between the 'political size' of a country and its market size does not totally disappear even in the absence of policy-induced trade barriers.

Another disadvantage is that a high degree of openness exposes the economy to external shocks and therefore the fate of the domestic economy is often conditioned by forces outside its control.

4 Luxembourg as an EU member state

4.1 Luxembourg and EU institutions

Luxembourg is one of the six founding members of the European Union and was signatory to the Treaty of Rome in 1957. In 1999 Luxembourg also joined the euro area. The country has long been a prominent supporter of the European project, and in general, its population have tended to be in favour of economic and political integration. In the Autumn 2014 Eurobarometer survey (European Commission, 2014a), 89% of the respondents stated that they feel that they are citizens of the EU, which was the highest favourable response in this regard within the EU. In the same edition of the Eurobarometer, 67% of the residents indicated that they are still optimistic about the future of the EU and highly supportive of the euro.

Luxembourg hosts several EU institutions and agencies. These include the European Court of Justice, the European Court of Auditors, a significant part of the European Commission administration, the Secretariat General of the European Parliament, the European Investment Bank, the European Financial Stability Facility (EFSF), the European stability mechanism (ESM) and the Statistical Office of the European Communities (Eurostat). The Secretariat of the European Parliament is located in Luxembourg, although the Parliament itself usually meets in Strasbourg.

Currently the President of the European Commission, Jean-Claude Juncker, hails from Luxembourg. The country, like all other member states has representatives in the EU institutions including the European Parliament, the European Economic and Social Committee and on the Committee of the Regions, with six representatives in each of these institutions.

4.2 Luxembourg benefits from the EU

Luxembourg benefits from its EU membership in many ways. Many of these, such as peace and security, political stability, safeguarding of democracy, freedom of movement and access to a large single market, are enjoyed by all EU member states.

Luxembourg pays more into the EU budget than it receives from it. However, given its central geographical position between founding members, Luxembourg was chosen to host the EU institutions and agencies listed above. For this reason, the largest share of the money that Luxembourg receives from the EU budget (amounting to 85% in 2013) is associated with the administration of these entities. This creates considerable employment in the country, generating direct, indirect and income multiplier effects on the economy.[4]

A considerable proportion of EU funds is spent on projects associated with economic capacity building, supporting agriculture, research and regional development.

The funds received by Luxembourg are also partly spent to support research, which is considered crucial for promoting competitiveness, economic growth and job creation. Targeted investment in this regard is directed at biomedicine, information and communications technology (ICT), green technologies, logistics and outer space research.

4.3 Threats arising from EU membership

The internal market and the breakup of the eurozone are the two major threats to the future of Luxembourg as an EU member state.

Economic and Monetary Union, which was hailed as major leap of European integration, was not suitably structured to deal with the banking and financial crisis and the large fiscal, financial and structural imbalances that had accumulated in the euro area over the years. Following the global financial crisis, a full-blown sovereign debt crisis occurred in 2011–2012, without rules and mechanisms to deal with it (Sapir and Wolff, 2015). As the fierce debates relating to the rescue programme for Greece have shown, these imbalances threaten the very existence of the monetary union. Even though the debt crisis has now abated, an economic crisis, mostly due to feeble growth and near-zero inflation, has been ushered in. Some authors argue (e.g. Klinkers, 2012) that to keep the euro zone intact, more federalism may be needed, meaning more transfers of cross-border wealth, stricter and centrally fixed rules in areas like taxation, social security and labour standards, a reform that would very likely be politically difficult (Keleman, 2007: 52).

The second challenge, relating to the imbalances of the euro area, is the possibility of re-erecting barriers to the free movement of goods and services of the internal market. As the history of the independence of Luxembourg has made obvious, a respect for the sovereignty of a small state and access to a large market is a recipe for economic success. The 1992 'single market' programme was enthusiastically embraced by Luxembourg (Allegrezza, 1993) and is often considered as one of the most important advantages enjoyed by the EU small states.

5 The economic challenges ahead

5.1 The danger of 'secular stagnation'

According to the Organisation for Economic Co-operation and Development (OECD, 2015b) and the IMF (2015) there is the possibility of long-term stagnation in the EU and this will, inevitably, affect the economy of Luxembourg. Secular stagnation may be the outcome of two main forces, emanating from the supply side (such as an ageing population and slow rate of technical progress) and/or from the demand side (such as reduced income leading to reduced consumption and rising income inequalities).

Regarding the demand side, De Grauwe (2015) argues that the eurozone's secular stagnation may also be attributed to the asymmetric way external imbalances within the eurozone were corrected between the southern countries, as debtors, and the northern countries as creditors. The latter imposed tough austerity measures on the former, pushing them into quick and deep spending cuts and intense recessions.

There may, however, be some light at the end of the tunnel as important steps are being taken by the European Commission, notably the creation of the ESM and the establishment of a European banking union, as well as the Investment Plan for Europe (European Commission, 2014b).

In the particular case of Luxembourg, the problem of low productivity is especially relevant with regard to potential growth, which, for Luxembourg, has been revised downwards compared with the period before the crisis. It is estimated that this would just attain 2%, dragged down by the drop in the labour contribution, as well as by the drop in factor productivity, that has turned negative since 2009 (European Commission, 2015). One factor that may have contributed to a fall in productivity relates to the financial sector, where the potential has been dented by the rather strict regulatory framework which was imposed on the sector by the regulators, notably the European Commission and the European Central Bank.

5.2 Diversification of the economy

Private investment in research and development (R&D) remains relatively low in Luxembourg, although progress towards a more diversified, knowledge-intensive economy is seen as a political priority. Indeed, while the quadrupling of public sector R&D intensity since 2000 reflects the authorities' resolve to build up public research capacities, Luxembourg is not on track to reach its R&D intensity target of 2.3–2.6% of GDP by 2020. R&D intensity was at 1.2% in 2013, a relatively low level compared with the EU average (2.0%). This is due to the sharp drop in business investment from 1.46% of GDP in 2000 to 0.71% in 2013 (European Commission 2015). In Luxembourg, cooperation between public research institutions and private firms is well below the EU average, reflecting the current disconnect between private sector R&D

and the public research system. However, one has to bear in mind that the huge financial and business service sectors do not invest in traditional R&D, although they do launch new or improved services.

5.3 Skills shortage, migration, education, training

The Programme for International Student Assessment (PISA) tests, organized by the OECD, triggered a series of empirical analyses of the performance of the Luxembourg school system. Socio-economic factors play a significant role in educational outcomes with pupils from a migrant background achieving in general worse results than non-migrants. While multilingualism represents a strength of Luxembourg's school system, it can also constitute a barrier for pupils not having one of the three national languages as a mother tongue. The system selects pupils at a very early stage, placing them into vocational streams and classic secondary education. This early tracking accentuates the educational gap caused by differences in socio-economic status and immigration background (Langer, 2007).

With regard to early school leavers, Luxembourg registers a relatively low rate, with about 6% of the population aged 18–24 compared to the EU average (11%) in 2014.

The tertiary education attainment rate (52.2% of the 30 to 34 year-olds) in 2013 is progressing towards the very high national 2020 target of 66%. However, the rate reflects to a large degree the highly educated immigrant population living and working in the country, but not necessarily the outcome of Luxembourg's education system. The employment rate for recent tertiary graduates is higher than in the EU as a whole (83.8% compared to 80.7% in 2013). An area of concern is that the employment rate of 20–34 year olds among recent graduates has dropped from 89.5% in 2010 to 79.1% in 2013 (European Commission, 2015).

5.4 Competitiveness

In 2003, Luxembourg's social partners, meeting during the traditional crisis management forum known as 'tripartite', decided to set up a 'competitiveness observatory' to monitor and benchmark the development of the position of the Luxembourg economy. A very general definition of competitiveness has been retained by the social partners, referring to factors conducive to productivity, while taking care of inclusiveness and catering for environmental protection.

Almost 80 indicators were chosen and classified into ten groups, namely macroeconomic performance, employment, productivity and labour costs, market operations, institutional and regulatory frameworks, entrepreneurship, education and training, knowledge economy, social cohesion and environment. The individual indicators were normalized and added up to form a composite index, and summarized as a general competitiveness score (see Figure 6.3).

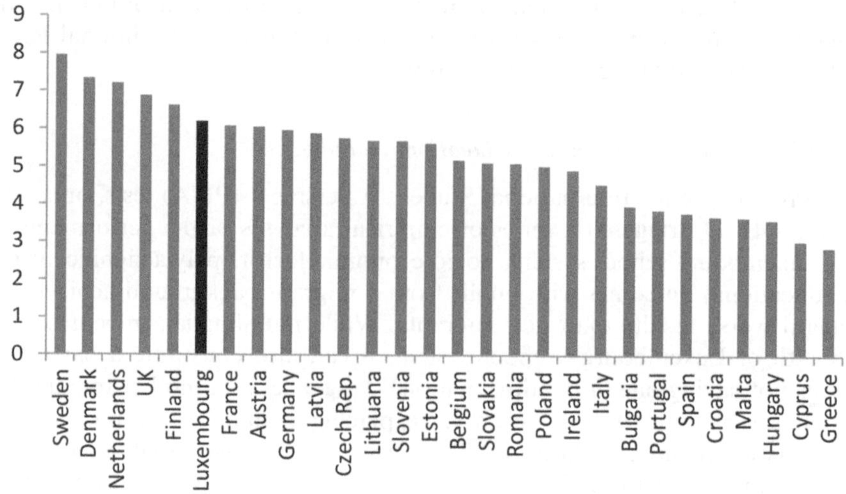

Figure 6.3 Final score of the national competitiveness composite indicator
Source: Observatoire de la compétitivité (2014).

The results of the scoreboard, together with 30 international benchmarks and assessment of potential macroeconomic disequilibria, issued by the European Commission, the IMF and the OECD, are included in a major report ('*Bilan compétitivité*'), which is discussed in a special parliamentary session on competitiveness and growth.[5] According to this index, Luxembourg receives a relatively high score when compared to other EU members.

Luxembourg also performs relatively well in terms of competitiveness, as measured by other well-known productivity scoreboards, including the competitiveness indicators of the World Economic Forum (WEF) and the IMD World Competitiveness Center (IMD), as shown in Table 6.1.

It should be stated here that the productivity picture for the whole economy has to be interpreted with caution (STATEC, 2014c). In the case of financial services, productivity is difficult to measure due to the complications in the definitions of the outputs and the inputs in the production in financial activities. Another problem is that the service industries in general are characterised by a single production technology and again in this case there are complications regarding the measurement of outputs and inputs. Furthermore, the inclusion of physical capital as an input for banking and financial intermediation activities is not appropriate. This is a very difficult problem for national accountants and economists who have to make sense of data to judge productivity developments. This is particularly true for Luxembourg, which has a relatively large financial sector.

Table 6.1 Adjusted ranking with the top ten European countries

Rank	*WEF*	*IMD*	*Heritage Foundation*	*European Commission*
1.	Switzerland	Switzerland	Switzerland	Switzerland
2.	Finland	Sweden	Ireland	Sweden
3.	Germany	Germany	Denmark	Denmark
4.	Netherlands	Denmark	Estonia	Germany
5.	UK	Norway	UK	Finland
6.	Sweden	**Luxembourg**	Netherlands	**Luxembourg**
7.	Norway	Netherlands	**Luxembourg**	Netherlands
8.	Denmark	Ireland	Germany	Belgium
9.	Belgium	UK	Finland	UK
10.	**Luxembourg**	Finland	Sweden	Ireland

Source: Observatoire de la compétitivité (2014).

5.5 *Wage cost and automatic indexation*

The wage system in operation in Luxembourg is often criticized by international organizations such as the OECD and the IMF as a driver of labour costs and inflation and hotly debated among unions and employers' federations (*Luxemburger Wort*, 2013). The wage setting system is based on collective bargaining, covering almost half of the employees at the national level, and on a mandatory wage increase for all employees, triggered automatically by an inflation threshold. On top of this, there is a minimum wage arrangement, which is supported by law.

In times of high inflation, to ward off the consequences of adverse shocks from the price of petrol, it was decided to introduce a temporary 'adjustment' of the automatic wage indexation. The last adjustment took place during the period 2012–2014, limiting it to one wage increase ('tranche') per year, and this has helped contain labour cost increases to some extent.

There is some evidence that the link between the mechanism of indexation, inflation and wages at a macroeconomic level is much more complex than usually depicted. A recent study by the University of Luxembourg (Sneesens et al., 2014), comparing the determinants of wage costs in Luxembourg, Belgium, France and Germany could not show, all else remaining equal, any significant difference due to the automatic indexation mechanism. Another study (STATEC, 2015) found that contrary to the findings of the IMF (2014), the wage differential of inflation (measured by the national consumer price index) with the inflation of the eurozone as well as the level of the inflation in Luxembourg are not driven significantly either by automatic indexation nor by the minimum wage developments. It is likely that if inflation would accelerate in Luxembourg, the arguments on inflation and its links to competitiveness will emerge again and may once again dominate the public debate.

5.6 The balance of payments

The current account balance has remained in surplus in recent years, though lower than the average surplus of around 10% of GDP recorded during the period 2001–2007. The surplus is projected to shrink even further from 2015 – as VAT on e-commerce, paid to the country of residence of consumers, will be deducted from the export of services (European Commission, 2015).

The current account surpluses are mostly driven by financial services and make up for a persistent and gradually increasing deficit in the merchandise trade balance. The deficit in merchandise stems more from weak export growth than from an increase in imports, as is reflected in the significant loss in export market share for goods, which accelerated in the aftermath of the financial crisis.

The current account surplus is also dragged down by the widening deficit on the primary income balance. This net outflow increased to 31% of GDP in 2012 (from 14.8% of GDP in 2002), mirroring the increasing success of the financial services industry in placing its products abroad and the large number of cross-border and migrant workers.

5.7 Sustainability and well-being

The financing of social security is at the heart of the Luxembourg business model, where social contributions as well as tax on wages are kept very low (OECD, 2015a), guaranteeing social peace and cohesion, overseen by the social partners, and rendering Luxembourg a very attractive place to live. According to the latest stability and convergence programme posted by the Ministry of Finance (2015), gross public debt is projected to remain at less than 25% of GDP, well under the 30% limit set by the government. The balance of the general public sector was in surplus during the past decade, except in 2003 (internet bubble), 2009 and 2010 (global recession). This made it possible for Luxembourg to retain its AAA rating by major rating agencies.

However, the budgetary impact of an ageing population poses a challenge to long-term fiscal sustainability, in particular in the area of pensions and long-term care and health expenditures. The system relies on huge transfers from the central government to social security, financed by tax receipts and contributions paid by an increasing proportion of relatively young workers, particularly by immigrants and cross-border workers. The sustainability of the system requires a fast rate of employment increase or in technical progress. The pension system is pre-funded by a considerable amount (about 30% GDP) which could cushion the impact of a protracted slow growth.

The reform of the pension system in 2012, encompassing both the general and special retirement schemes, took effect on 1 January 2013. It is based on aligning retirement age with increased life expectancy and adapts pensions to the budget situation. Movements in pensions will be conditioned by the income from the scheme's contributions. If contributions fall short, the scheme's reserves will be topped up to make up the difference. Adjustments to pensions in response to wage rate variations will be partially or completely suspended. In the latter case the only changes will be cost of living adjustments. Regardless of the growth scenario, the reform permits the financing of social security expenditures on the basis of funds accumulated in reserves beyond 2040, even without increases in contributions.

5.8 Financial sector re-engineering

Luxembourg's financial sector weathered the financial crisis of 2008–2009 fairly well, broadly due to the high degree of its diversification and its limited links with the domestic economy. Combined with the relatively small scale of the domestic banking sector, these features have helped to shield Luxembourg's financial sector from unfavourable developments in international markets, despite its importance in the economy. Indeed, the majority of banks in Luxembourg are foreign-owned and engage only in fund administration, private banking, or act as a conduit for lending abroad.

The tightening of capital requirements for banks in Europe and elsewhere, accompanied by more effective risk control in the EU Banking Union (see below) might put deleveraging pressures on banks, possibly reducing the size of international bank groups and their affiliates in Luxembourg.

Recent research by the OECD (Cournède and Denk, 2015) found a hump-shaped relationship between the size of an economy's financial sector and economic growth. An already large financial sector can be associated with growth slowing down due to resource misallocation, rent seeking, implicit government guarantees, exposure to financial shocks and raising income inequality. These results suggest that Luxembourg might have reached a size where the growth contribution of the financial sector may be turning negative. However, in Luxembourg, a large share of financial sector output is exported, potentially reducing this negative risk.

These possibilities call for measures that foster the diversification of the economy. The government has invested in alternative economic activities, notably bio- and health-technologies, logistics, as well as information and communication technologies. In many cases investment relating to technological advance has been undertaken in partnership with the university of Luxembourg, research institutes and public private partnerships.

5.9 Social cohesion: the challenge of 'national identity'

Social cohesion, which goes beyond the distribution of income, is the most important challenge for Luxembourg and has rightly attracted considerable attention in recent years.

The 'at risk of poverty' rate of Luxembourg is about the average of the EU, and the distribution of household income is relatively equitable (Eurostat, 2015), even if inequality has increased during the last decade.

Small European countries are often characterized by close links between the political class and the economy (Becker, 2011). This is also true in Luxembourg which has a type of arrangement labelled the 'Luxembourg social model' based on an institutionalized dialogue between the government, the employers and the unions on economic and social issues in the context of a welfare state, with the aim of attaining a consensus. Some scholars (Hirsch, 2003) have criticized this arrangement as a rent seeking oligopoly, with the danger of bypassing Parliament, and generating a tendency of cronyism and muddling through instead of clear and transparent decision processes.

It should be recognized, however, that this institutional feature in Luxembourg has permitted an orderly structural change of the economy, from a high reliance on the manufacturing sector to an economy with a relatively large financial sector, and has prevented potential conflicts relating to the hosting of a large and growing non-national population.

To avoid the danger of having an electorate which is not representative of the whole population, the government is allowing the possibility of a 'double nationality' to foreigners (Allegrezza, Thill and Pelletier, 2015). This has led to a slowdown in the increase of the share of foreigners in the population by integrating them as full citizens. Since this approach was judged insufficient, the government launched a referendum in June 2015 asking nationals to state whether they were ready to give voting rights at general election to non-Luxembourgers, provided they had resided for more than ten years in the country. This proposal was rejected by a vast majority of the citizens.

Although the vote was not directed against foreigners, and was probably influenced by a raft of spending cuts and tax hikes in order to keep the budget in surplus, the image of the quiet and open society may have been tainted.

This result brought back memories of the referendum results in connection with the European Constitutional Treaty of 2005, when only a relatively small majority voted in favour of the new Treaty, the biggest opposition coming from the south of the country, where the steel industry dominated. This underscores the latent malaise of 'grass root' Luxembourgers who seem to feel more and more marginalized by the development of a globalized economy and a foreign population which is increasing at a fast rate.

The Luxembourg language (Letzebuergesch), which has been standardized and received the status of national language in 1984, is seen by many as an essential part of the country's identity. This might put multilingualism (French, German and progressively English) at risk, until now a distinctive feature of the country's historical identity and a testimony of the open mindedness since its inception (Pigeron-Piroth and Fehlen, 2014). For the time being, as the census of 2011 has shown, French remained the most important working language, almost at par with Luxembourgish (STATEC, 2014b).

Although the Luxembourg public sector is quite lean – amounting to 12% of total employment – about half of the 'national' workforce, that is excluding foreigners and cross-border workers, are employed in the public service. Pieretti, Marchiori and Zu (2015) argue that a public sector, reserved mostly for nationals, mastering the three administrative languages (French, German and Luxembourgish) shields the natives from competition in the labour market and protects them from low-skilled immigrants, leading to upward wage pressures, especially in the highly skilled category of workers.

6 Conclusion

Luxembourg has not fared too badly after the great recession. The financial sector, the most prominent contributor to the country's value added, was not exceedingly shaken by the travails of the international banking crisis, which was followed by a wave of mergers and acquisitions and other forms of restructuring.

Now the sector is in need of reengineering against a backdrop of new tax harmonization rules, transparency reviews and a stringent regulatory surveillance by OECD and the European Commission.[6] Speedy diversification of this sector and of the economy as a whole is therefore called for.

Luxembourg now faces two major challenges. The first, common to all small countries, is that due to its inherent vulnerability, the country must keep alert regarding developments in the outer world, in order to seize new opportunities, building on the creativity of its diverse labour force. The second challenge, given the diversity of its population and its workforce, is to continue nurturing social cohesion domestically, through the construction of a shared identity and a feeling of 'we-ness', while guaranteeing a high standard of living.

Notes

1 The medieval town developed around a natural defensive promontory which served as a fort for the Romans and which developed into a castle. The castle's old name, Lucilinburhuc ('Little Fortress'), is the origin of the name of the country.
2 The standardized unemployment rate, published by Eurostat, is somewhat lower than the national unemployment rate by 1% point.
3 In this study (Allegrezza 2015) used GNI per capita as the dependent variable with population size and a composite index of competiveness (compiled by the Observatory for Competiveness of the Ministry of Economy of Luxembourg,). The composite index of competitiveness was statistically significant while the variable measuring country size (measured by population size) was not. The regression was tested for heterogeneity (Breusch-Pagan test) and for outliers.
4 Information derived from: http://ec.europa.eu/budget/mycountry/LU/index_en.cfm.
5 The 2015 edition of the *Bilan compétitivité* is available at: http://www.odc.public.lu/publications/perspectives/PPE_030.pdf.
6 The tax rulings, while legal and widely used by almost all member states, have been highlighted in international media in the so-called LuxLeaks affair. This uproar accelerated the adoption of principles by the OECD and subsequently the European Commission to make sure that all potentially harmful tax practices should be made transparent or forbidden. The Luxembourg government has committed to cooperate and abide by these new rules. The motive for this is to prevent companies from making secret tax deals with individual governments and shifting profits for tax avoidance.

References

Alesina, A. and Spolaore, E. (2005) 'Trade, Growth and the Size of Countries', in P. Aghion and Durlauf (eds), *Handbook of Economic Growth*, Vol. 1B, Chapter 23. Available at: http://www.anderson.ucla.edu/faculty_pages/romain.wacziarg/downloads/handbook.pdf (accessed 23 January 2016).

Allegrezza, S. (1993) 'The Case of Luxembourg', in A. Jacquemin and D. Wright (eds), *The European Challenges Post-1992: Shaping Factors, Shaping Actors*, Cheltenham: Edward Elgar Publishing.

Allegrezza, S. (2015) *Note on GNI per Capita, Population Size and Competitiveness – Data and Regression Results*, mimeo, Luxembourg: STATEC.

Allegrezza, S., Thill, G. and Pelletier, F. (2015) *Regards/07: Sur ses électeurs potentiels*, STATEC, May 2015. Available at: http://www.statistiques.public.lu/catalogue-publications/regards/2015/PDF-07-2015.pdf (accessed 23 January 2016).

Alouini, O. and Hubert, P. (2010) 'Country Size, Growth and Volatility,' Working Paper no. 2010–2018, July 2010, Paris: OFCE. Available at: http://www.ofce.sciences-po.fr/pdf/dtravail/WP2010-18.pdf (accessed 23 January 2016).

Becker, U. (2011) *The Changing Political Economies of Small West European Countries*. Amsterdam: Amsterdam University Press.

Cournède, B. and Denk, O. (2015) *Finance and Economic Growth in OECD and G20 Countries*, OECD Working Paper No. 1223. Available at: www.oecd-ilibrary.org/docserver/download/5js04v8z0m38.pdf?expires=1448609659&id=id&accname=guest&checksum=18A1AC543B053A13EE690227A7E18EA6 (accessed 23 January 2016).

De Grauwe, P. (2015) *Secular Stagnation in the Eurozone. CEPRs Research-based Policy Analysis and Commentary from Leading Economists*, VOX CEPR's Policy Portal. Available at: http://www.voxeu.org/article/secular-stagnation-eurozone (accessed 23 January 2016).

Doyle, E. and O'Connor, F. (2013) 'Innovation Capacities in Advanced Economies: Relative Performance of Small Open Economies', *Research in International Business and Finance* (Firm Level Aspects of International Integration), 27(1): 106–123.

Easterly, W. and Kraay, A. (2000) 'Small States, Small Problems? Income, Growth, and Volatility in Small States', *World Development*, 28(11): 2013–2027. Available at: https://williameasterly.files.wordpress.com/2010/08/25_easterly_kraay_smallstatessmallproblems_prp.pdf (accessed 23 January 2016).

European Commission (2014a). *Eurobarometer* (Autumn). Available at: http://europa.eu/rapid/press-release_IP-14-2702_en.htm (accessed 23 January 2016).

European Commission (2014b). *Quarterly Report on the Euro Area*, 13(4): 23–29. Available at: http://ec.europa.eu/economy_finance/publications/qr_euro_area/2014/pdf/qrea4_section_2_en.pdf (accessed 23 January 2016).

European Commission (2015) *Country Report Luxembourg 2015*, Staff working document, 18 March. Available at: http://ec.europa.eu/europe2020/pdf/csr2015/cr2015_luxembourg_en.pdf (accessed 23 January 2016).

Eurostat (2015) *Demography Report*, Short Analytical Web Note 3/2015. Available at: http://ec.europa.eu/eurostat/documents/3217494/6917833/KE-BM-15-003-EN-N.pdf/76dac490-9176-47bc-80d9-029e1d967af6 (accessed 23 January 2016).

Favaro, E.M. (2008) *Small States, Smart Solutions: Improving Connectivity and Increasing the Effectiveness of Public Services*. Washington, DC: The World Bank.

Hirsch, M. (2003) 'Le modèle luxembourgeois et ses limites', in S. Allegrezza, M. Hirsch and N. Von Kunitzski (eds), *L'histoire, le présent et l'avenir du modèle luxembourgeois*, Luxembourg: Institut d'études européennes et internationales du Luxembourg.

IMF (2013) 'Macroeconomic Issues in Small States and Implications for Fund Engagement', IMF Policy Paper, 20 February. Available at: https://www.imf.org/external/np/pp/eng/2013/022013.pdf (accessed 23 January 2016).

IMF (2014) *Luxembourg Article IV Consultation Staff Report*, 18 April 2014. Available at: https://www.imf.org/external/pubs/ft/scr/2014/cr14118.pdf (accessed 23 January 2016).

IMF (2015) *World Economic Outlook: Uneven Growth Short- and Long-Term Factors*. Available at: http://www.imf.org/external/pubs/ft/weo/2015/01/pdf/text.pdf (accessed 23 January 2016).

Kelemen, R.D. (2007) 'Built to Last? The Durability of EU Federalism?' in S. Meunier and K. McNamara (eds), *Making History: State of the European Union*, Vol. 8, Oxford: Oxford University Press. Available at: http://aei.pitt.edu/7932/1/kelemen-r-07a.pdf (accessed 23 January 2016).

Klinkers, L. (2012) *European Federalist Papers* (1, 2 and 3). Available at: http://www.europeanfederalistpapers.eu/index.php/en/papers (accessed 23 January 2016).

Langer, W. (2007) 'The End of Equal Opportunities? A Multilevel Analysis of the Luxembourg PISA 2003 Data', *Economie et statistiques* N° 17/2007, working papers du STATEC. Available at: http://www.statistiques.public.lu/catalogue-publications/economie-statistiques/2007/17-2007.pdf (accessed 23 January 2016).

Luxemburger Wort (2013) 'Premier Meets Labour Unions and Employers for Bilateral Talks (5 April 2013)'. Available at: http://www.wort.lu/en/luxembourg/premier-meets-labour-unions-and-employers-for-bilateral-talks-515ed321e4b018cd52acf143 (accessed 23 January 2016).

Ministry of Finance, Luxembourg (2015) *16th Update of the Stability and Growth Program*. Available at: http://www.mf.public.lu/publications/programme/16th_update_stability_growth_programme.pdf (accessed 23 January 2016).

Observatoire de la compétitivité (2014) 'Competitiveness Report: A Resilient Economy', *Perspectives de politique économique*, No. 29, Ministry of the Economy, Grand Duchy of Luxembourg. Available at: http://www.odc.public.lu/publications/perspectives/PPE_029bis.pdf (accessed 23 January 2016).

OECD (2015a) *Economic Survey of Luxembourg 2015*. Available at: http://www.oecd.org/luxembourg/economic-survey-luxembourg.htm (accessed 23 January 2016).

OECD (2015b) *Escaping the Stagnation Trap: Policy Options for the Euro Area and Japan*. Available at: http://www.oecd.org/japan/escaping-the-stagnation-trap-policy-options-for-the-euro-area-and-japan.pdf (accessed 23 January 2016).

Pieretti, P., Marchiori, L. and Zu, B. (2015) 'Immigration, Occupational Choice and Public Employment', *Cahier d'études BCL*. Available at: www.ferdi.fr/sites/www.ferdi.fr/files/evenements/presentations/luca_marchiori.pdf (accessed 23 January 2016).

Pigeron-Piroth, I. and Fehlen, F. (2014) 'Les langues dans les offres d'emploi au Luxembourg (1984–2014)', IPSE Working Paper, Université du Luxembourg. Available at: http://www.statistiques.public.lu/fr/publications/thematique/population-emploi/langues/etude.pdf (accessed 23 January 2016).

Sapir, A. and Wolff, G.B. (2015) 'Euro-area Governance: What to Reform and How to do it', Bruegel Policy Brief, Issue 2015/1. Available at: http://bruegel.org/wp-content/uploads/imported/publications/pb_2015_01_270215_01.pdf (accessed 23 January 2016).

Sneessens, H., Bourgain, A., Shadman, F. and Mehta, K. (2014) *Formation des salaires et indexation automatique. Analyse comparative de quatre pays européens*,

Perspectives de politique économique, No. 28, juillet, Ministère de l'économie, Luxembourg. Available at: http://www.odc.public.lu/publications/perspectives/PPE_028.pdf (accessed 23 January 2016).

STATEC (2014a). *Note de conjuncture. No 2: La situation économique au Luxembourg: Evolution récente et perspectives.* Retrieved from www.statistiques.public.lu/catalogue-publications/note-conjoncture/2014/PDF-NDC-02-14.pdf (accessed 23 January 2016).

STATEC (2014b). *La société luxembourgeoise dans le miroir du recensement de la population.* Retrieved from http://www.statistiques.public.lu/fr/publications/series/livre-recensement-2011/index.html (accessed 23 January 2016).

STATEC (2014c). *Cahier économique. No. 118: Dynamique des entreprises du Luxembourg.* Available at: http://www.statistiques.public.lu/catalogue-publications/cahiers-economiques/2014/PDF-Cahier-118-2014.pdf (accessed 23 January 2016).

STATEC (2015) *Note de conjoncture. La situation économique au Luxembourg – Évolution récente et perspectives.* Available at: www.statistiques.public.lu/catalogue-publications/note-conjoncture/2015/PDF-NDC-01-15.pdf (accessed 23 January 2016).

7 The Macedonian economy and the European Union[1]

Igor Velickovski, Marjan Petreski and Branimir Jovanovic

1 Introduction

The Republic of Macedonia is located in the central Balkan Peninsula in Southeast Europe. It is one of the successor states of the former Yugoslavia, from which it declared independence on 8 September 1991. It became a member of the United Nations in 1993 under the provisional description of 'the former Yugoslav Republic of Macedonia'. It is a landlocked country, bordering Greece in the south, Albania in the west, Bulgaria in the east and Kosovo and Serbia in the north. The country's capital is Skopje. According to the State Statistical Office, a little more than two million inhabitants live on 25,713km^2. However, as Macedonia lately faces fairly large emigration rates and in the absence of an official census since 2002, it is believed that the total population is below that figure.

The country is organized as a parliamentary republic. It is a multi-ethnic country, with approximately 25% of the people with Albanian ethnic background, 4% with Turkish, 3% with Roma and 2% with Serbian. Macedonia was the only Yugoslav republic that was not involved in the wars after the breakup of Yugoslavia. However, there was an inter-ethnic internal conflict in 2001, which lasted for several months.

This chapter describes the structure and performance of the Macedonian economy and puts them in the context of the Macedonian accession to the European Union (EU). The chapter is organized into five sections. Section 2, which follows this introduction, presents information about the structure and performance of the Macedonian economy since the introduction of the market economy. Section 3 gives an account of the process relating to Macedonia's bid for EU membership. Section 4 discusses, through figures, the economic dependence of Macedonia on the EU. Section 5 assesses Macedonia's prospects of forming part of the euro area. The last section concludes the chapter with some comments on future prospects.

2 The Macedonian economy

2.1 Developments and challenges in early transition

Macedonia was severely hit by the breakup of Yugoslavia. The fall in the gross domestic product (GDP) after the break-up was more persistent than in other republics, despite the fact that it did not experience a war. Moreover, the recession following the transformation was very prolonged in Macedonia. The first year in which GDP started growing was 1996, whereas in Slovenia it started growing in 1993, in Croatia, Bosnia and Herzegovina and Serbia in 1994, and in Montenegro in 1995. Also, the loss in production in the early transition years was the highest in the region (excluding Bosnia and Herzegovina, Croatia, Serbia and Montenegro, which were involved in wars). Real GDP in 1996 was 14% lower than in 1990, which is a much bigger fall than in Slovenia, Albania, Romania and Bulgaria (Figure 7.1).

Several factors may help explain the dismal performance of the economy in the early transition years. First, the Macedonian economy was heavily dependent on Yugoslavia for the placement of its products. The organization of production in Yugoslavia was such that Macedonia, as a less developed and more agriculture-oriented republic, was mainly engaged in the production of intermediary goods, which were then used for producing final goods in the more developed republics, such as Slovenia. As a result, with the breakup of Yugoslavia and the subsequent wars, Macedonian firms lost their traditional markets. Second, Macedonia had a rather rapid privatization. Of all the countries from the region, only Croatia had a similar pace of privatization (Figure 7.2). This led to a collapse in production, employment and aggregate

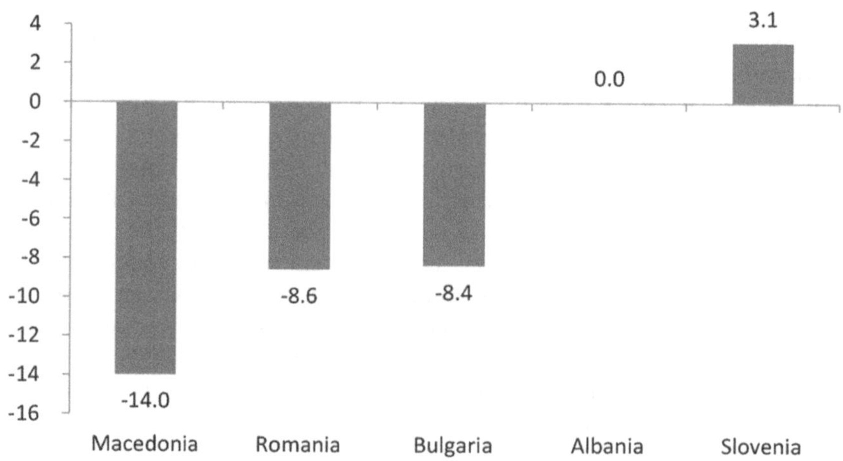

Figure 7.1 Real GDP in 1996 compared to GDP in 1990 (%)
Source: Penn World Tables.

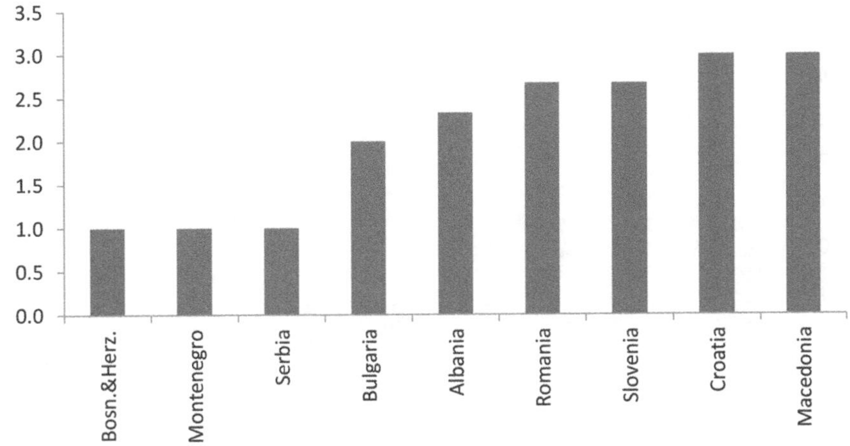

Figure 7.2 Large scale privatization index in 1996 (higher values = faster privatization)
Source: European Bank for Reconstruction and Development.

demand, which consequently depressed the economy (Daskalov et al., 2003). Indeed, of all the countries from the region, Macedonia had the highest increase in unemployment in the early transition (Figure 7.3). Finally, the country faced a trade embargo from Greece in 1994, which lasted for 19 months, and in addition severely felt the consequences of the UN embargo on the Federal Republic of Yugoslavia.

The early transition years were also marked by very high inflation. End-of-year retail price inflation (the official measure of inflation in that period) exceeded 200% every year until 1994 (Petrevski, 2005).

The high inflation rate during this period was fed by the persistent devaluation/depreciation of the currency. Although the country followed a policy of fixed exchange rate, as from the monetary independence in April 1992 until May 1993, the currency was devalued several times during this period. Then, in May 1993, the country moved to a policy of a floating exchange rate, which made the currency depreciate severely for several months. After the currency stabilized in 1994 and 1995, it was pegged to the German mark in October 1995, which resulted in low inflation in the subsequent years (Figure 7.4). It has remained fixed to the mark/euro ever since, with only one devaluation, in July 1997, by 16% (Figure 7.5).

2.2 Developments and challenges after 1996

Despite the achievement of macroeconomic stability by 1996, the economy continued to underperform in the following years. Average annual GDP growth for the period 1996–2014 was only 2.2%, which was the lowest in the

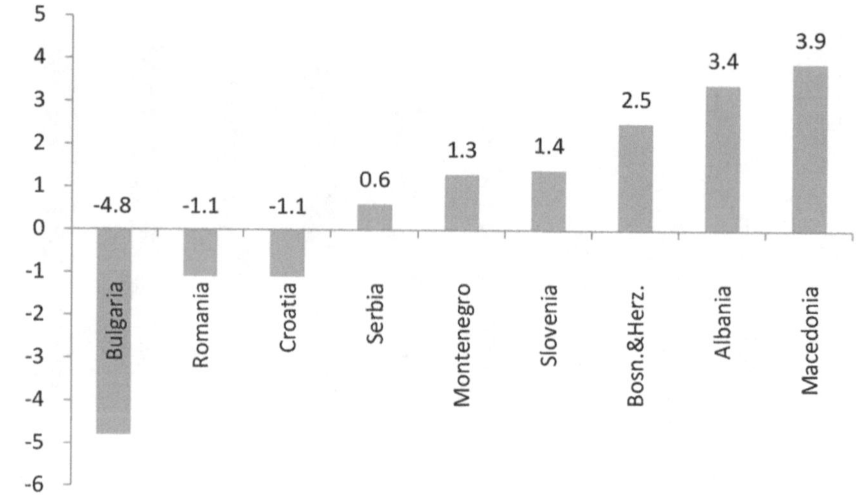

Figure 7.3 Change in unemployment between 1991and 1996 (percentage points)
Source: International Labour Organization.

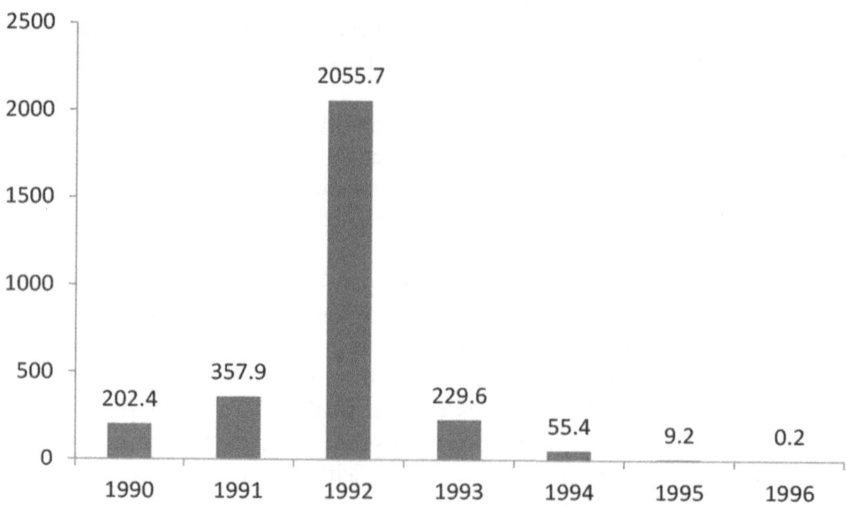

Figure 7.4 End-of-year inflation (%)
Source: National Bank of the Republic of Macedonia.

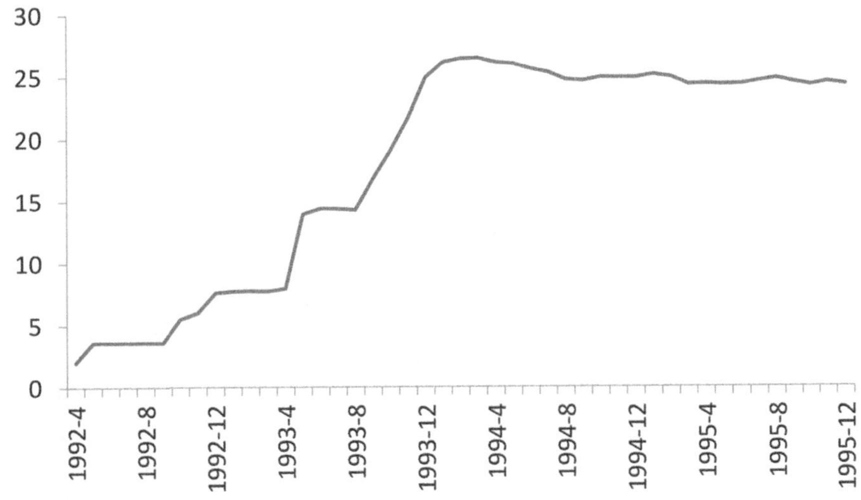

Figure 7.5 Exchange rate of the denar against the German mark
Source: National Bank of the Republic of Macedonia.

region (Figure 7.6). This low growth rate was partially due to the internal inter-ethnic conflict in 2001. Growth, during this period, never exceeded 6% per annum, and exceeded 5% only in 2007 and 2008 (Figure 7.7).

In addition to being low, growth has also been very unequally distributed. Income distribution became increasingly uneven after independence and is currently by far the most uneven in the region (Figure 7.8). The inequality of income increased significantly in the early transition, and stabilized itself afterwards, until 1999. Then, it started rising again, especially after 2005 (Figure 7.9).

Unemployment has remained high during the period under consideration. It has fallen slightly in recent years, to 29% in 2013 (Figure 7.10), though this may be attributed to the shift from informal to formal employment (Jovanovic, 2015). The average rate of unemployment for the period 1991–2013 was 33%, which is much higher than in the other countries in the region (Figure 7.11).

The poor economic performances initiated a wave of emigration from the country. Approximately 220,000 people left the country between 1990 and 2010, which is 11% of the current population (Petreski and Petreski, 2015). From the region, only Albania and Bosnia and Herzegovina have had higher emigration in the same period (Figure 7.12). Albania has one of the highest rates of emigration in the world, while Bosnia and Herzegovina had a severe war, which produced a wave of refugees.

Several observations may be helpful for gaining better insights into the causes of the poor economic performances of the Macedonian economy (Daskalov et al., 2003). To begin with, as a small economy with limited natural resources, Macedonia is very dependent on the external sector. The

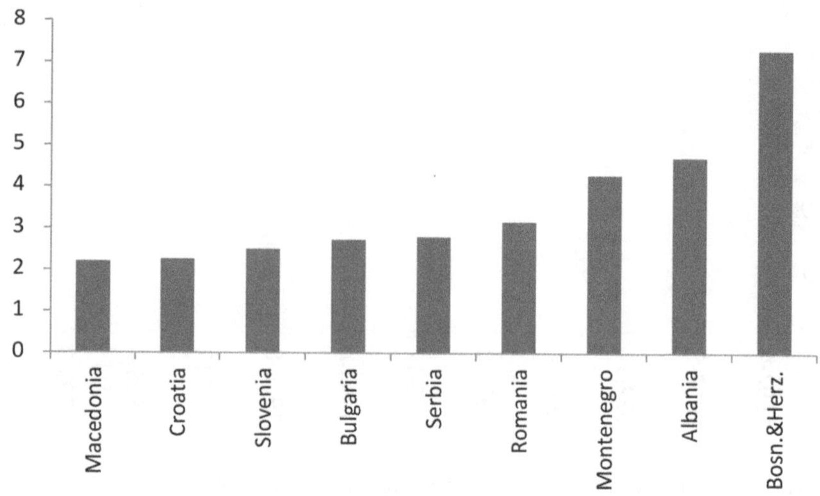

Figure 7.6 Average annual real GDP growth in the region between 1996 and 2014 (%)
Source: Penn World Tables and World Economic Outlook.

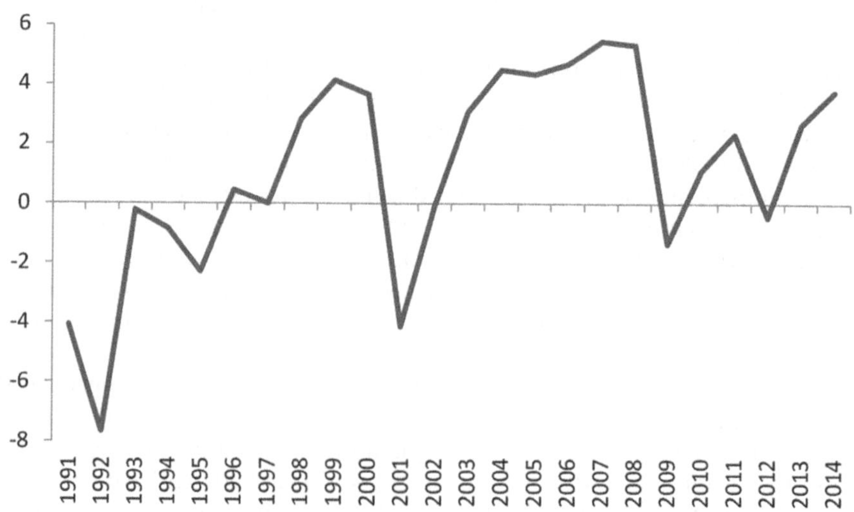

Figure 7.7 Year-on-year GDP growth in Macedonia between 1991 and 2014 (%)
Source: Penn World Tables and World Economic Outlook.

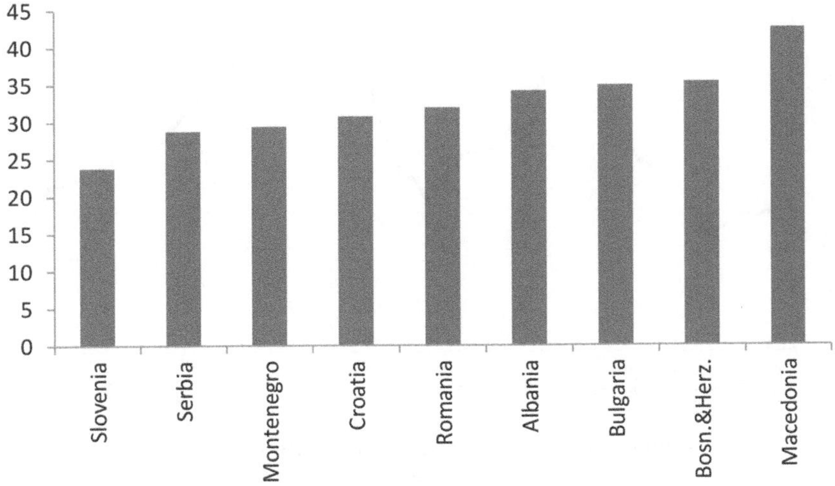

Figure 7.8 Income inequality in the region, last available year (Gini coefficient)
Source: Standardized World Income Inequality Database of Solt (2014).

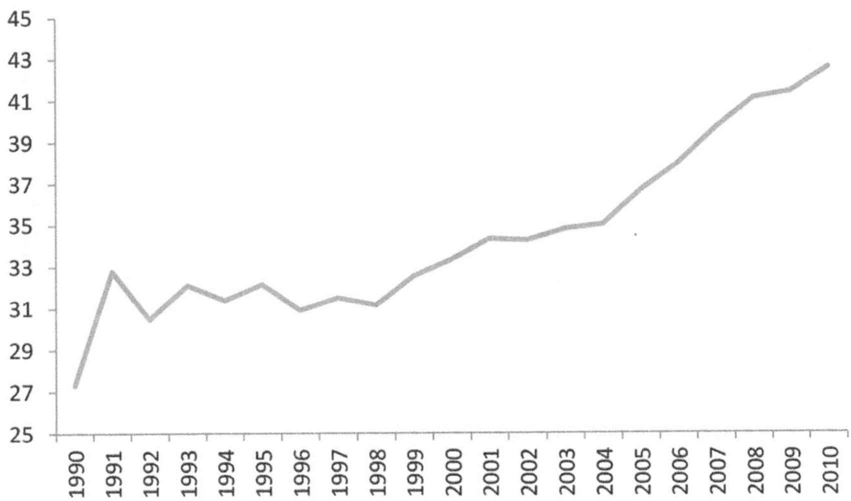

Figure 7.9 Income inequality in Macedonia between 1990 and 2010 (Gini coefficient)
Source: Standardized World Income Inequality Database of Solt (2014).

Figure 7.10 Unemployment in Macedonia between 1991 and 2013 (%)
Source: International Labour Organization.

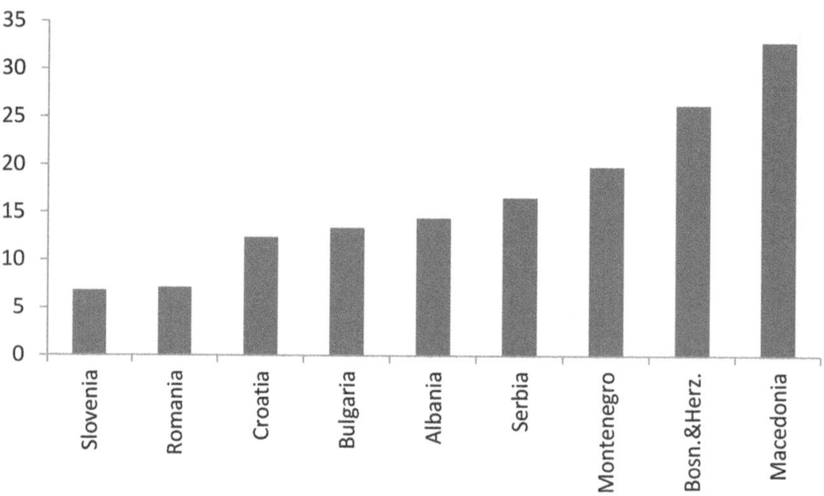

Figure 7.11 Average unemployment in the region between 1991 and 2013 (%)
Source: International Labour Organization.

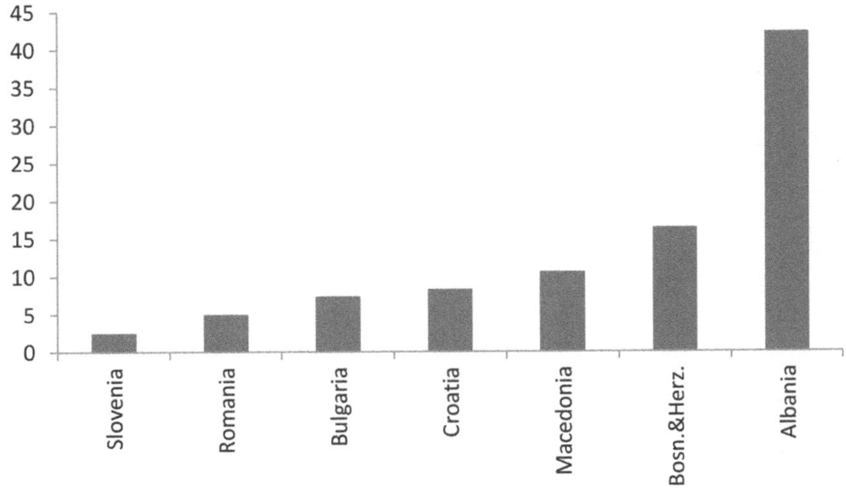

Figure 7.12 Emigration in the region between 1990 and 2010 (percentage of population in 2010)
Source: World Bank, Global Bilateral Migration Database & Migration and Remittances Factbook 2011.

external sector itself has underperformed heavily since independence. Exports, as a share of GDP, have increased over the course of time, but their increase has been more than offset by the increase in imports. The overall result, hence, has been that the trade deficit widened (Figure 7.13), by far the highest widening in the region (Figure 7.14).

Furthermore, the country proved relatively unattractive for foreign direct investment (FDI), which may be due to its small size (see Jovanovic and Jovanovic, 2015). The average level of FDI in the 1995–2014 period was 3.8% of GDP, which is one of the lowest in the region (Figure 7.15).

On the positive side, the country receives sizeable amount of remittances every year, averaging 3.2% of GDP between 1996 and 2014, slightly lower than the FDI (which include several major privatizations, like those of the telecommunication and electricity companies). Furthermore, there has been an upward trend in remittances in recent years (Figure 7.16). Still, remittances are used mostly for consumption, and very little for investment. This may be attributed to the high poverty rate in the country (see Petreski and Jovanovic, 2014).

There has been no stimulus coming from the public sector, the size of which has remained modest, one of the smallest in the region (Figure 7.17). In addition to being small, it has also been rather ineffective, similar to that of Albania, Serbia and Romania, and better only than Bosnia and Herzegovina (Figure 7.18).

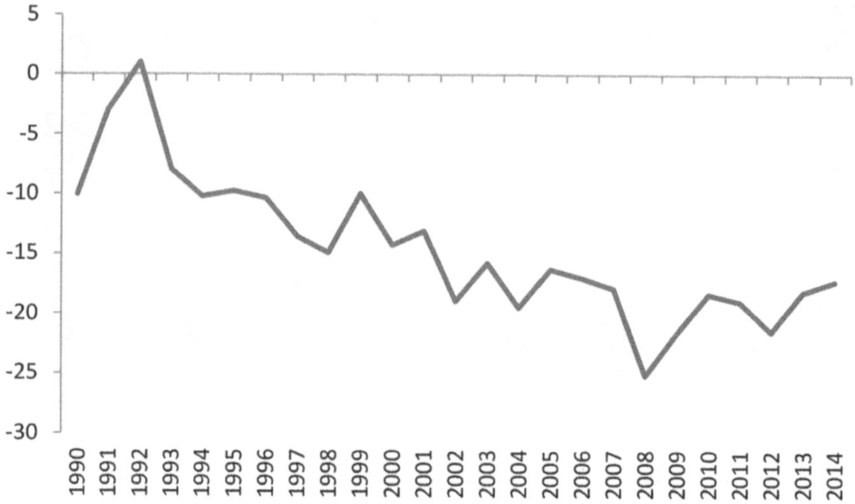

Figure 7.13 Trade deficit in Macedonia between 1990 and 2014 (percentage of GDP)
Source: World Bank's World Development Indicators.

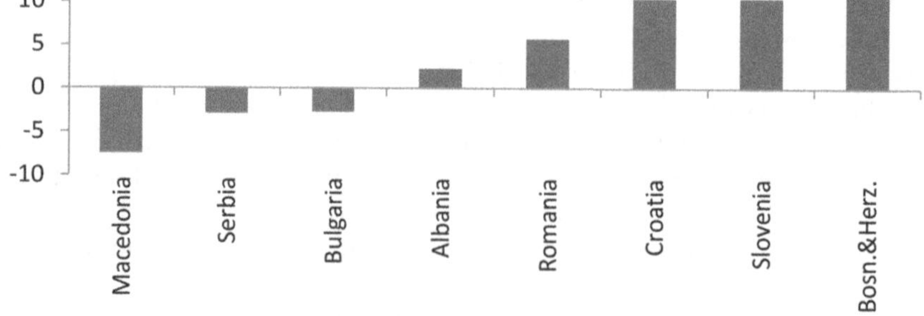

Figure 7.14 The trade deficit between 1996 and 2014 in the countries from the region (%)
Source: World Bank's World Development Indicators.

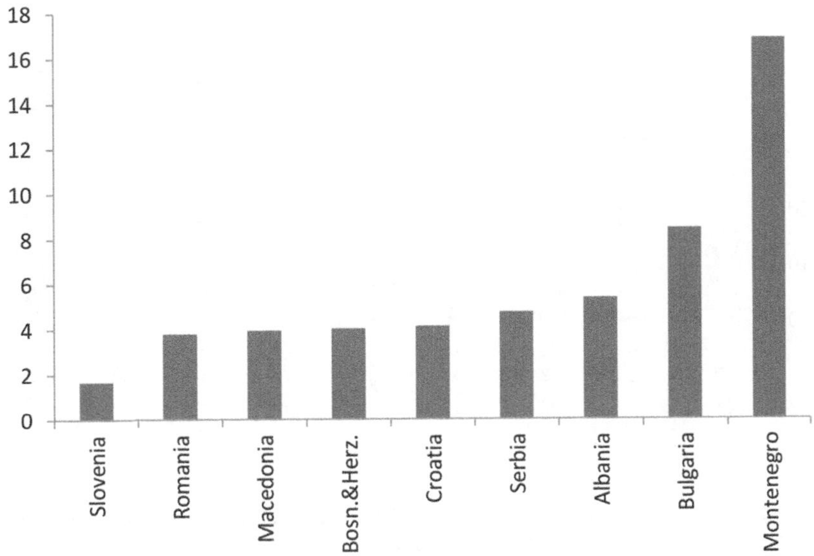

Figure 7.15 Average FDI inflows in countries from the region from 1996–2014 (percentage of GDP)

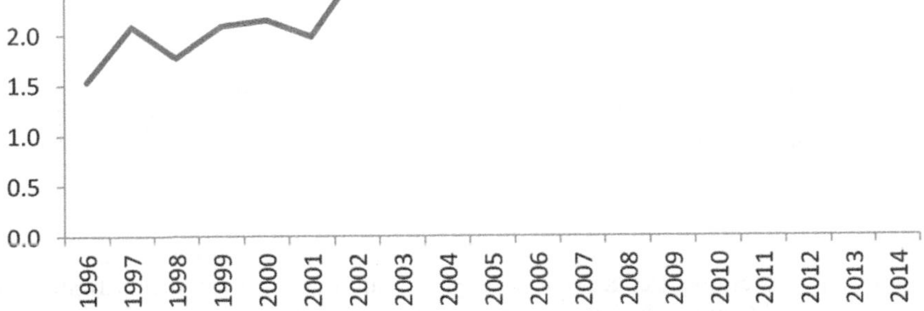

Figure 7.16 Remittances in Macedonia between 1996 and 2014 (percentage of GDP)

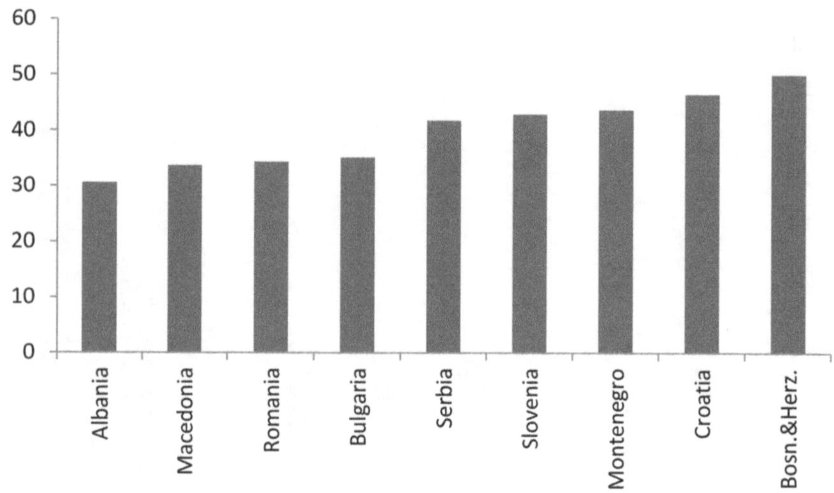

Figure 7.17 General government total expenditure in countries from the region from 1996–2014 (percentage of GDP)
Source: World Economic Outlook Database, International Monetary Fund.

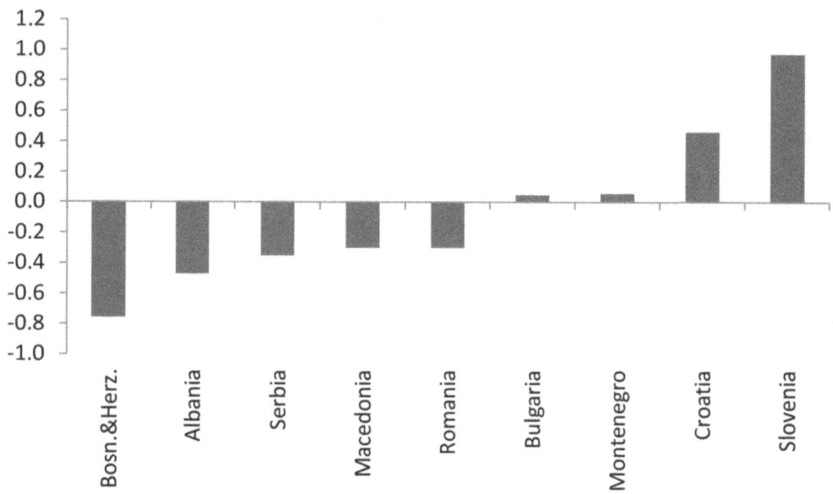

Figure 7.18 Government effectiveness index in countries from the region from 1996–2013 (index, higher value = higher effectiveness)
Source: Worldwide Governance Indicators, World Bank.

The need for greater involvement of the public sector in the economy becomes clear when one takes a look at the infrastructure. Macedonia has one of the poorest infrastructures in the region (Figure 7.19), better only than Romania, Albania and Bosnia and Herzegovina.

Macedonia has invested very little in infrastructure and the improvement in infrastructure is one of the lowest in the region (Figure 7.20), similar only to the improvements in Croatia and Slovenia, which have a much smaller need for improvement, given the higher quality of their infrastructure.

3 Macedonia and the EU

3.1 The Stabilization and Association Process

Macedonia approached the European Union in 2000, after nine years of its independence from Yugoslavia, and after a decade of political and economic turmoil. The first step towards joining the EU was the initiation of the Stabilization and Association Process, the result of which was the Stabilization and Association Agreement (SAA) signed on the 9 April 2001 in Luxembourg, which entered into force on 1 April 2004. The parts regulating trade and trade-related issues entered into force earlier on 1 June 2001, through a special Interim Agreement between the Republic of Macedonia and the European Community.

The objective of EU's SAA was to establish bilateral contractual relationships between the European Commission and the countries of the Western

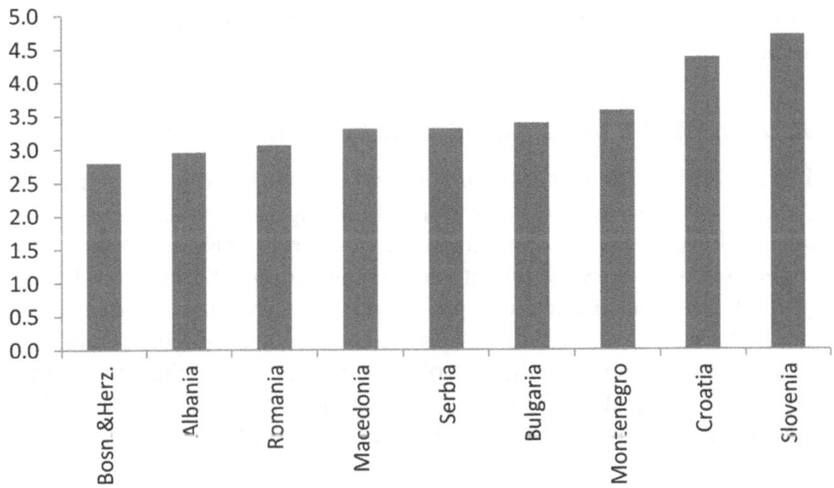

Figure 7.19 Quality of overall infrastructure in the region, 2006–2014 (index, higher value = better infrastructure)

Source: Global Competitiveness Report, World Economic Forum.

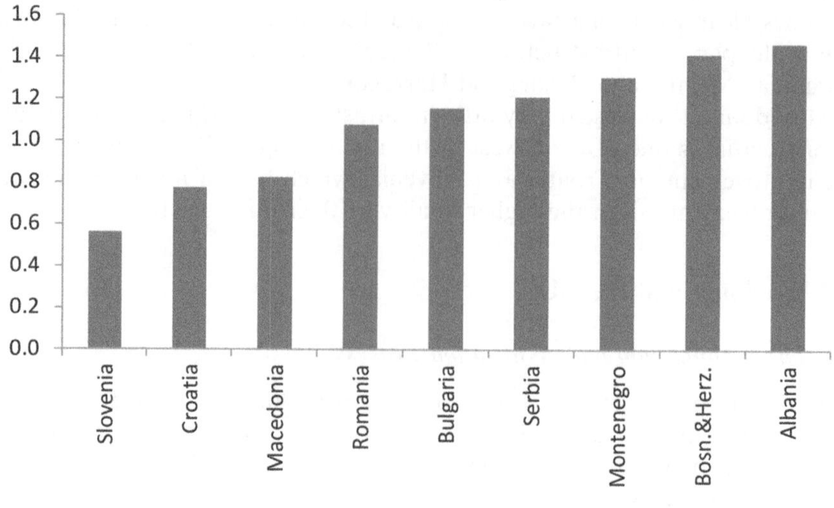

Figure 7.20 Improvement in the infrastructure in the region from 2006–2014 (index, higher value = better infrastructure)
Source: Global Competitiveness Report, World Economic Forum.

Balkans, Macedonia being the first country to sign the Agreement. It provided a forum for political dialogue, strengthened regional cooperation and promoted economic relations. In particular, the SAA stipulated provisions concerning the free movement of goods, services, labour and capital. Hence, a free trade area (FTA) was created between the EU and Macedonia, with a maximum transition phase of ten years.[2]

3.2 Recommendation to open negotiations for admission to the EU

Having established the grounds for political dialogue and economic cooperation, the SAA also paved the way for submitting the application to join the European Union. This step was taken on 22 March 2004, in Dublin, Ireland. Later the same year, the government adopted the National Strategy for European Integration and commenced the procedure for answering the questionnaire of the European Commission relating to many aspects for country's preparedness for accession and the compliance with the Copenhagen criteria. On 17 December 2005, after the successful completion of the questionnaire, the European Council officially granted the country a candidate status.

3.3 Blockage of the accession process

Since the official granting of a candidacy status in 2005, the European Council has been reiterating this decision each year until the present time, but the opening up of the negotiations was not possible because of the country's dispute with Greece about the name 'Macedonia'. The official name of Macedonia is 'the Former Yugoslav Republic of Macedonia' and it is the name used in the entire multilateral communication, including the one with the European Union. It is still considered to be only a 'provisional reference' introduced by the United Nations in 1993.

The 'name dispute' is a disagreement between Macedonia and Greece on who can rightfully use the name 'Macedonia'. The Greek government argues that the use of the name 'Republic of Macedonia' by Macedonia presents a direct expression of territorial intentions toward Greece, the northern region of which is also called Macedonia. The dispute commenced after the Republic of Macedonia's independence from Yugoslavia in 1991 and continues to exist until the present day. Efforts to resolve the issue have been constantly under way under the auspices of the United Nations, but the opposing positions have not been reconciled. Hence, Greece vetoed the Republic of Macedonia's membership in NATO in 2008 and continues to state that it will block its accession to the EU and the opening up of negotiations. Since 2008, the EU officially added the resolution of the name issue to the list of preconditions for accession. The European Commission recommended the opening up of negotiations between the EU and Macedonia in 2009, but, as anticipated, Greece vetoed this process in the European Council and has done so on six occasions.

Greece was not alone in hampering the opening up of negotiations between the EU and Macedonia. Some bilateral issues with Bulgaria on the shared part of the country history in the nineteenth and twentieth centuries also emerged as an obstacle on the way to the EU accession. As an EU member, Bulgaria utilized its power to veto the commencement of negotiations between the EU and Macedonia in 2012.

3.4 Advantages and disadvantages of joining the EU

Despite the fact that the Macedonian dream for the EU membership has been fading in recent years – due to various reasons including the non-resolution of the name issue and the European economic crisis – the advantages and disadvantages of joining the EU have been occasionally debated in Macedonian society.

On political grounds, undoubtedly, it is argued that EU membership would bring about a higher degree of stability and stronger governance. Macedonia is situated in a geographical area characterized by conflicts in the past: the 1992–1995 War in Bosnia, the 1999 Kosovo War and the subsequent refugee crisis, as well as the 2001 internal Macedonian conflict. The latter stemmed from ethnic Albanian claims for having larger constitutional rights, as they represent around a quarter of the entire population. This evolved into internal conflict in 2001 which was resolved by the Ohrid Framework Agreement of August 2001, which largely accepted the claims and introduced ethnic

Albanians as a constitutional nation in the country. The inter-ethnic tensions have now subsided but fragilities remain, including that there are political instabilities originating from Macedonia's relationships with other neighbours.

The possible membership in the EU (as well as in NATO) would bring about a positive environment for settling the inter-ethnic conflicts, and could also improve the relationships with Macedonia's neighbours. In addition, EU membership could be a form of guarantee for institutional quality and governance, which should then translate into a better place to live for citizens, accompanied by better living standards.

On social grounds, it appears from public debate that there is a general belief that EU membership would usher in many social advantages. However, specific social attitudes, prevalent in many EU countries, are likely to find opposition in Macedonia, if the country were to join the EU, due to ideas rooted in the Macedonian mentality, often fed by the government's position on certain matters, including abortion, the rights related to the sexual orientation and other liberal attitudes.

From the economic perspective, EU membership could open up a vast export market for Macedonia. Despite the fact that the major part of tariffs and quotas have already been dismantled (not only due to SAA, but also due to Macedonia's membership in the World Trade Organization), it is expected that the economy may further benefit from the complete opening up of the EU market, i.e. of the complete merging with the European Common Market. A support in this process may be lent by the nominal convergence the economy achieved due to the pegged denar (see Section 5.1), as well by the high trade and financial integration with the EU which might strengthen the business cycle synchronization (see Section 5.3).

Furthermore, the utilization of EU structural funds may bring faster restructuring of the economy and support regional development, hence increasing productivity and competitiveness. Moreover, EU membership may improve the functioning of the institutions through better public governance and lower corruption, although this remains questionable given the experiences of some new member states (e.g. Bulgaria and Romania) that did not manage to make significant progress in the fight against corruption after they joined the EU.

Finally, if EU membership is assumed to bring larger political stability in the country, hence reducing country risk, then EU membership would also bring a higher credit rating for the economy, lower interest rates imposed on the foreign debt, downward pressure onto domestic interest rates, and larger inflow of FDI, which all together would be beneficial to growth, investment, export and public finance.

There may also, however, be some disadvantages. First, if EU membership, supported by the usage of structural funds, pushes the economy more than FDI and government investment, then under a pegged exchange rate, prices may be pushed up, which if not slowed by exchange rate appreciation, or blocked by preventing wage growth, may actually lead to a deterioration of economic conditions and threaten macroeconomic stability. Second, the prospective full liberalization of the capital account could pose potential problems for the sustainability of the fixed exchange rate regime also. Third, complete EU integration may further stir emigration from the country, possibly leading to a brain drain. Fourth, the EU Common Agriculture Policy (CAP) may prevent the government from distributing subsidies for agricultural production, a system which has become quite popular during the last decade.

Overall, there are both advantages and disadvantages of Macedonia's prospective EU integration, but public debate would seem to assign more weight to the former.

4 Dependence of the Macedonian economy on the EU

4.1 Trade, remittances and financial dependence

As explained in the introduction, Macedonia is a small, landlocked and open economy. As such, it is heavily dependent on the European Union in economic terms. Table 7.1 presents the trade shares (export plus import) of Macedonia with the EU and the Western Balkan countries. It is evident that the share has grown over the decades: first, because over time Macedonia became more and more dependent on the EU in trade terms, substituting for the traditional lost eastern markets after gaining independence from Yugoslavia; second, because the EU has been enlarging itself (mainly with the large wave of enlargement in 2004). Presently, the trade share with the EU amounts to about two thirds of the whole trade volume. Interestingly, an additional 12% to 25% of total trade is conducted with the other countries of the Western Balkans, which now form CEFTA-2006.[3] Given that these countries are themselves very much dependent on the trade with the EU, it appears that in trade terms Macedonia is almost entirely dependent on the EU. Germany tops the list, with a growing share approximating a quarter of total trade volume, and followed by Great Britain, Italy, Greece and Bulgaria (Petreski, 2013a).

Macedonia heavily depends on the EU in financial matters also. The banking system is composed of 15 banks, of which 11 are owned by foreign banks. These hold about 75% of banking assets, of which more than 80%

Table 7.1 Trade shares of Macedonia with the EU and the Western Balkans

	1994	*2004*	*2014*
European Union	36.2%	67.9%	68.8%
out of which: Germany	15.6%	20.1%	23.3%
Western Balkans	18.1%	25.0%	11.8%

Source: State Statistical Office of Macedonia.

originate from the EU. The largest bank, however, is domestically owned. The second-largest bank is Greek owned, while the third-largest is Slovenian-owned. France, Bulgaria, Austria and Germany hold the ownership of the remaining part of the banking system (NBRM, 2015). Similarly, the insurance system, albeit being considerably smaller than the banking system, is dominated by foreigners as 14 out of 15 insurance companies are foreign-owned, of which 11 are owned by insurance groups residing in the EU (ISAM, 2014).

Also, a major part of the total FDI flowing into the economy originates from the EU. As Table 7.2 suggests, the share of EU-based FDI in Macedonia has been increasing over time (even if the enlargement in 2004 is controlled for), suggesting that the dependence of Macedonia on the EU in financial terms has also been strengthening.

Last but not least, Macedonia has a large diaspora and hence is a recipient of a large amount of remittances. Petreski and Jovanovic (2013) estimate that the pure cash transfers entering the economy each year range between 4% and 10% of GDP, outweighing the size of FDI (which is less than 4% of GDP) and totalling between USD 400 million and USD 1 billion. Out of these, it has been estimated that about half originate from the EU, as the largest part of the Macedonian diaspora is based in Germany, Italy, Sweden and other EU member states. However, the dependence on the EU here is not dominant as with the trade and financial flows, since large contingents of Macedonians also live in the USA, Canada, Australia, Switzerland, and more recently in Iraq and Afghanistan.

4.2 European sovereign debt crisis

Given the large trade with and financial exposure of the Macedonian economy to the economy of the European Union, the business cycles between the two have synchronized to an extent over time (as discussed in Section 5.3), leading to almost immediate transmission of any shocks hitting the European Union (and more precisely, the economy of the eurozone) onto the Macedonian economy. The Great Recession of 2007 was first felt in Macedonia in the last quarter of 2008, being mainly transmitted through the halting of export and overall reduction of trade. The foreign demand, especially that stemming from the EU dwindled and has remained depressed over the subsequent European sovereign debt crisis (since 2010).

Contrary to trade, the Macedonian banks remained quite unaffected by the Global Financial Crisis/European sovereign debt crisis due to the predominance

Table 7.2 FDI shares of Macedonia with the EU

	1997	*2004*	*2014*
European Union	39.0%	77.1%	84.3%

Source: National Bank of the Republic of Macedonia.

of traditional banking activities, the conservative lending policies and the high capital ratios. However, the period of the Great Recession and the European sovereign debt crisis coincided with increased government spending and an intense government campaign to attract FDI under favourable conditions in the so-called technological-industrial development zones. These efforts have to an extent compensated for the lost foreign demand, preventing large output drops that might have been caused by the crisis. However, in the wake of the crisis, institutional investors, mainly within the region and mostly Slovenian, immediately withdrew.

4.3 The Greek crisis and the Macedonian economy

The European sovereign crisis was of major concern for Macedonia, not wholly because of the impact on trade and financial flows in general, but rather because of Macedonia's neighbourhood and economic relationships with the most severely hit economy – Greece. Despite the name dispute that Macedonia has with Greece, economic cooperation with Greece since the economic embargo of 1994 has been expanding. The trade volume with Greece ranks it third or fourth place among Macedonia's trade partners. Despite the decline in Greek FDI into Macedonia in recent years, Greece still remains an important investor in the economy. The second-largest bank, the oil refinery, a large concrete factory and other important companies in Macedonia are Greek-owned.

However, trade with Greece has been severely hit (Table 7.3), first shortly after the Great Recession, and second, after 2012 until the present, when Greece encountered major liquidity problems and a potential exit from the common currency.

While many believe that the riskier channel for contagion of the Greek crisis is the banking sector, this is precluded through Greek-owned banks being regulated by the domestic jurisdiction, which prevents a direct withdrawal of the company's capital except through open sale. To further shield the economy, the National bank of Macedonia disallowed other transactions to be conducted until the crisis is resolved and the Greek economy stabilized.

Overall, the exposure of the Macedonian economy to the economy of the European Union, and in particular to that of the eurozone, remains high judging by the trade and financial linkages. As a result, shocks hitting the European economy directly are swiftly transmitted onto the domestic economy, primarily through reduction of trade and capital inflows. However, direct withdrawal of the capital base out of the economy is not possible, acting as a shield to the current turmoil in the eurozone.

Table 7.3 Trade volume with Greece (percentage of total trade)

2005	*2006*	*2007*	*2008*	*2009*	*2010*	*2011*	*2012*	*2013*	*2014*
11.6%	10.8%	9.7%	9.6%	9.4%	7.9%	6.8%	9.4%	8.4%	7.3%

Source: State Statistical Office of Macedonia.

5 Macedonia and the euro

5.1 Nominal and real convergence criteria

Reaching the high degree of sustainable nominal convergence defined in the Maastricht Treaty is a necessary condition for joining the euro area. Assessment of the nominal convergence is conducted on the basis of fulfilment of the four main Maastricht criteria: (i) price stability; (ii) long-term interest rate convergence; (iii) exchange rate stability; and (iv) public finance sustainability.

Starting from around 2,000% annual inflation in 1992, when the Republic of Macedonia proclaimed its independence, the inflation rate was successfully reduced to the one-digit level within a few years. Since 1996, when price stability was achieved, the inflation rate has averaged 2.4%, reaching its highest value of 8.3% in 2008 due to the one-off transmission effect of the rise of food and energy prices worldwide (Davidovska and Kadievska 2008). The inflation rate has been fluctuating closely around the reference value of inflation calculated according to the requirement of the Maastricht Treaty since the inception of the euro (Figure 7.21). The recorded low inflation has been achieved by the maintenance of a stable exchange rate in an environment of relatively low credibility of monetary policy at the initial stage of transition, a high level of openness and a euroized economy. However, on the basis of historical data, it cannot be fully concluded that the fulfilment of the price stability criterion will not be a challenge in the future. Indeed, the expected speed-up of the real convergence of Macedonia toward the EU is expected to set in motion the Balassa-Samuelson[4] effect which may drive the inflation rate to a higher level exceeding the Maastricht reference value.

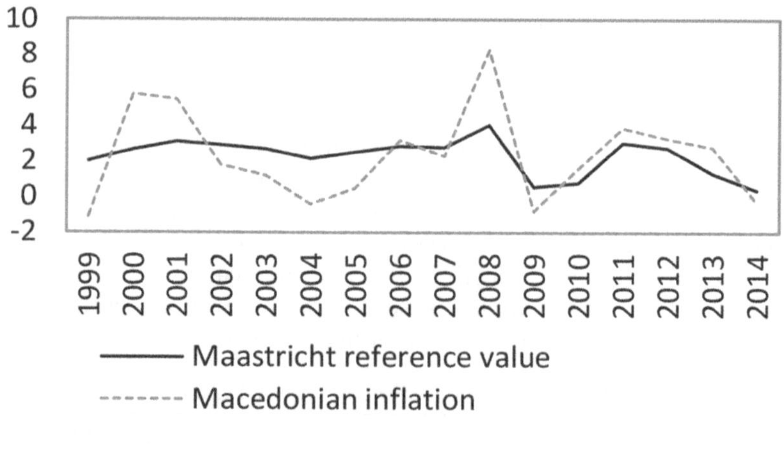

Figure 7.21 Inflation rate of Macedonia and the reference value of the price stability criterion[5]

Source: National Bank of the Republic of Macedonia and Eurostat; own calculations.

Inflation convergence is expected to enhance the interest rate convergence, since inflation expectations are a component of nominal interest rates. Thus, a relatively low inflation rate contributed to maintaining lower yields of the Macedonian government securities after the inception of five-year bonds in Macedonia in 2011 in comparison to the reference interest rate calculated according to the Maastricht criterion (Figure 7.22). Although the maturity of the government securities in Macedonia is shorter and thus not completely appropriate for comparison with the reference interest rate (ten-year maturity), such comparisons may still be indicative for the future movement of interest rates. In 2014, for the first time, the government issued a ten-year bond yielding 4.65% which is also below the reference interest rate.

Regarding the criterion of exchange rate stability, the National Bank of the Republic of Macedonia has been maintaining a stable exchange rate since 1995 by pegging the denar to the euro (Figure 7.23). Having the exchange rate maintained within the narrow band of less than 2% since the inception of the euro suggests that Macedonia is not expected to face substantial difficulties in fulfilling the criterion of exchange rate stability. However, there are potential challenges for achieving this criterion in the future as discussed in Section 5.2.

In assessing the sustainability of the public finance, attention is paid to the ratio of government deficit to GDP and the ratio of public debt to GDP, which should not exceed the Maastricht reference values of 3% and 60%, respectively. As for the fiscal deficit criterion, the government of Macedonia has achieved a ratio of below 3% of GDP for most of the time since 1999 (Figure 7.24). The first exception occurred in 2001 and 2002 as a result of

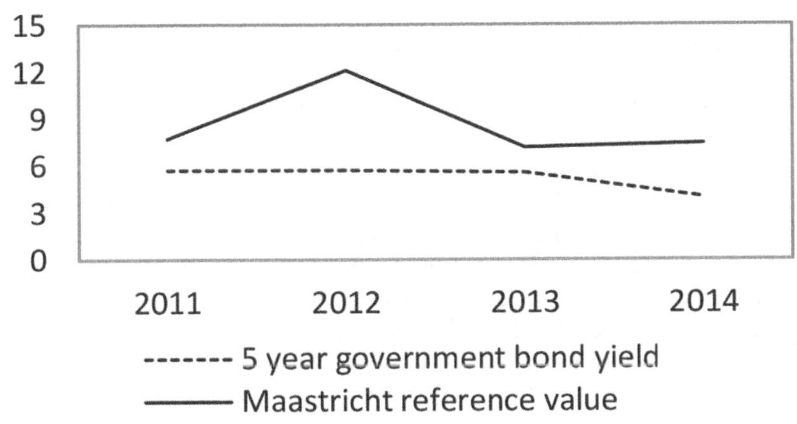

Figure 7.22 Macedonian government bond yield and the Maastricht interest rate criterion[6]

Source: National Bank of the Republic of Macedonia and Eurostat; own calculations.

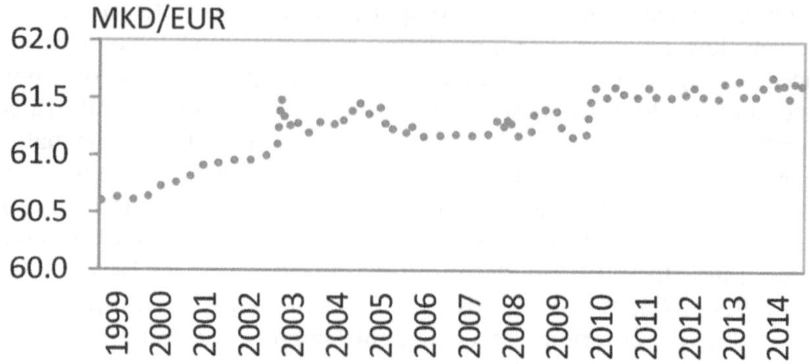

Figure 7.23 Movement of the exchange rate of denar pegged to euro
Source: Eurostat.

rising budgetary expenses associated with the inter-ethnic conflict. Nevertheless, the budgetary position was consolidated in the following years and maintained close to a balanced budget until the beginning of the global crisis. However, since 2012, the budget deficit has constantly exceeded the ceiling of 3%. Furthermore, the April 2015 edition of the *World Economic Outlook* predicts that the deficit will persistently remain above 3% until 2020. The low budget deficit before the crisis contributed to the reduction of the public debt-to-GDP ratio, which registered the lowest value of 23% in 2008 (Figure 7.25). Then, a sharp reversal happened during the crisis resulting in a doubling of the level of the public debt-to-GDP ratio to 46% in 2014. Although the indicator was below the reference value of 60% during the analysed period, its sharp increase in the aftermath of the crisis may compromise the fulfilment of this criterion in the future.

Despite the relatively satisfactory status on the nominal side, some indicators of real convergence reveal a different picture. Macedonian GDP per capita, based on purchasing power standard (PPS), was only 36% of the EU27 average in 2011 (Figure 7.26). Although a degree of real convergence has been under way during the recent decade, its pace is quite slow and much remains to be done to achieve full real convergence in the long run. In addition, the comparative price level indicator reveals a similar conclusion since the Macedonian price level in terms of final consumption expenditure is around 40% of the average price level in the EU28 (Figure 7.27).

5.2 Fixed exchange rate of the denar

After acquiring monetary independence in April 1992, the National Bank of the Republic of Macedonia chose a managed float supported by monetary targeting

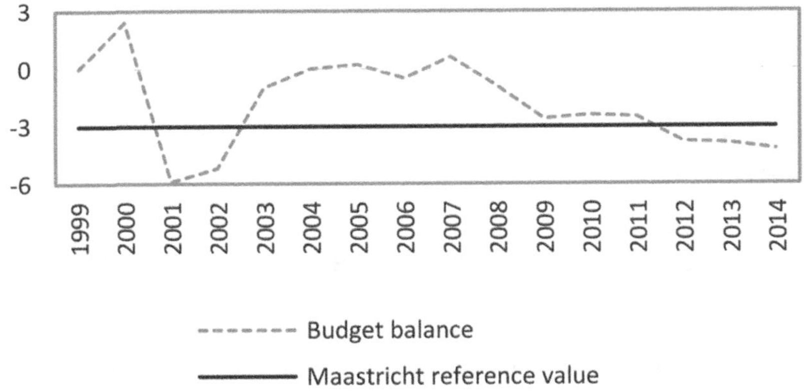

Figure 7.24 General government balance as percentage of GDP
Source: National Bank of the Republic of Macedonia and Ministry of Finance of the Republic of Macedonia.

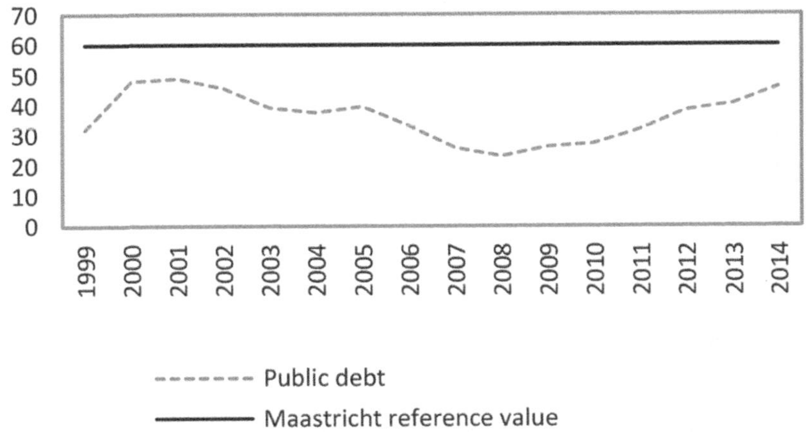

Figure 7.25 Public debt as percentage of GDP
Source: National Bank of the Republic of Macedonia and Ministry of Finance of the Republic of Macedonia.

which proved successful in curbing hyperinflation. However, this monetary policy strategy was not completely successful in anchoring inflation expectations given the high level of trade openness and euroization, which led consequently to higher exchange rate pass-through (Velickovski and Pugh, 2011). Therefore, in October 1995, the monetary policy switched to a de facto pegged exchange rate regime, pegging the Macedonian denar initially to the

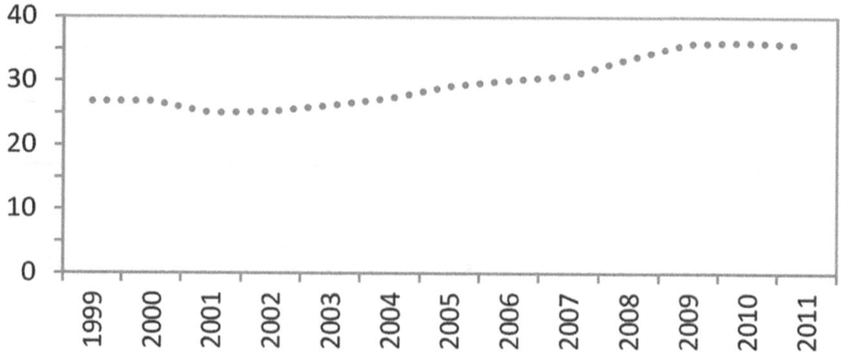

Figure 7.26 GDP as a percentage of EU27 total (based on PPS per inhabitant)
Source: Eurostat.

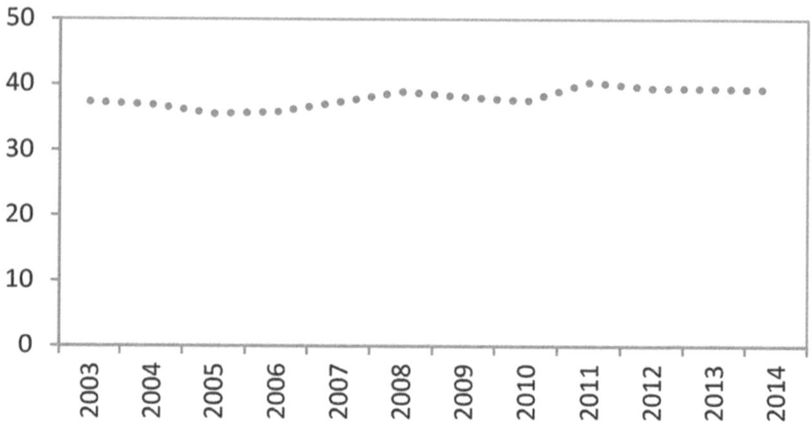

Figure 7.27 Price level index (EU28 = 100) in terms of final consumption expenditure
Source: Eurostat.

Deutsche Mark and, since 2001, to the euro. Anchoring inflation expectations by pegging the exchange rate appears to have been a key factor in stabilizing and maintaining low inflation. Since 1995, only one devaluation has taken place, in July 1997. The 16.1% devaluation still maintained a low and stable inflation rate, which consequently supported the exchange rate stability in the following period. Since 1999 when the euro currency was launched, the exchange rate has fluctuated on a daily basis as well as over longer periods largely within ±1%, which is narrower than the ERM II fluctuation margins around central rates.

A stable nominal exchange rate accompanied by low and relatively stable inflation rates contributed to remarkable stability of the real effective exchange rate (Figure 7.28). At the same time, the equilibrium real effective exchange rate was estimated as broadly in line with the fundamentals (Gutierrez, 2006). On the other hand, Jovanovic (2007) suggests that the fundamental equilibrium exchange rate of the denar exhibits a tendency to appreciate over time which is driven by the rise in the net current transfers. Yet, strong evidence for misalignment of the denar has not been provided by other studies (Petrevski, 2007; Égert et al., 2008).

The empirical evidence supports the existing exchange rate regime given that pegs and intermediate regimes significantly outperform floats in terms of economic growth in transition countries, including Macedonia, according to Petreski (2014a).[7]

However, some specifics of the Macedonian economy create uncertainty about the continued sustainability of the exchange rate. The most apparent is the high trade deficit as a percentage of GDP, which has been around 20% for a long period, as explained above, exposing the economy to external shock vulnerability. Although, the current account deficit as a percentage of GDP fluctuated around a sustainable level most of the time (Unevska and Jovanovic, 2011), the trade deficit is largely covered by private transfers, which are not a stable source of finance, thereby putting pressure on the foreign exchange reserves and jeopardizing exchange rate stability. Moreover, the high level of euroization of the banking balance sheets influenced by the volatile sentiment of their depositors – households – brings significant risks reflected in foreign exchange market pressures. The success in attracting

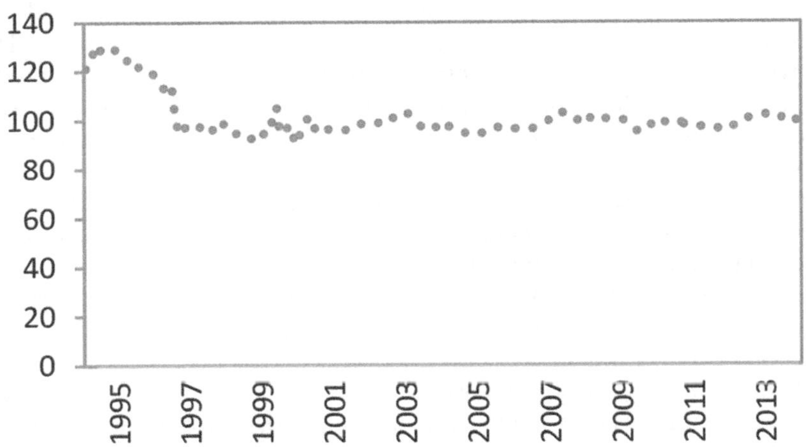

Figure 7.28 Real effective exchange rate (CPI-based; 2007 M12 = 100)
Source: Bruegel.

foreign direct investments, which were low in the past albeit improving slightly during the last few years, will be crucial for facilitating the task of the National Bank of the Republic of Macedonia of maintaining a stable exchange rate in the future.

5.3 Advantages and disadvantages of adoption of the euro

Due to the blockage of the Macedonian integration in the EU, as explained above, a vivid debate about the costs and benefits the country may face from potential monetary integration has not started yet. Nevertheless, having a de facto pegged exchange rate to the euro inspires a discussion on whether the advantages outweigh the disadvantages of joining the euro area.

On microeconomic grounds, the Macedonian highly open economy is expected to benefit from the elimination of transaction costs arising from foreign exchange transactions. One type of transaction cost are financial costs, which are related to the fees in the form of the bid-ask spreads for conversion of domestic into foreign currency. Moreover, elimination of transaction costs in combination with disappearance of the exchange rate risk can reduce uncertainty of importers' and exporters' future profit, leading to greater trade activity. However, the additional trade-enhancing effects of the euro may not be substantial given the already achieved high level of trade integration which was influenced to some extent by the fixed exchange rate.

The microeconomic gains would obviously translate into macroeconomic effects affecting economic growth via various channels such as trade intensity, trade and production structures as well as lower interest rates and encouraged foreign direct investments due to eliminated exchange rate risk and likely credit risk. Although Macedonia's trade and financial linkages with the EU improved over time as discussed in Section 4, yet trade and production structures have not sufficiently converged with the euro area. Thus, the Krugman index of specialization supports convergence of the production structure of Macedonia towards that of the EU in terms of both value added and employment; however substantial differences are still evident (Figure 7.29).

On the other hand, trade with the EU is dominantly one-way (inter-industry) while the two-way (intra-industry) trade does not register a convergence trend, which fluctuated around 20% during the analysed period (Figure 7.30). The largest part of the two-way trade is of vertical type whereas the horizontal intra-industry trade, which is more relevant for the business cycle/shock synchronization, is small.

All these factors affect the business cycle synchronization of Macedonia with the euro area. The economic developments in the eurozone have significant and relatively strong output and inflation effects on the Macedonian economy (Petrevski, Bogoev and Tevdovski, 2015), which supports to some extent the business-cycle synchronization with the euro area as estimated by Petrovska (2012). Yet, only a small portion of domestic output variation can be explained

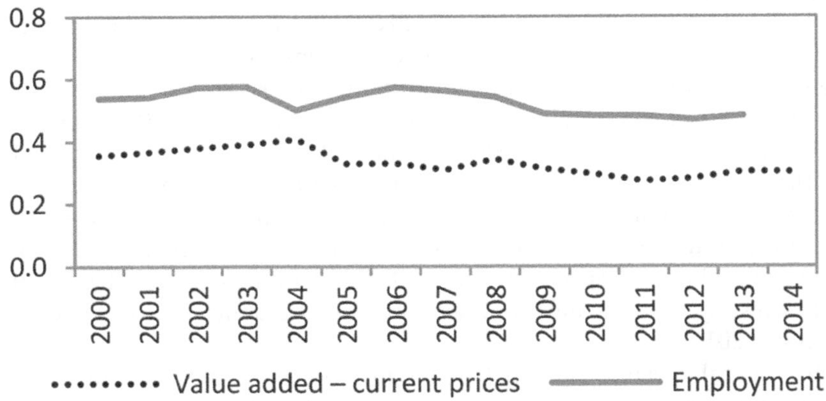

Figure 7.29 Krugman index of specialization of the production structure with the EU28[8]
Source: Eurostat.

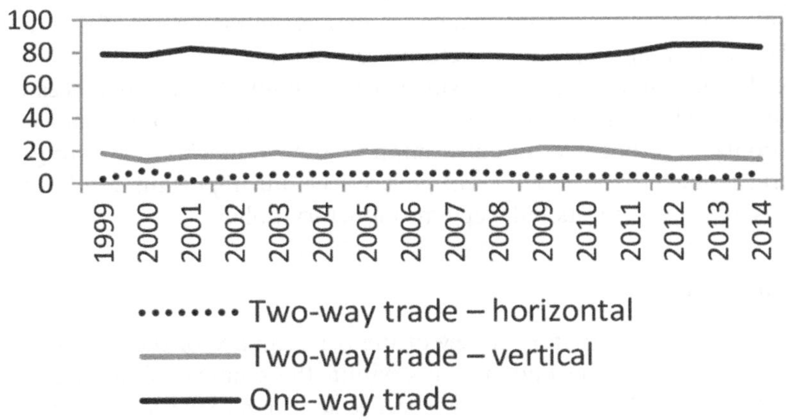

Figure 7.30 Indices of the structure of trade with the EU28[9]
Source: Eurostat.

by the euro area demand (Andonova and Petkovska, 2011), inducing low synchronization between shocks hitting the Macedonian economy and the euro area on both the supply and the demand side, as estimated by Velickovski (2010) and Velickovski and Stojkov (2014). This indicates that there will be potentially high costs to losing independent monetary policy for Macedonia.

Although the need for an independent monetary policy at this stage is accentuated by the finding of a very low synchronization of supply and demand shocks between Macedonia and the euro area, the ability to conduct an independent monetary policy is also relevant when assessing the disadvantages of adopting a single currency. Empirical research in this area suggests that the effectiveness of domestic monetary policy measured via the interest rate channel is quite limited (Bogoev and Petrevski, 2012; Velickovski, 2013). In addition, the exchange rate channel has also been constrained due to the de facto pegged exchange rate regime which restrains monetary policy, in particular, in times of crisis (Jovanovic and Petreski, 2014). Nevertheless, despite the fixed currency, monetary policy conduct strengthened over time, enlarging the space for the possibility of achieving other domestic objectives, apart from inflation, such as output stabilization (Jovanovic and Petreski, 2012).

In general, despite the relatively tight room for independent monetary policy in the past due to the fixed exchange rate, relinquishing the interest rate and exchange rate instrument might be costly for Macedonia at this stage since the shock synchronization with the euro area is still low. In this light, the problems that Greece is experiencing currently due to its inability to depreciate the currency is very relevant evidence for the size of costs a country may face when it abandons its monetary independence.

Overall, it appears that the benefits may outweigh the costs of the adoption of the euro if appropriate structural reforms are undertaken resulting in longer-lasting financial inflows, which would diminish the differences in production structures and trade patterns. This would not only enhance shock synchronization, but it would also improve the country's credit rating which, in turn, is likely to improve fiscal governance, an important condition for a country that gives up its independent monetary policy.

6 Conclusion

The chapter has given an overview of the performance of the economy of the Republic of Macedonia and put this within the context of the accession of the country to the EU, as well the prospective accession to the common European currency. The chapter has explained the difficult time Macedonia went through after gaining independence from Yugoslavia, faced with bad privatization, trade collapse, high inflation and a stagnant economy, flavoured with intense corruption, political instability, embargo and internal conflict later. It has argued that a light at the end of the tunnel has been the dedication to accede to the EU, although it has remained stuck as an EU candidate country, facing a continuous blockade by Greece, due to the name dispute.

Macedonia's EU membership is likely to be beneficial for the country, due to enhanced trade and financial integration within the Union, and in particular, within the eurozone. Such membership could also lead to higher political stability and better governance. In the case of Macedonia, nominal convergence has been already achieved to a sufficient extent, while progress has also been registered in real convergence. Further structural reforms in the economy may smooth the way to adopting the euro when and if the country becomes a member of the EU. This is, however, brought into question by the problems that Greece is experiencing currently with the inability to depreciate its currency.

The Macedonian prospects for EU membership will depend on its progress in the establishment of a functioning society and economy. Corruption still represents a big problem in society, as well as bad governance, which then leads to severe misuse and abuse of public resources. Intensified and more productive and efficient public investments are needed in order to improve the infrastructure. This, coupled with an improved business regulation framework, may stimulate investment, both domestic and foreign, which in turn could contribute to stronger export diversification and sustainable employment. The latter will particularly depend on a better alignment of workers' skills with labour demand, which requires proper reforms of the education system. Such changes are likely to enhance the economy's ability to cope with competitive pressures in EU markets, in the medium-term.

Yet, the two key challenges facing Macedonia with regard to its possible accession to the EU relate to the uncertainties in the domestic political scene and the resolution of the 'name issue' deadlock with Greece. Although the domestic political challenges are mounting, the 'name issue' dispute is likely to prove very difficult to settle.

Notes

1 The views expressed herein do not necessarily reflect the views of the National Bank of the Republic of Macedonia and the University American College Skopje. The authors would like to thank Lino Briguglio and Goran Petrevski for helpful comments.
2 Further details on SAA can be found in Daskalov et al. (2003).
3 CEFTA, the Central European Free Trade Agreement, was extended and enlarged in 2006 after the original member countries joined the EU and as a result left CEFTA.
4 The Balassa-Samuelson effect relates to the possible increase in wage rates in the production of tradable goods of a fast growing economy, which would then lead to higher wage rates in the non-tradable sector of the same economy. This, in turn, would lead to relatively high inflation rates and an appreciation of the exchange rate of the domestic currency.
5 The price stability criterion requires the average rate of inflation observed over a period of one year before the examination not to exceed the average rate of inflation of, at most, the three best performers by more than 1.5 percentage points.
6 The criterion for convergence of long-term interest rates requires that the level of the average nominal long-term interest rate on government bonds of the euro area candidate country over the 12 months before the examination does not exceed by more than two percentage points that of the unweighted arithmetic average of the three best-performing member countries in terms of price stability.
7 There are, however, in both the empirical papers and the public debate, advocates of the introduction of inflation targeting, which may bring some benefits over tight exchange rate pegging, especially if the Balassa-Samuelson process gains intensity in Macedonia in the future (e.g. Petreski, 2013b; 2014b).
8 The index takes value zero if a country has an industrial structure identical to the reference group of countries, indicating that the country is not specialized, and

takes a maximum value of 2 if it has no sectors in common with the reference group, reflecting strong sectoral specialization. The indicators are constructed using annual national accounts data compiled in accordance with the European System of Accounts 2010 (ESA 2010) based on the Statistical classification of economic activities in the European Community (NACE Rev. 2) and detailed breakdown into ten aggregates.

9 The indices of intra-industry trade are calculated according to Fontagné and Freudenberg (1997) using annual data at the five-digit level, which gives 3,530 commodity groups.

References

Andonova, U.D. and Petrovska, M. (2011) *The Transmission of External Shocks to the Macedonian Economic Activity.* National Bank of the Republic of Macedonia. Working Paper.

Bogoev, J. and Petrevski, G. (2012) 'Interest Rate Pass-Through in a Small Open Economy with a Fixed Exchange Rate – The Case of Macedonia', *Procedia – Social and Behavioral Sciences*, 44: 125–133.

Daskalov, S., Petkovski, M., Petrevski, G. and Biljanoska, J. (2003) 'Country Study: FYR Macedonia', in *Trade Policies and Institutions in the Countries of South Eastern Europe in the EU Stabilization and Association Process – Background Country Studies*, Document of the World Bank. Washington, DC: The World Bank, 20 April, pp. 109–146.

Davidovska, S.B. and Kadievska, V.M. (2008) *Food Prices and Inflation in the Republic of Macedonia*, National bank of the Republic of Macedonia, Working Paper.

Égert, B., Bogoev, J., Terzijan, S.B. and Petrovska, M. (2008) 'Real Exchange Rate Dynamics in Macedonia: Old Wisdoms and New Insights', *Economics E-Journal* 02/2008, 2(18):1–19.

Fontagné, L. and Freudenberg, M. (1997) 'Intra-Industry Trade: Methodological Issues Reconsidered', CEPII Working Paper No. 97–01.

Gutierrez, E. (2006) 'Export Performance and External Competitiveness in the Former Yugoslav Republic of Macedonia', International Monetary Fund. Working Paper No.06/261.

ISAM (Insurance Supervision Agency of Macedonia) (2014) *Annual Report 2014 of the Insurance Supervision Agency of Macedonia.* Available at: http://www.aso.mk/dokumenti/izvestai/godisni/Godisen% 20izvestaj% 20za% 20pazarot% 20na% 20osiguruvanje_2013_finalen_26.06.2014.pdfv (accessed on 12 July 2015).

Jovanovic, B. (2007) 'Calculating the Fundamental Equilibrium Exchange Rate of the Macedonian Denar', MSc Dissertation. Economics for Business Analysis. Staffordshire University.

Jovanovic, B. (2015) 'Kalman Filter Estimation of the Unrecorded Economy in Macedonia. National Bank of the Republic of Macedonia', Research Paper, 2015.

Jovanovic, B. and Jovanovic, B. (2015) 'Ease of Doing Business and FDI in the Ex-Socialist Countries', Mimeo, National Bank of the Republic of Macedonia

Jovanovic, B. and Petreski, M. (2012) 'Monetary Policy in Small Open Economy with Fixed Exchange Rate: The Case of Macedonia', *Economic Systems*, 36(4): 594–608.

Jovanovic, B. and Petreski, M. (2014) 'Monetary Policy, Exchange Rates and Labor Unions in SEE and the CIS during the Financial Crisis', *Economic Systems*, 38(3): 309–332.

NBRM (National Bank of the Republic of Macedonia) (2015) 'Quarterly Report on the Banking System of Macedonia Q1–2015', National Bank of the Republic of Macedonia. Available at: http://nbrm.mk/WBStorage/Files/Regulativa_Kvartalen_31_3_20141.pdf (accessed on 12 July 2015).

Petreski, M. (2013a). 'South East European Trade Analysis: A Role for Endogenous CEFTA-2006?' *Emerging Markets Finance and Trade*, 49(5): 26–44.

Petreski, M. (2013b). 'An Overhaul of a Doctrine: Has Inflation Targeting Opened a New Era in Developing-country Peggers?' *Eastern European Economics*, 51(5): 46–68.

Petreski, M. (2014a). 'Grooming Classifications: Exchange Rate Regimes and Growth in Transition Economies', *Eastern European Economics*, 52(1): 5–33.

Petreski, M. (2014b). 'Inflation Targeting at the Crossroads: Evidence from Post-communist Economies during the Crisis', *Communist and Post-Communist Studies*, 47(2): 247–260.

Petreski, M. and Jovanovic, B. (eds) (2013) *Remittances and Development in the Western Balkans: The Cases of Macedonia, Kosovo and Bosnia-Herzegovina*, Scholars' Press.

Petreski, M. and Jovanovic, B. (2014) 'Do Remittances Reduce Poverty in Macedonia?' Mimeo, Munich: MPRA.

Petreski, M. and Petreski, B. (2015) 'Dissatisfied, Feeling Unequal and Inclined to Emigrate: Perceptions from Macedonia in a MIMIC model', *Migration Letters*, 12(2): 152–161.

Petrevski, G. (2005) 'Macedonia: A Decade of Stabilization Policy', *South East Europe Review for Labour and Social Affairs*, 8(1): 97–116.

Petrevski, G. (2007) 'Equilibrium Real Exchange Rate in Macedonia', *International Journal of Monetary Economics and Finance*, 1(1): 5–17.

Petrevski, G., Bogoev, J. and Tevdovski, D. (2015) 'The Transmission of Foreign Shocks to South Eastern European Economies', *Empirica, Journal of European Economics*. DOI: 10.1007/s10663–10014–9275-x.

Petrovska, M. (2012) 'Business Cycle Regimes in a Group of South East European Economies. Evidence from a Threshold SUR Approach', *International Journal of Economic Policy in Emerging Economies*, 5(3): 272–292.

Solt, F. (2014) 'The Standardized World Income Inequality Database', *Social Science Quarterly*. Available at: http://myweb.uiowa.edu/fsolt/swiid/swiid.html (accessed on 12 July 2015).

Unevska, D. and Jovanovic, B. (2011) 'Sustainability of Macedonian Current Account', National Bank of the Republic of Macedonia. Working Paper.

Velickovski, I. (2010) *Potential Costs of Euro Adoption for Transition Countries: A Case Study for Macedonia*. VDM Verlag Dr. Müller.

Velickovski, I. (2013) 'Assessing Independent Monetary Policy in Small, Open and Euroized Countries: Evidence from Western Balkan', *Empirical Economics*, 45(1): 137–156.

Velickovski, I. and Pugh, G. (2011) 'Constraints on Exchange Rate Flexibility in Transition Economies: A Meta-Regression Analysis of Exchange Rate Pass-Through', *Applied Economics*, 43(27): 4111–4125.

Velickovski, I. and Stojkov, A. (2014) 'Is the European Integration Speeding Up the Economic Convergence Process of the Central and South-Eastern European Countries? A Shock Perspective', *Empirica*, 41(2): 287–321.

8 The Maltese Economy

Structure, performance and European Union membership

Lino Briguglio

1 Introduction

Malta,[1] located south of Italy in the middle of the Mediterranean Sea, consists of two inhabited islands, namely the main island, also called Malta, and Gozo, which hosts around 8% of the country's population. A third island, Comino, is a tourist resort.

1.1 Malta and Gozo

The total population of Malta was estimated at about 429.3 thousand at the end of 2014, of which about 27.4 thousand were foreign persons. With a land area of 316km^2, the population density of the Maltese islands was about 1,360 persons per square kilometre, which is one of the highest in the world for an independent state.

Malta has had a long and variegated history dating back to the dawn of civilization. The islands were colonized by many European powers, with the most recent one being Britain (1801–1964). Maltese is the national language and an official language of Malta and of the European Union (EU). The language is Semitic but written in the Roman alphabet, and a large proportion of the vocabulary comes from Sicilian and Italian.

During the nineteenth and the first half of the twentieth century, the Maltese economy was dominated by the provision of services associated with the British armed forces, including its military and naval installations. Malta became an independent state in 1964 and a republic in 1974.[2] It acceded to the European Union in 2004, became a member of the Schengen area in 2007 and of the euro area in 2008.

This chapter describes the structure and performance of the Maltese economy and explains how the economy was affected by Malta's accession to the EU. The chapter is organized into five sections. Section 2, which follows this introduction, presents information about the structure and performance of the Maltese economy. Section 3 gives an account of the advantages and disadvantages for Malta as an EU member state. The main constraints faced by the Maltese economy are discussed in Section 4. The last section concludes the chapter with a brief summary and some comments relating to future prospects.

2 Structure and performance of the Maltese economy

The Maltese economy is one of the smallest in the world. In 2014, the Maltese gross domestic product (GDP) at market prices amounted to approximately €7,960m., equivalent to around 0.05% of the GDP of the European Union, and around 0.07% of the eurozone. Malta's GDP per capita in 2014 amounted to approximately €18,700, as a result of which Malta is classified as a high-income country by the World Bank. Malta is also categorized as a country with very high human development (in the top quartile) by the UN Development Programme.

2.1 The economy in the 1950s and 1960s

As indicated earlier, Malta was for a very long period of time heavily dependent on British military expenditure. Because of this, the structure of the Maltese economy was grossly unbalanced, with the livelihood of the Maltese people highly dependent on the defence interests of a foreign country.[3] During the 1950s, the growing awareness that the importance of Malta as a strategic base of the British forces was due to decline led to attempts by the Maltese authorities to seek alternative sources of income and employment.

During the second half of the 1950s, it became clear that the run-down of the British military presence in Malta was going to lead to massive unemployment and the need was felt to draw up and implement a development plan to diversify the economy, so as to reduce dependence on military and naval occupations and to create new employment opportunities in industrial production, tourism and agriculture. Since Malta's domestic market is very small, industrial expansion had to be achieved through increased reliance on exports and therefore the promotion of competitiveness was considered of paramount importance.

The first five-year development plan based on these objectives was launched in 1959. The plan did not produce good results as the economy could not expand enough to make up for the slack created by the run-down of the British military establishments. By 1964, an atmosphere of pessimism prevailed particularly following the Stolper Report (Stolper, Hellberg and Callander, 1964)[4] which painted a bleak picture of Malta's economic future. The British government's reluctance to maintain the naval dockyard, which at that time employed thousands of Maltese workers, was expected to lead to further unemployment.

The second five-year development plan, launched in 1964, the year Malta became independent from Britain, was therefore based on pessimistic projections. However, the actual performance of the economy did not bear out the bleak projections of the Stolper Report and by 1969 the economy had expanded rapidly, leading to relatively low unemployment rates even though the rate of emigration was much lower than anticipated.

By 1986, six development plans had been launched by governments of different ideologies, but the basic objective of all these plans was the same, namely that of promoting economic viability, so that Malta, by its own efforts, would produce jobs for all those who sought them.

2.2 Major structural changes in the economy

An important change that occurred in the structure of the Maltese economy after it became independent in 1964 related to the phasing out of the bases of the British forces stationed in Malta. British military establishments reduced their share of GDP from an average of 22% in the second half of the 1950s to zero in 1979, the year that these establishments were totally dismantled, in line with Malta's 1972–1979 development plan.[5]

Another significant change was the rapid expansion of the manufacturing sector up to the end of the 1970s. Manufacturing accounted for just 10% of GDP during the second half of the 1950s and increased to about 33% during the late 1970s. The share of this sector declined during the 1990s and continued to do so during the 2000s. The sector has been transformed structurally over the years, with the major change being that the clothing industry, which was relatively large in the 1970s and 1980s, and depended mostly on low wage rates, declined. On the other hand, while technologically based industries, with high per worker value added, such as the electronic components industry, increased their relative share of the sector.

The services sector, including domestic property income, increased its share after 1964 and was also transformed mostly due to the development of tourism, transportation and financial services.

Looking at Maltese foreign trade in general between 1960 and 2014, some tendencies emerge: essentially, Malta experienced a relatively large deficit in its merchandise trade and a positive, but smaller, surplus in its services trade. Thus, with the exception of 2011–2014, the balance between exports and imports of goods and services taken together (the resource balance) was generally negative. This gap tended to increase into the 2000s, but had not threatened the stability of the exchange rate of the Maltese lira, when this was the domestic currency, due in part to net foreign currency inflows in the capital account of the Maltese balance of payments.[6]

2.3 The economy in 2014

Table 8.1 shows the contribution of major sectors to the Maltese GDP at basic prices between 2011 and 2014. It can be seen that in 2014 the GDP share of manufacturing amounted to about 10%. The services sector, including domestic property income, amounted to about 63% of GDP in 2014. During the same year, 1.3% of GDP was contributed by agriculture and

Table 8.1 The main sectors of the Maltese economy (€ million)

Sector	*2011*	*2012*	*2013*	*2014*	*Shares in 2014*
Agriculture, forestry and fishing	92.9	95.7	97.3	91.8	1.3%
Mining and quarrying	83.9	25.9	113.7	100.2	1.5%
Manufacturing	789.8	793.7	727.7	707.6	10.2%
Construction	285.4	280	274	275.7	4.0%
Market services	3,643.90	3,939.50	4,142.00	4,383.00	63.5%
Public administration and defence	1,115.20	1,183.30	1,253.80	1,348.10	19.5%
Total: gross value added	**6011.1**	**6318.1**	**6608.5**	**6906.4**	**100%**

Source: National Statistics Office, Malta (retrieved in November 2015).

fisheries, 4% by construction and 1.5% by quarrying. The remaining 20% represented the share of government. For a nation of its size, Malta's economy is relatively diversified, although there are a number of specific industries dominated by one firm or a few large firms.

A characteristic of the Maltese economy is its relatively large financial sector, with the assets of banks, insurance companies and investment funds amounting to about nine times GDP in 2014. The so-called core domestic banks of Malta are highly conservative in terms of capital adequacy and liquidity ratios. They provide most of their loans to and collect most of their deposits from residents in Malta. The non-core banks are mostly international banks highly dependent on wholesale funding and non-resident deposits, and therefore do not pose significant risks to financial stability in Malta (IMF, 2015).

Another important characteristic of the Maltese economy is its high degree of openness. Like many other small economies, Malta depends heavily on imports for its industrial supplies and consumer goods. The import content of total final sales was about 61% in 2014 as can be seen in Table 8.2. At the same time, since the domestic market is extremely small, the economy relies to a large extent on exports of goods and services, which amounted to some 58.5% of final sales in that year.

With the growth of export-oriented services and the relative decline of the need for industrial supplies for the manufacturing industry, the resource balance narrowed and was mostly positive between 2011 and 2014.

Exports of merchandise, excluding re-exports which are dominated by transhipment of fuel, are dominated by electronic and electrical equipment. Other important merchandise exports include chemicals, instruments and printing. In 2014, about one-third of Maltese exports of merchandise were directed towards the EU, primarily to France, Germany, Italy and the United Kingdom. Maltese imports of merchandise originate principally from the EU,

Table 8.2 Expenditures in the Maltese GDP and rate of real GDP growth (€ million)

Final expenditure	*2011*	*2012*	*2013*	*2014*
Household final consumption expenditure	4,025.5	4,116.1	4,241.2	4,361.8
General government consumption expenditure	1,344.5	1,447.6	1,479.6	1,611.7
Total gross capital formation	1,333.7	1,280.5	1,290.8	1,463.1
Exports of goods and services	10,989.8	11,857.8	11,852.0	11,864.7
Total final expenditure	**17,693.5**	**18,701.9**	**18,863.7**	**19,301.3**
Imports of goods and services	10,800.7	11,497.0	11,330.0	11,360.0
GDP at market prices at current prices	**6,892.8**	**7,205.0**	**7,533.6**	**7,941.3**
GDP at constant 2010 prices	10,800.7	11,497.0	11,330.0	11,360.0
Real GDP growth		**2.5%**	**2.6%**	**3.5%**

Source: National Statistics Office, Malta (retrieved in November 2015).

with the same four countries being the most important countries of origin. Trade with non-EU Mediterranean states (including North African countries) is relatively low. Imports and exports of electronic equipment to and from Asia and the USA are important.

Exports of services are relatively diversified and consist principally of tourism, transportation, financial services, remote gaming, and information and communications technology (ICT) activities. Malta's trade in services occurs mostly with the EU.

The Maltese islands have few natural resources, and most raw materials and industrial supplies have to be imported. Petroleum exploration has been undertaken on several occasions but, so far, its extraction has not been found to be commercially viable. Malta's climate and its cultural and historical heritage are important resources for attracting tourists to the islands.

2.4 Economic growth

Between 1964 and 2004, the year Malta joined the EU, the Maltese economy went through a cyclical pattern of change, tending to register relatively rapid growth during the second half of each decade, and relatively slow, even negative, growth during the first half of each decade (see Briguglio, 1988).

Malta was one of the slowest-growing economies in the EU when it acceded to the Union in 2004, with real GDP growth standing at only 0.9%. This was mostly because of the difficult international trading environment, which Malta was not meeting with sufficient competitiveness, compounded by the short-term effects of fiscal consolidation. However, there was an upturn in 2005–2008, with real GDP growing at a rate of 4.7% in 2005, 2.1% in 2006, 4.4% in 2007 and 5.3% in 2008, as supply-side policies were put in place to enable Malta to enhance its potential rate of growth and to converge with average EU levels. However, in 2009 the Maltese economy contracted by 2.7%, mostly owing to the effects of the global recession.

It subsequently recovered rapidly, and grew in real terms at an average rate of 2.9% annually between 2011 and 2014, as can be seen in Table 8.2.

2.5 Economic governance

Economic governance has undergone major changes since independence. In the 1970s and the first half of the 1980s the country was administered by a socialist Government (led by the Malta Labour Party – MLP, which later changed its name to Partit Laburista – PL), with widespread state intervention and stringent price and import controls. After 1987, the Partit Nazzjonalista (PN – Nationalist Party) was returned to power and, although upholding a conservative ideology, ushered in a radical change in economic policy, based on liberalization in the domestic market, the removal of import controls and a policy of privatization. The PL was returned to power in 2013, but the Government's economic policies remained broadly the same as those pursued by the PN, while focusing on major investment projects to bring reforms and development mainly in energy, tourism and international real estate development.

As a result of the country's accession to the EU in 2004, Malta had to adopt a body of EU legislation, which upgraded its institutional capacity, albeit at a significant cost, and markedly improved its regulatory frameworks. By joining the EU, access to the European market for Maltese exports improved. This also led to the country adopting an economic strategy that promoted domestic competition and international competitiveness, leading to a more efficient allocation of resources. Furthermore, Malta benefited from EU regional funds for economic and social development.

2.6 Malta's performance in a global context

Table 8.3 shows the rankings of Malta in terms of global indicators, expressed in relative terms that is as a percentage of the total number of countries covered by the respective index.[7]

It can be seen from Table 8.3 that in terms of political governance (WGI) Malta received relatively high rankings, where the highest rank possible was set at 1 (so the smaller the percentage, the higher the relative rankings), placing the country amongst the top 12% of all countries covered by the index, a ranking higher than the EU average. In terms of GDP per capita and the HDI, Malta also received a relatively high ranking globally, but somewhat lower than the EU average.

With regard to competitiveness, Malta ranked among the top 33% of countries but had a much lower ranking than the EU average. Malta's ranking in terms of GDP growth between 2010 and 2014 (i.e. following the post-2009 recession) was relatively low in a world-wide context[8] but on the high-side when compared to the EU average.

Table 8.3 Malta's ranking in global indicators (1 being the highest ranking)

Indicator	*Malta's rank*	*Number of countries*	*Malta's relative rank (%)*	*Average EU-28 relative rank (%)*
Worldwide Governance Indicators (WGI) (2013)	23	189	12.2%	15.5%
GDP per capita (2013)	35	184	19.0%	17.7%
Human Development Index (HDI) (2013)	39	187	20.9%	15.3%
Global Competitiveness Index (GCI) (2014–15)	47	144	32.6%	23.5%
Real GDP growth (2010–2013)	81	184	44.0%	53.6%

3 Malta and the EU

3.1 The Association Agreement

Malta's first attempt to associate itself with the EU occurred in 1967, and exploratory talks followed in 1968. An agreement setting up a formal association between Malta and the EU came into being in 1971. It was agreed that as a first stage, which was to last five years, the EU was to reduce by 70% its common external tariff for most of Malta's manufactured exports, subject to the rules of origin. In return, Malta was to accord, amongst other things, a phased tariff reduction reaching 35% by the fifth year of the agreement. At the end of the first stage, there was to be another five year stage, leading to the formation of a customs union between Malta and the EU. Subsequently the European Community (EC) tariff rates on Malta's industrial exports were reduced to zero and some modifications were made regarding the rules of origin. The agreement was also broadened to include financial cooperation.

The second stage of the agreement never came into being, so that by 1987, the 1971 agreement still represented the major arrangement through which Malta derived the tariff-free access of its manufactured products into EU markets, with some amendments deepening the relationship between Malta and the EC, including technical and financial assistance in the 1976 amendment.

In 1988, the newly elected Nationalist government sought and obtained an extension of the EU association agreement until 1990, stating that it was seeking eventual EU membership under the right conditions.

3.2 Malta applies to join the EC

On 16 July 1990, Malta, then under a Nationalist government, formally applied for EC membership, and this was followed by the publication of a favourable opinion by the European Commission in June 1993. However, in 1996, there was change of Government, following the Labour Party's general elections victory. The Labour government suspended Malta's application for EU membership and as a result Malta was excluded from the pre-accession preparations in which Cyprus and a number of Central and Eastern European states were participating.

However the Labour government lasted only two years, and, as a result of a change in government following a Nationalist Party win at the general elections of September 1998, EU accession negotiations recommenced and membership was re-activated. In February 1999 the European Commission updated the 1993 opinion on Malta's application for EU membership (European Commission, 1993). This led to the screening of Malta's laws so as to identify discrepancies with EU law, following which accession negotiations commenced in 2000, together with five other candidate countries (Latvia, Lithuania, Slovakia, Bulgaria and Romania).

In December 2000, at the Nice Summit, it was decided that Malta would have one Commissioner in the European Commission,[9] five seats in the European Parliament;[10] one Judge in the European Court of Justice; one judge in the European Court of First Instance;[11] one member in the Court of Auditors and five members in the Committee of Regions.

During the accession negotiations the Maltese government maintained a strong link with civil society through the Malta–EU Action and Steering Committee (MEUSAC), which also had to prepare Malta's position in the negotiation process. The negotiations with the EU were concluded in 2002. As a result of these negotiations, Malta was granted a number of transitional arrangements and derogations. Comparing the number of transitional arrangements and derogations secured by the ten new member states in the negotiations, Malta secured the largest number, the longest transitional arrangements, and some highly important permanent derogations – notably on the acquisition of secondary residencies by EU nationals, restrictions on the free movement of persons and the management of a fishing conservation zone.[12]

The justification for many of the concessions that were made – such as the restrictions on the purchase of property and on the free movement of persons, and the special treatment given to the island of Gozo – was Malta's small size (Buttigieg, 2004). Some concessions, however, were linked to, or, in a few cases, were largely a result of, other factors. For example, environmental, conservation and economic arguments all fed into the fishing zone agreement; the declaration on Malta's neutrality was linked to the manner in which Malta sees itself in world affairs and the need to maintain the national consensus on this issue; the transitional arrangements on the dockyards was driven by a mixture of economic goals and a need to mitigate the negative social implications of unemployment.

3.3 Disadvantages of joining the European Union

In the run-up to the 2003 referendum relating to Malta's EU membership, there was a lively debate about the advantages and disadvantages of Malta's accession to the EU.[13] Those who did not favour Malta's joining the EU cited as a major economic disadvantage the fact that import controls against EU member countries would have to be dismantled and this would give rise to a loss of output and employment in firms enjoying protection. Right up to the 1990s, a large number of domestically oriented firms depended on import controls to remain in existence.

Another economic disadvantage that was associated with EU membership was that food prices were likely to increase because of the EU Common Agriculture Policy (CAP). The CAP worked through a system of minimum prices in EU member states, maintained by intervention buying within the EU itself, and by import levies on products entering the member states from outside the EU. Operators in the agricultural sector also feared that imports from Sicily would displace local produce, if import controls were to be dismantled.

Another source of concern related to the possible inflow of foreign workers that could have resulted due to the freedom of movement of labour within the EU. It was argued that such inflow could destabilize Malta's small labour market. Yet another drawback that was often mentioned by those who opposed EU membership was that the Maltese government would lose revenue from import duties, and would therefore have to find alternative sources of revenue, such as by increasing value added tax (VAT) rates.

In the political sphere, the most important disadvantage that was identified related to the loss of sovereignty. As an EU member, Malta would cease to be able to act independently in a number of economic and political areas. On joining the EU Malta, being the smallest state, could not expect to influence the policies of the EU in the same manner that West Germany, France, Britain and Italy could, and as a result its future depended on the interests of the larger members.

Disadvantages associated with social factors also featured in the debate. For example the fact that in many EU countries divorce and abortion were legally allowed, and civil rights with regard to sexual and religious orientation were more liberal in many EU countries, was a source of worry in a section of the Maltese population.

The Labour Party, which opposed EU membership, and which had the support of about half the Maltese electorate in the 2002 general elections, proposed an alternative model, which was labelled 'Switzerland in the Mediterranean', whereby, it was argued, Malta could benefit from a special form of political and economic relationship, without taking on all the burdens associated with membership, especially loss of sovereignty.

3.4 Advantages of joining the European Union

The major arguments put forward in the run-up to the 2003 referendum in favour of Malta's accession to the EU related to opportunities in having access to a very large market, free of import barriers. The Maltese economy was and still is very closely linked to the EU – a large percentage of its exports were directed towards Germany, England, Italy, Belgium and France, and a large percentage of Malta's imports come from these same countries. Foreign-owned firms in Malta were to a large extent European. In a way, it was argued, Malta was already tied to Europe, but not being a full member, Malta could not reap the benefits that members enjoyed. In this regard, the pro-membership proponents argued that non-membership was to be increasingly disadvantageous for Malta, mostly due to the trade harmonization that was expected to occur within the EU.

Another economic advantage that was identified was that, as a full member, Malta could also attract more investment from non-member countries wanting to use Malta as a platform from which to penetrate the European market. Ireland had benefitted to a large extent from foreign investment of this type, and there was no reason, it was argued, why Malta should not also benefit in this regard, given of course that financial and physical infrastructural constraints were reduced as much as possible. Malta is also strategically placed to attract investment from European countries in their bid to expand their North African and Middle Eastern markets. With the increased harmonization of commercial legislation and political attitudes, which full membership would entail, Malta could attract a considerable amount of this type of investment.

Another argument put forward by the pro-membership campaigners was that Malta would stand to gain from transfers from the EU Regional Development Fund, Cohesion Fund and the Social Fund, which are mainly intended to decrease disparities between countries and regions in the EU. Being on the lower end of the per-capita income scale, compared to the 12 existing members, Malta would undoubtedly have access to these funds, as of right, and would have the possibility of influencing decisions as to the allocation of EU funds.

A pro-accession argument was that the Maltese economy would benefit as this would force Malta to change its import control policy which, to an extent, promoted inefficiency. This policy, which developed at a fast pace during the 1970s, and which had not been fully dismantled at that time, gave rise to an elaborate, bureaucratic machinery intended to encourage import substitution. If Malta joined the EU as a full member, it was contended, Maltese firms would be forced to utilisze economic resources in the most efficient manner and this would enable them to enhance their competitiveness.

At the political level, it was argued that by participating in the EU institutions Malta could influence the policies and decisions which affect it directly and indirectly and could also have direct access to EU services in matters relating to governance.

The voting power of small states in the EU is small but still more than proportional to their population size, leading to degressive proportionality, which, at that time in some ways even gave the possibility of a veto to a small state like Malta.[14]

As a result of EU membership, the EU body of laws that were to be transposed as a result of membership were expected to lead to better economic governance, including the setting up of independent regulatory authorities in such vital sectors as telecommunications, product standards, the environment, transport and competition.

Membership was also expected to benefit trade unions, business organizations and non-governmental organizations, as they would find it possible to cooperate closely with their European counterparts, thereby enriching social dialogue within Malta and extending it to the EU platform.

Local government was also expected to benefit, since local councils would be able to communicate directly with 'Brussels' on issues that were of concern to them.

It was therefore evident that EU membership had both advantages and disadvantages. Subsequently, the outcome of the referendum was in favour of Malta's accession, possibly indicating that although the disadvantages were recognized, these were outweighed by the perceived benefits.[15] Malta acceded to the EU in May 2004, following a transition period during which Malta's legislation and economic governance were transformed in line with the so-called *acquis communautaire* (the body of legislation relating to the EU).

3.5 Malta accedes to the EU

Malta acceded to the EU in May 2004. Membership has led Malta to liberalize its markets and has improved access to EU markets. As a result of Malta's accession to the EU the economy underwent a rapid transformation of its regulatory and operational structures, leading to the harmonization of Malta's laws with those of the EU. Competition in the domestic market was enhanced as the result of improved enforcement of competition law, overseen by the EU Commission. The removal of import controls against EU members promoted efficiency in production and government intervention in the form of state aid was controlled, so that, in general, resources were more efficiently allocated. Environmental regulation and environmental management was considerably improved. Access to regional and social funds was substantial, enabling Malta to enhance its physical infrastructure and undertake educational and social projects.[16]

The feared loss of jobs from domestically oriented firms resulting from the removal of trade barriers and free movement of labour from nearby Sicily did not materialize – on the contrary, following EU accession, the unemployment rate in Malta remained relatively low.[17]

Accession to the EU led to the adoption of the euro in January 2008 following a very successful transitional period characterized by wide consultation with and among stakeholders.[18] The monetary authorities cited among the advantages of joining the euro the fact that over 50% of Malta's trade, was, at that time, with eurozone countries.

The adoption of the euro ushered in better economic governance in the island, in line with the Stability and Growth Pact, increased price transparency, and reduced transaction costs for Malta's dealings with other members of the area. The adoption of the euro might also have led to an increase in Malta's attractiveness to foreign direct investment.

4 Prospects for the Maltese economy

According to a recent European Commission Country Report for Malta (European Commission, 2015) the Maltese economy and the Maltese labour market was performing well with strong labour market fundamentals and low unemployment rates. Economic and employment growth were projected to continue to outpace the euro area average in 2015–2016. Positive reviews were also drawn up by the IMF, which, in its Article IV report of February 2015 stated that Malta has weathered the crisis well and its economic outlook is stronger than that of the euro area as a whole.[19]

However, the economy faces various constraints, some of which are inherent, such as its small size, and others are self-inflicted, and can therefore be addressed through appropriate policy responses.

4.1 Inherent constraints associated with small economic size

The Maltese economy faces various limitations in view of the very small size and the insularity of the country – physical characteristics that will remain regardless of the economic policies it adopts.

The country's small size leads to a very high dependence on imports, mostly due to limited natural resource endowments, and on exports, mostly due to a small domestic market, rendering the economy highly exposed to external shocks. Insularity brings additional problems associated with international transport, which is a major concern given that Malta depends so heavily on exports.[20]

Problems associated with Malta's small size also include constraints associated with limited ability to reap the benefits of economies of scale and limitations on the degree of domestic competition.[21]

4.2 Constraints and problems that can be addressed by policy choices

4.2.1 Fiscal sustainability

Given the large welfare outlays, substantial expenditure on government services (which tend to be relatively high per capita due to the problem of overhead expenditure indivisibility) and claims by public sector employees for higher salaries, the Maltese Government will have to be continually on its guard to ensure sustainable public finances. As a member of the euro area, the Maltese Government is subject to relentless external pressure to control both its budget deficits and its national debt, in line with the requirements of the EU's Stability and Growth Pact (Von Brockdorff and Falzon, 2014). Between 2013 and 2015, the government budget deficit as a ratio of GDP was, on average, within the 3% parameter set by the Stability and Growth Pact but its debt to GDP ratio was not, and averaged about 70%.[22]

4.2.2 Demographics and pensions

The Maltese population is an ageing one, and as a result the current 'pay-as-you-go' pension system (whereby retirees receive pension benefits out of contributions by current workers) is not sustainable (Formosa, 2014). The options for reform range from extending the retirement age (a change that is already being implemented), requesting people to save more while they are still working, and directly tying current savings with future pension payments. One way of reducing the dependency of the older segment of the population on the working age population would be to introduce a mandatory pension pillar to accompany the current pay-as-you-go system while gradually phasing out the existing system to one that directly links an individual's pension to his or her savings during the working period. However, there is no consensus in Malta as to how the pension system is to be further reformed.

4.2.3 Labour market participation

Labour market participation in Malta is among the lowest in Europe, mostly because of the low activity rate of women. Given that Malta's main resource is its labour force, policies directed towards increasing labour market participation are of utmost importance. Policies towards this end have been put in place with a degree of success, so much so that the participation rate of women increased from 42% in 2010 to 51% in 2014. This issue is also particularly important given the underlying challenge that the economy faces because of its ageing population. By 2030 the number of workers supporting one pensioner is expected to fall from the current figure of four persons to two, assuming current participation rates. Therefore, an increased participation rate of women in the workplace would also be desirable in this regard.

4.2.4 Balancing wage rates and productivity

According to the IMF (2015) unit labour costs in Malta are rising faster than in trading partners, posing competitiveness risks. This problem relates to the link between wage rates and productivity. In order for Malta's GDP per capita to further converge with the EU average, wage rates will have to increase, given that a large proportion of GDP is income from employment. However, unless wage rate increases are matched by improvements in labour productivity, the end result will be an increase in per unit costs, leading to a loss of competitiveness.

4.2.5 Trade gap

Malta depends highly on imports of industrial supplies and these increased rapidly during the 2000s, leading to unprecedented merchandise trade deficits in absolute and relative terms. This was exacerbated by the low growth rate of exports of merchandise. However, growing reliance on services, rather than manufacturing, has resulted in a reduction in the ratio of imports to final sales. It should be noted that, despite the relatively large gap in merchandise trade, the resource balance (i.e. the difference between exports and imports of goods and services) was mostly positive between 2011 and 2014, indicating that the surplus on services trade more than compensated for the deficit in merchandise trade.

4.2.6 Financial riskiness

The fact that Maltese core banks (notably Bank of Valletta and HSBC) rely mostly on deposits originating from Malta, and that government bonds are mostly purchased by Maltese residents, renders Malta somewhat sheltered from external financial instability. In addition, the Maltese core banks are generally profitable, with high solvency and liquidity ratios. For these reasons, Malta was not highly exposed to the 2008–2009 financial turmoil.

The major element of riskiness in the Maltese financial system is that a very high proportion of the lending of the Maltese core banks is secured by real estate collateral, leading the system to depend very highly on the construction sector and on purchase of property. However, this risk is mitigated by the fact that the rate of mortgage repayments in Malta is high. In addition exposure of banks to speculative property trading is very small as it is normal practice by Maltese banks to ensure that the value of the secured property exceeds the loan tied to it by a substantial percentage.

4.2.7 High cost of borrowing funds

In Malta credit institutions are very underdeveloped and the cost of borrowing funds for business is high relative to the euro area average, sometimes rendering it difficult for businesses, particularly smaller firms, to access credit. IMF (2015) attributed this to various factors, including limited domestic competition and a high rate of non-performing loans, which adds to cost of the lending agencies. Policies that encourage cross-border financing to stimulate competition among lenders and that lead to a reduction in the rate of non-performing loans are therefore called for to reduce rate of interest on lending. IMF (2015) also suggests that a credit registry should be created to reduce financing costs and to help facilitate other forms of market financing, such as securitization.

Malta also lacks an institutional arrangement for long-term financing of risky projects. For this purpose the creation of a development bank could help in making available this type of lending.

4.2.8 Education

Malta faces major challenges relating to education. The percentage of early school-leavers is relatively high when compared to that of other EU member states. Early school-leavers tend to find it difficult to find employment and, if they do find a job, their earnings are likely to be relatively low. Another challenge in the educational sphere is that in Malta enrolment rates in tertiary education are relatively low, and the proportion of persons with tertiary education attainment is one of the lowest in the EU. However, the Maltese authorities are addressing these problems and the rate of early school-leavers is falling as a result of policies adopted by the educational authorities. In addition, tertiary educational opportunities have significantly increased, as a result of new courses being offered at the University of Malta and at the Malta College of Arts, Science and Technology.

4.2.9 Irregular migration

A fairly recent development in Malta is the influx of irregular migrants mostly originating from Africa and more recently from Syria, most of whom reach Malta by sea via Libya. Legal migrants have also increased, either retiring in Malta, or joining the labour force and therefore adding to the productive capacity of the country, thereby also contributing to government finances. Irregular migrants, on the other hand, are often a burden on the economy and in addition create social problems mostly due to hurdles they encounter in properly integrating in society.

Addressing the problem of irregular migration has become one of Malta's top policy priorities. The Maltese government has often called for a fairer burden-sharing mechanism within the EU, given that Malta is often considered as a stepping stone into the EU. Recent negotiations within the EU have attempted to create a burden sharing arrangement, but there is not sufficient consensus between the EU member states on this matter. Even if such an arrangement were to be put into place, Malta is likely to continue facing problems associated with irregular migration as long as Libya, located just 220 miles south of Malta, remains in a state of civil strife.

5 Conclusion

This chapter has given an overview of the structure and performance of the Maltese economy since the 1950s and identified the major constraints faced by the Maltese economy, including those associated with its very small size, rendering the economy very exposed to external shocks, and limiting its ability to reap the benefits of economies of scale. Other major challenges currently faced by the economy identified in this chapter relate to public financing, particularly given the difficulties in securing pension sustainability, and to the labour market, particularly the need to balance wage increases with labour productivity.

This study has also discussed the economic benefits and downsides of Malta's EU membership. It was argued that a major benefit was the marked improvement in economic governance, which, most probably, would not have occurred had Malta not joined the EU. It was shown that, overall, the economy has performed well since Malta joined the EU, and the outlook, according to the IMF (2015) and the European Commission (2015), looks positive.

Notes

1 In this chapter the terms Malta and Maltese Islands are used interchangeably. When referring to the largest island of the Maltese archipelago the term 'Malta Island' is used.

2 The political system is Malta is a parliamentary democracy.

3 An early report on the Maltese Economy was that produced by Balogh and Seers in 1955. See Brincat (2009) for a discussion on this report.

4 Stolper, who was the Head of the United Nations mission for Malta, recommended that a solution for Malta was to encourage mass emigration. Emigration from Malta was actually subsidized at that time.

5 A list of development plans for Malta up to 1987 is given in Briguglio (1988: Ch. 18).

6 For an overview of the Maltese economy during different periods following Malta's independence in 1964 see Waldorf (1969), Metwally (1977) and Briguglio (2011).

7 The sources of the table are the following: GDP per capita and real GDP growth (2009–2003) were sourced from: IMF World Economic Outlook Database, available at: http://www.imf.org/external/pubs/ft/weo/2015/01/weodata/index.aspx. The source of the Global Competitiveness Index (GCI) is the Global Competitiveness Report available at: http://www.weforum.org/reports/global-competitiveness-report-2014-2015. The GCI leaves out many countries, most of which are low income countries, and therefore if all countries were included the relative ranking of Malta would be higher. The Human Development Index was sourced from the *Human Development Report*: available at: http://hdr.undp.org/en/content/table-1-human-development-index-and-its-components. The data pertains to 2013. The Worldwide Governance Indicators are available at: http://info.worldbank.org/governance/wgi/index.aspx#home. The data pertains to 2013. There were 215 countries and territories in the list but non-independent territories were excluded from the relative ranking shown in the table.

8 Like many other developed countries, Malta's real GDP growth rate was much lower than that of many developing countries.

9 The Commissioner nominated by Malta to the European Commission is currently Karmenu Vella, who is responsible for Environment, Maritime Affairs and Fisheries.

10 This was extended to six members following the entry into force of the Lisbon Treaty in December 2009.

11 After the Lisbon Treaty came into force, this court became known as the General Court.

12 For an account of the results of the negotiations on the accession of Malta see http://ec.europa.eu/enlargement/pdf/negotiations_report_to_ep.pdf.

13 See Briguglio and Cordina (2002).

14 Eventually, however, the Lisbon Treaty reduced the vetoing power of a single state through the introduction of three types of votes: a simple majority, which is used for procedural decisions; qualified majority voting (QMV), employed in many decisions concerning the internal market, economic affairs and trade; and unanimity which is required in decisions relating to foreign policy, defence and taxation.

15 The 2003 referendum asking whether the electorate agreed with Malta's accession to the EU is discussed in Cini (2003).

16 For an overview of major changes resulting in Malta from EU membership see Cachia Caruana (2007). See also Pace (2002) and Pace (2006).

17 One of the transitional concessions granted to Malta on accession was that Malta was to retain its work permit system and to impose restrictions on the free movement of persons for the first seven years of membership. These measures were hardly resorted to and the labour market in Malta remained stable throughout the years of membership (see Tabone, 2014).

18 On 29 April 2005, Malta took the first step towards joining the single currency when it joined the Exchange Rate Mechanism (ERM) II, at a fixed parity rate of LM1 = €2.33. The country's external reserves, a main indicator of the sustainability of the exchange rate prior to the adoption of the euro, were on average equivalent to about eight months of imports between 1994 and 2004.

19 The IMF report is available at: http://www.imf.org/external/pubs/cat/longres.aspx?sk=42732.0.

20 For a discussion on characteristics of small island states see Briguglio (1995).

21 On the constraints faced by Malta as a small state see Briguglio and Buttigieg (2004).

22 The rules set by the Stability and Growth Pact are explained at: http://ec.europa.eu/economy_finance/economic_governance/sgp/index_en.htm.

References

Balogh, T. and Seers, D. (1955) *The Economic Problems in Malta: An Interim Report*. Malta: Government Printing Office.

Briguglio, L. (1988) 'Economic Changes since 1960', *Hyphen – Journal of Melitensia and the Humanities*, 5(5): 205–223. Available at: http://melitensiawth.com/incoming/Index/Hyphen/Hyphen.%205(1988)5/01.pdf (accessed 23 January 2016).

Briguglio, L. (1995) 'Small Island Developing States and their Economic Vulnerabilities', *World Development*, 23(9): 1615–1632. Available at: http://www.sciencedirect.com/science/article/pii/0305750X9500065K (accessed 23 January 2016).

Briguglio, L. (2011) *Macroeconomics and the Maltese Economy*. Malta: BDL Publishing.

Briguglio, L. and Buttigieg, E. (2004) 'Competition Constraints in Small Jurisdictions', *Bank of Valletta Review*, No. 30. Available at: https://www.bov.com/documents/bov-review-30-paper-1 (accessed 23 January 2016).

Briguglio, L. and Cordina, G. (2002) 'The Economic Effects of Membership in the EU for Malta', Economics Department of the University of Malta. Paper presented at the EADI General Conference, Ljubljana, September 2002.

Brincat, M. (2009) 'The Birth of the "Maltese Model" of Development, 1945–1959', *Journal of Maltese History*, 1(2): 34–52. Available at: http://www.um.edu.mt/arts/history/jmh/docs/2009/brincat-34-53-1.pdf (accessed 23 January 2016).

Buttigieg, E. (2004) 'Challenges Facing Malta as a Micro-State in an Enlarged EU', *Bank of Valletta Review*, No. 39. Available at: http://www.wbaonline.co.uk/abstract.asp?id=45548 (accessed 23 January 2016).

Cachia Caruana, R. (2007) 'The Accession of Malta to the EU', in G. Vassilour (ed.) *The Accession Story: The EU from Fifteen to Twenty Five Countries*, Oxford: Oxford University Press.

Cini, M. (2003) 'Malta Votes Twice for Europe: The Accession Referendum and General Election, March/April 2003', *South European Society and Politics*, 8(3): 132–146

European Commission (1993) 'Opinion (Avis) on Malta's Application for Membership, June 1993', *Bulletin of the European Communities*, Supplement 4/93. Available at: http://aei.pitt.edu/5761/ (accessed 23 January 2016).

European Commission (2015) *Country Report Malta 2015*. Available at: http://ec.europa.eu/europe2020/pdf/csr2015/cr2015_malta_en.pdf (accessed 23 January 2016).

Formosa, M. (2014) 'Socio-Economic Implications of Population Ageing in Malta: Risks and Opportunities', *Bank of Valletta Review*, No. 49. Available at: https://www.bov.com/pjazza/bov-review—49th-edition (accessed 23 January 2016).

IMF (2015) *Malta: 2014 Article IV Consultation*, Staff Report. Available at: www.imf.org/external/pubs/cat/longres.aspx?sk=42732.0 (accessed 23 January 2016).

Metwally, M. (1977) *Structure and Performance of the Maltese Economy*. Malta: AC Aquilina.

Pace, R. (2002) 'A Small State and the European Union: Malta's EU Accession Experience', *South European Society and Politics*, 7(1): 24–42.

Pace, R. (2006) 'Malta and EU Membership: Overcoming Vulnerabilities, Strengthening Resilience', *Journal of European Integration*, 28(1) (Special Issue: *The European Union's Member States: The Importance of Size*).

Stolper, W., Hellberg, R. and Callander, S. (1964) *Economic Adaptation and Development in Malta*. United Nations Department of Social and Economic Affairs.

Tabone, P. (2014) *Malta's EU Story: How Ten Years of EU Membership Have Changed the Country*. Malta: The Today Public Policy Institute. Available at: https://www.um.edu.mt/__data/assets/pdf_file/0011/223769/TPPI_Malta_EU.pdf (accessed 23 January 2016).

Von Brockdorff, P. and Falzon, J. (2014) 'Assessing the Impact of the European Fiscal Compact on Eurozone Mediterranean States, with a Focus on Malta', *Mediterranean Journal of Social Sciences*, 5(14): 1–17. Available at: http://www.mcser.org/journal/index.php/mjss/article/view/3124/3080 (accessed 23 January 2016).

Waldorf, W.H. (1969) *An Economic Model of the Maltese Economy*. Malta: Office of the Prime Minister.

9 Montenegro

A small economy on the road to European Union membership

Milorad Katnić and Tijana Stanković

1 Introduction[1]

Montenegro is a small state located on the Balkan Peninsula, with a population of 622,100 persons in 2015 (Eurostat). It is bordered by Croatia, Bosnia and Herzegovina, Serbia, Kosovo, Albania and by the Adriatic Sea.

The country has had a variegated history characterized by struggles for freedom and independence from various powers including the Byzantine, Ottoman, and Austria-Hungarian empires. It was recognized as the first independent state in the Balkans at the Congress of Berlin in 1878. Montenegro was annexed by the Kingdom of Serbia in 1918 and after the Second World War became one of the republics of the Socialist Federal Republic of Yugoslavia (SFRY).

When the SFRY disintegrated in 1991, the citizens of Montenegro became part of the two-member federation with Serbia under the name of 'Serbia and Montenegro'. The dysfunction of this federation, as well as ruinous Serbian nationalistic and economic policies, resulted in Montenegro again seeking political independence. Following a democratic referendum in 2006, Montenegro declared itself an independent state and became a member of the UN during that same year. In March 2007, Montenegro and the European Union (EU) initiated the Stabilisation and Association Agreement which was officially signed on 15 October 2007. In 2010, the European Commission issued a favourable opinion on Montenegro's application, granting the country candidate status.

This chapter traces developments in the economy of Montenegro during the twenty-first century, from a situation of bleak prospects as part of Serbia and Montenegro to the attainment of the status of an EU candidate country, with the prospect of becoming an EU member state sometime in the future. The chapter also deals with the advantages that the process of integration into the European Union has brought and is still bringing about to the country. The chapter also discusses the painful lessons learned by the Montenegro policy makers from the boom and bust period between 2006 and 2009.

The chapter is organized into seven sections. Following this introductory section, Section 2 gives a brief account of the economy of Montenegro until the twenty-first century leading to the collapse of SFRY. Section 3 describes the seeds of the transformation of Montenegro from a backward socialist economy into a dynamic market economy, during which time the country unilaterally adopted the euro and started to put in place a number of economic reforms. The section that follows explains how the economic boom of 2006–2008 led to an economic bust in 2009, when Montenegro was severely hit by the international global recession and paid the price of uncontrolled economic overheating. Section 5 presents the advantages and disadvantages associated with the possibility of Montenegro joining the EU, while Section 6 discusses the characteristics of Montenegro as a small state with a small open economy. The last section concludes the chapter with some comments on the future prospects of the country's economy.

2 The economy of Montenegro until the twenty-first century

2.1 The economy of Montenegro until the Second World War[2]

Prior to the industrialization process in socialist Yugoslavia and after the Second World War, Montenegro's economy was predominantly based on agriculture, particularly livestock breeding, olive growing, and production of fruits, vegetables and forestry. On the shores of the Adriatic Sea there was production of salt. International trade was predominantly conducted through the ports of Kotor and Bar (Đurović, 1958). Podgorica (now the capital of Montenegro) was the centre of trade and craft. The first industrial facilities were built in the late nineteenth and early twentieth centuries. They were mostly small private plants, such as breweries and mills. Up to the mid-twentieth century, Montenegro remained a poor country faced with mass starvation and emigration. Imports of goods were three times as much as exports, and the state was burdened with high and costly foreign debt (Andrijašević, 2010: 343–344).

The Second World War brought with it further economic decline. The war took the lives of more than 10% of Montenegro's population and more than 5% were left disabled. Also, during the war, about 80% of the livestock was destroyed and over 25% of people were left without a roof over their head. The war devastated the existing infrastructure and destroyed the little industry that had existed in Montenegro.

After the Second World War, the traditional system of economic relations was replaced by socialism. Private property was nationalized and agricultural land was expropriated to create cooperatives of rural workers, in line with the Soviet model. The centrally planned economy led to the accelerated industrialization, villages were depopulated and cities gained importance. As one of the poorer republics of the federation, Montenegro received generous funding from federal sources. The period of creation of the socialist system in the Federation brought to Montenegro a strong wave of economic development. Construction of hydropower plants and the aluminium industry transformed Montenegro from a predominantly agricultural economy to an industrial one. Before the Second World War almost 80% of the population was agricultural – in the early 1960s this share decreased to below 50%, and in the early 1980s it was below 15%.

Modern transport infrastructure, including ports, railways and roads, improved the communications within Montenegro and with the rest of Yugoslavia. Tourism, consisting mainly of visitors from Eastern Europe and the other republics of Yugoslavia, also became a significant industry. Due to its long-standing maritime tradition, a strong naval fleet was built during the socialist period and this played an important role in the economy.

Montenegro registered significant economic progress during the period 1945 to 1980, with an estimated annual growth rate of 6% (Andrijašević and Rastoder, 2010: 468). In spite of the financial support it received from federation funds and the significant investment in its infrastructure, Montenegro remained relatively backward economically and one of the poorest republics in the federation. In 1979, its gross domestic product (GDP) in relation to the average of the federation, reached a maximum of 71%. A devastating earthquake that hit Montenegro in 1979 severely damaged the coast and had major negative effects on the economy.

2.2 The collapse of the Federation

During the 1980s it became increasingly clear that the Yugoslav socialist project was not sustainable. State and citizens of socialist Yugoslavia lived beyond their means. Economic development of Yugoslavia was based on handouts from the West and borrowing from abroad. But even this was not sufficient to balance the accounts and the fiscal deficits were financed by printing money, which led to a high rate of inflation and periodic devaluations. In the early 1980s, there was stagnant economic growth and rising unemployment, which led to the emigration of a substantial proportion of the working-age population. In the early 1980s, the socialist expectations were shattered when Yugoslavia declared its inability to service its foreign debt.

The transition in Yugoslavia, from a centrally planned economy to a market economy, starting in the late 1980s, led to hyperinflation, which in 1989 reached alarming rates. The collapse of the federation was characterized by political instability, serious conflicts and even wars. Serbia and Montenegro[3] experienced international economic sanctions,[4] which left dramatic consequences on the economy of the two-member federation. In just a few years GDP was more than halved, from $2,847 per capita in 1991 to $1,330 per capita in 1993.[5] The hyperinflation that resulted in 1993 automatically depreciated all incomes denominated in the national currency – the dinar. Thus employees and pensioners at the beginning of the month were hurrying to exchange their income in billions of dinars for a few deutschmarks.[6]

For Montenegro, characterized by religious and ethnic tolerance, the wars in the region resulted in a large number of refugees, which constituted over 20% of the total population during the 1990s. This increase in the population brought about considerable economic pressures in a short period of time.

The disintegration of the Yugoslav common market, international isolation and sanctions destroyed the industrial sector including the aluminium and steel industries, wood processing, household appliances, construction machinery and others, built during the socialist period. The infrastructure was neglected and further damaged during the 1999 NATO bombings.[7] The infrastructure as well as tourist facilities were neglected too, and foreign tourism inflows, because of the security risks, declined dramatically. During the years of sanctions,[8] the naval fleet was destroyed, partly trapped and left to decay in foreign ports. All this caused massive unemployment of over 30% of the labour force. Grey and black markets replaced most of the formal economy. Even basic foodstuffs, medicines and fuel could only be found on the informal market.

The dramatic reduction in the tax base, with the increasing cost of financing the wars that Serbia-Montenegro was involved in, and the growing social needs, resulted in a high fiscal deficit, which was monetized. The high rate inflation contributed to the growth of the informal economy (Schneider, 2009), and this led to further reductions in the tax revenues. There was a vicious circle with the fiscal deficit being fed by inflation and inflation leading to higher deficits. The population and the overall economy suffered as a result, and poverty was widespread. In 2000, GDP per capita in Serbia-Montenegro, expressed in purchasing power parity, amounted to only 29% of the EU average in 2000.[9]

The depth of the economic problems that Montenegro faced at the beginning of the twenty-first century is difficult to describe and understand from today's perspective, even though only 15 years have passed. In 2000 the minimum wage was 72 deutschmarks (about €35), and the average net wage was €188 deutschmarks (about €93) per month. From over 600 thousand inhabitants, only about 141 thousand were formally employed. The number of unemployed persons increased from year to year, and reached over 81 thousand in 2000.

A large number of refugees, due to conflicts in neighbouring countries, temporarily or permanently stayed in Montenegro, and created additional pressure on social and health funds. Although Montenegro had introduced a stable currency, the deutschmark,[10] inflation in 2000 was over 25%. The budget deficit in 2001 amounted to about 7.5% of GDP and was mainly funded by donations from the USA and the EU. Public debt, by 2002, amounted to over 80% of GDP, thus Montenegro was not able to borrow on the international capital market. The domestic capital market did not exist. Due to hyperinflation and the collapse of banks in the 1990s, there were practically no savings or lending activities. Foreign direct investment was minimal. The misery of the population of Montenegro was further intensified as a result of daily restrictions on electricity and water.

3 Transformation into a market economy

3.1 Montenegro regains independence

The dire economic situation of Montenegro during the 1990s led the Montenegro authorities to distance the country from Serbia, which was still essentially run on socialist lines. With political distancing, in the early twenty-first century, Montenegro began to take economic policy into its own hands and to build an independent economic system. The most important step in this direction was the introduction of the deutschmark as parallel currency in November 1999, and as the sole legal tender in January 2001. In parallel with its own monetary policy, Montenegro began to construct independent financial and fiscal policies, liberalized trade and capital flows, and started the process of privatization. The economic transition however required a political transition, with appropriate governance institutions. Initially there was a period of political uncertainty and instability and under these circumstances solid economic progress could not be expected. The inflow of capital remained relatively modest and economic growth up to 2003 was slow (see Table 9.1).

During the period 2006–2008, economic growth in Montenegro was one of the fastest in Europe, a turnaround which was halted in 2009, the year of the global recession. Over a ten-year period, Montenegro was transformed from a backward socialist economy into a dynamic market economy, which attracted a relatively large amount of capital inflows.

The inflow of foreign direct investment (FDI) between 2005 and 2008, on average, amounted to 18% of GDP and, measured by this indicator, was one of the highest in Europe. FDI and other forms of foreign capital, which entered into Montenegro through the banking sector, highly affected economic conditions in the country.

During the same period, GDP per capita increased by about 67% and the average wage more than doubled. The number of employed persons increased by 15% (from 144.3 thousand to over 166.2 thousand), while the rate of unemployment was halved (from about 25% to about 13% of the labour force). Although tax rates were significantly reduced, budget revenues increased, which in 2006 and 2007 led to budget surplus. Write-off of part of the debt by the Paris Club, economic growth and prepayment, led to a fall in public debt, which in 2008 was below 30% of GDP.

This economic progress was, to a large extent, the result of economic reforms that were implemented as from 1999. The whole process was underpinned by the concept of economic liberalization, which generated a competitive business environment.

3.2 Euroization as the foundation of the reforms

The use of the deutschmark as the domestic unofficial means of payment and nonbanking saving by citizens and businesses had been in de facto operation decades before this currency was introduced as legal tender in 2001. That was even before the disintegration of the Yugoslav Federation. Serbia, the larger federal state, which by printing its national currency, the dinar, generated a high rate of inflation and a devaluation of its currency, was not as keen on using the deutschmark as Montenegro was.[11]

Table 9.1 Economic indicators for Montenegro (2000–2014)

	2000	*2001*	*2002*	*2003*	*2004*	*2005*	*2006*	*2007*	*2008*	*2009*	*2010*	*2011*	*2012*	*2013*	*2014*
GDP at current prices (€ million)	1,065.7	1,295.1	1,360.3	1,510.1	1,669.8	1,815.0	2,148.9	2,680.5	3,085.6	2,981.0	3,104.0	3,234.0	3,148.9	3,327.0	3,393.0
GDP per capita (€)	–	2,107	2,212	2,455	2,714	2,949	3,490	4,352	5,001	4,821	5,011	5,212	5,064	5,341	5,379
GDP real growth (%)	3.1	1.1	1.9	2.5	4.4	4.2	8.6	10.7	6.9	–5.7	2.5	3.2	–2.5	3.3	2.0
Population (thousand)	605.0	607.4	609.8	612.3	613.4	614.3	615.0	615.9	617.0	618.3	619.4	620.1	620.6	621.2	621.2
Average net wage per month (€)	93	108	149	174	195	213	246	338	416	463	479	484	487	479	477
Public revenue/GDP (%)	–	32.0	31.7	39.8	39.2	39.9	45.5	49.5	50.1	45.4	42.3	39.7	41.6	43.0	39.7
Public consumption/ GDP (%)	–	39.5	40.9	42.1	40.6	41.5	42.3	43.3	50.4	51.1	47.2	43.4	47.3	47.7	42.9
Inflation (yearly average) (%)	25.7	27.9	9.4	6.2	4.3	1.8	2	8	7.3	1.5	0.7	2.8	5.1	0.3	–0.5
Bank credit/ GDP (%)	10.7	9.6	9.2	13.3	16.9	20.7	50.2	93.1	95.9	88.7	81.1	72.9	74.4	72.6	69.8
NPL/total credits (%)	–	–	–	–	5.7	5.2	2.9	3.2	7.2	13.5	21.0	15.5	17.6	17.5	15.9
FDI/GDP (%)	–	0.8	6.4	2.6	3	21	21.7	21.2	18.9	35.8	17.8	12	14.7	9.7	10.4
Surplus/deficit of budget/ GDP (%)		–7.5	–9.2	–2.3	–1.3	–1.6	3.2	6.3	–0.4	–5.7	–4.9	–3.7	–5.6	–5.3	–3.2
Public debt/ GDP (%)	–	–	84.5	47.1	44.5	38.6	32.6	27.5	29	38.3	40.9	46	54	58.2	57.3

	2000	*2001*	*2002*	*2003*	*2004*	*2005*	*2006*	*2007*	*2008*	*2009*	*2010*	*2011*	*2012*	*2013*	*2014*
Exports of goods and services/GDP (%)	–	–	35.4	30.6	42.0	43.5	49.6	43.1	39.7	34.5	37.3	42.8	44.1	41.8	41.1
Imports of goods and services/GDP (%)	–	–	59.9	47.0	58.1	61.1	80.0	86.0	93.4	65.4	63.2	64.9	68.8	62.1	61.1
BoP Current Account/GDP (%)	14.3	23.6	12.9	–6.7	–7.2	–8.5	–24.7	–39.5	–49.8	–27.9	–22.9	–17.7	–18.7	–14.6	–15.3

Source of data and estimations: Ministry of Finance, Government of Montenegro and other official sources of data.

Note: NPL (non-performing loans); BoP (balance of payments).

After 2000, economically and politically, this meant a formal separation from the common policy of Serbia and Montenegro. The use of the deutschmark in Montenegro shielded the economy and the citizens of Montenegro from hyperinflation – an essential step towards economic independence, which eventually also led to political independence.

Subsequently, in 2002, Montenegro adopted the euro[12] which facilitated the economic reforms and which led to stabilization of the economic system, principally because of monetary stability and predictability. Inflation was significantly decreased and after a few years, in 2005, was at the same level as that of the eurozone (Lukšić, 2012).

In turn this led to the fostering of confidence in the banking sector. Deposits and credit grew gradually, while interest rates were decreased. Fiscal discipline improved. The euro also ushered in lower transaction costs in international trade and reduced currency risk in the trade between members of the eurozone, leading to a simplification and a lowering of costs in trade and investment procedures. Furthermore, the euro fostered stronger economic and financial integration with the eurozone states and had a positive impact on the tourism sector (Bogetić, 2000).

With no currency of its own, the focus of macroeconomic stabilization was on fiscal policy. In the first phase of fiscal policy reform, which started in 2000, the most important task was to increase revenue, to continue improving fiscal discipline and to introduce more transparent public resources management. Prior to the fiscal reform, not all state revenue was controlled by the central government and a significant proportion of this revenue was managed by different state bodies. As a result one of the first and most important tasks was to consolidate state revenues through a treasury account.

At the beginning of 2003, value added tax was introduced as a pillar of tax reform and as a replacement of the turnover tax. Proportional personal and corporate income taxation was replaced by progressive rates. The stage of tax reform that followed in 2004 related to the simplification of the system with one of the aims being the encouragement of inward investment. Starting from 2004, the concept of one digit flat direct tax rate was promoted and a corporate rate of 9% was introduced. Income tax was also decreased gradually to 9% and as a result, Montenegro became the country with the lowest rate of direct corporate tax and income taxes (Katnić, 2010).

3.3 Searching for greater economic freedom

Along with monetary and fiscal reform, Montenegro proceeded with its process of liberalization, including the removal of price controls and the freeing of trade. Restrictions relating to ownership of real estate by foreigners were removed gradually. In 2004, legislative arrangements for a system of free capital flows and free profit repatriation were introduced.

In parallel with the sale of majority or minority stakes in state companies during 2001–2002, there was a process of encouraging citizens to invest in companies through a voucher system – all adult citizens of Montenegro could become owners of vouchers which they could invest in six privatization funds of 221 companies, including telecommunication and oil distribution entities. The state retained ownership of corporations involved in strategic public utilities and infrastructure, mostly in energy production and transport, including railways, the main sea port (Bar), airports and the airlines.

4 Boom and bust

4.1 The economic boom

As from 2004, there was a huge inflow of capital directly in the form of foreign investment and indirectly through the banking sector. From 3% of GDP in 2004, foreign direct investment increased to 21% of GDP in 2005 and reached 35% of GDP in 2009. Credit activity also increased rapidly from 21% of GDP in 2005 increasing to 89% of GDP in 2009 (see Table 9.1).

There was also a rapid expansion of foreign trade. In 2005 total foreign trade of goods and services[13] amounted to 53% of GDP, while in 2008 this ratio reached 67% of GDP. Simultaneously, the deficit on the current account also increased from 8.5% of GDP in 2005 to 49.8% in 2008. The biggest share of exports were raw materials, mostly aluminium ingots, and exports were concentrated on a small number of countries, mostly Italy, Greece and Slovenia, which received over 50% of total exports in 2008.

For Montenegro, those were the times of easily accessed and cheap capital. The large inflows of capital ushered in a boom in the real estate market and fast growth of share prices, leading to a stock frenzy. The banks supported this rapid growth by easily approving loans for real estate and shares purchase no matter the solvency of the lender or the quality of the investment. People without experience and expertise were buying shares and real estate expecting that in a year their value would at least double. Over the first part of this cycle, most of those who invested in property or in shares ended up better off.

Public sector expenditure may also have played a part in the rapid economic growth during the period 2005 to 2008. In those years, government expenditure increased from about 41% to over 50% of GDP. This rate is extremely high in comparison to regional averages. At the same time, the number of employees per capita in the public sector was among the highest in Europe. This reality is indicated in the analyses of the IMF (2009) and World Bank (2008). At the same time there was an increase of capital expenditure mostly in infrastructural projects. All this resulted in a pro-cyclical push, further leading to an overheated economy.

For the first time in history, in 2006, Montenegro recorded budget surplus amounting to 3.2% of GDP, which was almost doubled in the following year and reached 6.3%. Higher state revenues led to higher expenditures, leading to a pro-cyclical fiscal policy. Earnings in the public sector and pensions were doubled in a very short time. Increased demand for labour accompanied by a decline in unemployment led to fast growth of earnings in the private sector as well. One outcome of all this was an inflation rate which reached 8% in 2007.

Between 2006 and 2008, Montenegro was one of the fastest growing economies in Europe with average growth rate of GDP of 8.7% (see Table 9.1). At the same, income per capita in Montenegro increased by more than 60% and reached 42% of the EU average, expressed in purchasing power parity. Many Montenegrins came to believe, naively, that this phase was going to continue for many years.

4.2 The financial crises

The financial crisis hit Montenegro in the second half of 2008. Foreign investors started to withdraw capital, and banks started to restrict credit and impose stricter conditions. Prices on the stock exchange and real estate dramatically declined, leading to a situation of excess supply, with few buyers and a large number of sellers. Panic quickly spread, bringing back memories of the bank crisis of the 1990s. In just a few months, hundreds of millions of euros, amounting to more than 20% of deposits, were withdrawn from the banks. Prices of the most important export products such as aluminium and steel were halved in the international market. To make matters worse, there was a sharp decline in international and internal trade. Export of goods and services in 2009, compared to 2008, nominally declined by 16%, and import by 32%. The consequence of all this was a decline of GDP of 5.7% in 2009.

There was a subsequent heavy decline of government revenue, and this at a time when the Government decided to support the banking sector and certain companies that required additional resources to keep afloat and were considered to be important for the economy. This resulted in relatively high fiscal deficits, which between 2009 and 2014 averaged about 5% of GDP. This in turn led to an increase in public debt, which doubled from about 30% of GDP in 2008 to about 57% of GDP in 2014 (see Table 9.1).

This was because the changes in government expenditure occurred at a time of rapid declines in government revenue due to the slowdown of the economy, accompanied by decreases in investment and consumption expenditures. Government revenue decreased from 50% of GDP in 2008 to 45% in 2009 and by 2011 it was below 40% of GDP. This reality required fast fiscal adjustment. The government did try to adjust its expenditure, as such expenditure decreased from 51% of GDP in 2009 to about 43% of GDP in 2011, however fiscal deficits remained relatively high, which also led to a growing public debt.

Earnings in the public and private sectors, as well as pensions, did not remarkably decrease during the years of crisis. During these years, GDP per capita in nominal terms increased slightly. However, unemployment increased rapidly pushing many families below the poverty line. Individuals who had taken loans to buy real estate, or to acquire shares, found themselves in a very difficult situation. As a result of the crisis, the value of assets decreased significantly, while the related commitments remained at relatively high interest rates.

The 2009 global recession exposed an important limitation of Montenegro's economy, namely its high degree of vulnerability due to high exposure to economic forces outside its control, mostly as a result of its small size.

A major characteristic of small economies is their vulnerability to exogenous shocks due to the high degree of trade openness and high dependence on strategic imports such as industrial supplies, food and fuel. In addition, the exports of small economies tend to be concentrated on a few categories of goods or services. Furthermore, they tend to depend highly on a few larger countries for their exports. This means that small countries tend to be highly affected by changes outside their borders (Katnić, 2010).

However the effect of the crisis in Montenegro was to an extent also self-inflicted, because the absence of a well-structured fiscal policy over the years of the boom, rather than stabilizing the economy, led to further instability.

4.3 Structural reforms as a tool for recovery and higher competitiveness[14]

At the beginning of the crisis, which primarily affected the banking sector through the withdrawal of deposits and reduction in lending, the Government, together with the Central Bank of the country, implemented a set of measures aimed at stabilizing the economy, particularly the banking sector. Legislation relating to deposit guarantee schemes was quickly put in place and this helped to decrease psychological pressure and to prevent panic, factors that often lead to bank runs.

Another piece of legislation, defining measures and instruments available to the Government and the Central Bank to support endangered banks, was adopted. In addition, the Central Bank was given a stronger role as regulator through the amendment of regulations, accompanied by a new institution, the Council for Financial Stability, to oversee the orderly working of the financial sector. Altogether, these measures led to the stabilization of the banking sector, as a result of which deposits and therefore the liquidity of banks improved and this was further boosted by additional capitalization of banks by the Government. The sector still suffered from a high level of non-performing loans (see Table 9.1), a legacy of the boom period, and this dampened the banks' capacity for new lending.

The reform measures adopted in the aftermath of 2009 were necessary to stabilize the economy, particularly the banking sector, and brought about a rapid recovery, so that in 2010 a growth rate of 2.5% was registered followed by a rate of 3.2% in 2011. Although in 2012 there was negative growth of −2.5%, the economy recovered again between 2014 and 2015. Growth is expected by 4.1% in 2016 and an average of 3.5% in 2017 and 2018.[15] The set of structural reforms were in accordance with the requirements of the European Commission, emphasizing the fiscal impact and consistency in implementing the reforms, as explained in the Montenegro Economic Reform Programme 2016–2018[16] (Government of Montenegro, 2016).

4.4 Social and labour market reforms

Montenegro has an aging population, due to a low birth rate and increased life expectancy. While in 1971 persons younger than 20 years made up 42.8% of total population, in 2011 this ratio had been reduced to 26.3%. During the same period, the population older than 65 amounted to 7.6% of total population and this percentage increased to 12.8%. Montenegrin demographic trends indicate that life expectancy by 2060 will reach 83.6 years from the present 74, while the number of persons older than 65 as a ratio of the working population will reach 38% from the present 20.4%, during the same period.

These demographic trends, if not accompanied by appropriate reforms, will lead to an unsustainable pension system due to the additional pressures on the already fragile public finances. This problem is exacerbated by the low rate of gainful employment which is about 50% of the working age population, a much lower rate than the EU average of 65%.

In 2010, the Government of Montenegro adopted an Action Plan of Structural Reforms[17] containing measures relating to the labour market, pensions, healthcare and education. The reforms associated with the labour market were mostly designed to solve problems of rigidities in this market. Reforms in the field of pension schemes were aimed at improving the sustainability of the system based on the principle of intergenerational solidarity. Pension reform in Montenegro had started in 2004, with the introduction of the concept of a three-pillar pension system, of which, however, the mandatory saving second pillar was not implemented. The third pillar, which involved voluntary saving for pension, was added to the Pay-as-you-go system already in place. The pensionable age was extended to 67 years for men and women, and conditions for early retirement became more rigid. Reform of the social welfare system was mostly intended to incentivize persons to join the labour force. The reforms in healthcare and education encouraged a higher degree of involvement of the private sector in providing the services, and introduced measures aimed at quality improvement (Lukšić, 2012).

These reforms, though important, turned out to be insufficient, as pointed out by the IMF (2015) and the European Commission (2014). The Programme of Economic Reforms 2015–2017[18] adopted by the Government of Montenegro in January 2015 was drawn up with the intention of strengthening the reforms just listed. This will be a major challenge for the government of Montenegro as these reforms attempt to change patterns of behaviour of various interest groups, and it is expected that there will be strong resistance against these processes.

5 The advantages and disadvantages of EU membership

5.1 EU membership as a strategic goal

Montenegro has had a vision of integration into the European Union as from 1997, one which became more clear following independence. It became a strategic goal of Montenegro mostly because, in the eyes of most Montenegrins, for a small post-socialist country, EU membership was expected to bring about political and economic improvements, as well as stability and democracy within the region. The experience of other countries in Central and Eastern Europe showed that the process of accession and actual membership brought about fast economic modernization, GDP growth, decline in unemployment and transition to a developed-country status.

The signing of the Stabilisation and Association Agreement in 2007 was the first official document that signalled Montenegro's willingness to integrate with the EU.[19] In 2010, the European Commission issued a favourable opinion on Montenegro's application,[20] identifying a number of priorities that needed to be addressed before accession negotiations were to begin, and Montenegro was granted candidate-country status. The accession process was initiated in December 2011 and accession negotiations with Montenegro started on 29 June 2012.

5.2 The upsides and downsides of EU membership

Membership in the EU provides various advantages for a small country like Montenegro, including that the country would have a voice in the political, economic and social governance of the European continent through its vote in the European Parliament, the possibility of having an EU Commissioner, and the participation of its political leaders in the highest committees, particularly in the European Council which defines the EU's overall political direction and priorities.

Joining the EU would also permit Montenegro to become part of the EU internal market, with freedom of movement of goods, services, people and capital. This in turn would intensify competition, in theory leading to improvements in standards and control of monopolistic practices, through the transposition of competition law. Consumers would have a better choice of goods and their prices. Montenegrin citizens would have the opportunity to study abroad and work in the EU labour market. There would also be a greater possibility of inflow of regional funding from the EU. In terms of political governance, EU membership is likely to lead to increased respect to the rule of law and more transparency in public procurements, and therefore a reduction in corruption. In turn this could lead to improved public sector efficiency and productivity.

One of the most important downsides of EU membership is that the country would have to share aspects of its sovereignty with the EU institutions, and would be obliged to transpose directives and regulations in its body of legislation, even if these appear not to be entirely in the interest of the country.

Montenegro is not there yet and is currently passing through a transition phase as a candidate country. The process which leads to the integration of a country within the EU consists of a number of focused reforms over an agreed period, formally organized into so-called negotiation chapters. The changes associated with this process are mostly intended to enhance international competitiveness, internal competition, improved transparency and other political, economic and social improvements. Sometimes this requires painful adjustments on the part of the government and the people of the country wishing to join the EU. In the case of Montenegro, certain EU laws may hurt sections of the population. In reality it is easy to copy the text of the EU law and transpose the text into the domestic body of laws, but its implementation and enforcement is not always a simple task, particularly when these affect certain traditions or an entrenched way of life.

The experience in Montenegro shows that it is very important to educate people to understand the changes of the system and to weigh the benefits of EU membership against the drawbacks of the transposed legislation. This requires careful explanation of the purpose of the reforms. Montenegro is conducting a strong public campaign that focuses on raising awareness of the advantages of joining the European Union, although this need not mean that as a candidate country, Montenegro should accept EU rules unconditionally. In fact, at the time of writing this chapter, negotiations are taking place so as to secure the best mutual outcome for Montenegro and the EU, in the interests of both sides. An important requisite, on the part of Montenegro, should be that the process of integration preserves the Montenegrin authenticity in the European context.

6 The constraints and opportunities of a small state

Small states are sometimes defined as those with a population of 1.5 million persons or fewer, according to the Commonwealth Secretariat[21] and the World Bank.[22] Montenegro, with a population of about 620 thousand inhabitants, falls within this category.

Some strands of the literature on small states argue that it is an advantage for a country to be small (Baldacchino and Bertram, 2009), while others argue that small size is a disadvantage, but that policy measures can overcome such disadvantages (Briguglio et al., 2010). Montenegro certainly faces a number of disadvantages in view of its small size, but the economic reforms adopted by the country and those yet to be adopted during the process of EU accession could enable the country to overcome them.

6.1 Characteristics of small states

A major characteristic of small states relates to their high degree of economic exposure. Montenegro, as an open economy, is very vulnerable to exogenous influences and is exposed to both positive and negative economic trends and the consequences they carry. Montenegro has experienced these effects since renewing its independence in 2006. The world economic crisis was a good lesson for Montenegro in that being a small state is a two-edged sword. The need to further open up the economy is good for growth, but this at the same time increases exposure to exogenous shocks, and therefore sound macroeconomic governance is of major importance for a small state to enhance its economic resilience.

Another disadvantage of small size is the limited ability to reap the benefits of economies of scale. A small state therefore has to be careful not to attempt to compete in areas which require large scale production, because, generally speaking, it will not succeed in competing with larger states.

However, by observing the economic performance of many small states, one can conclude that these states can succeed economically, in spite of their constraints and vulnerabilities. This is supported by the fact that today there are many small states that are included among the economically advanced countries with a relatively high GDP per capita and well-developed institutional framework. The process of globalization has turned the world into practically a single market and the barriers of state borders for the supply of products, services and capital have been to a large extent dismantled. One advantage of being a small state is that such a state can speedily take advantage of the opportunities presented by the globalization process, due to the flexibility in decision making and economic orientation, something that larger states may lack.

In addition, the flexibility of a small system may enable a small state to respond quickly to the negative effects of economic shocks, as was the case of Montenegro after the 2009 crisis.

6.2 The voice of small states in the EU

Small size also has political implications. Within the EU, a small country like Montenegro is likely to have a relatively weak voice in the block's institutions. The larger member states have more clout than smaller ones when it comes to decision making, and a small country has to recognize its limitations in this regard.

However, when and if Montenegro joins the EU, the country will benefit from the so-called degressive proportionality, in that the country will be allocated a proportion of seats in the European Parliament higher than the proportion of its population to the EU population, which is just about 0.1%. However, its voice will still be minimal in a Parliament of over 750 members.

As a member of the EU, Montenegro would have a representative in all decision-making institutions including the European Commission and the Council, again with a representation likely to be larger than its proportion of the EU population. However, here again, its voice will not be strong enough to change the direction of EU decisions. However, even in such circumstances, the influence of Montenegro in European affairs would be much greater than it would be if the country were to remain a non-EU member state.

It is of major importance for a small state within a union of states, such as the EU, that it does not lose its identity and authenticity, and, as stated, in the case of Montenegro this is an important aspect of the negotiations for EU membership.

7 Conclusion

This chapter has given an overview of the economy of Montenegro which, as shown, has experienced major changes since the dissolution of the Yugoslav federations (FSRY and FRY) and the gaining of the country's political independence in 2006.

It has been shown that even in a short span of nine years, the economy of Montenegro experienced a boom and bust cyclical pattern, with practically uncontrolled growth up to 2008, a sudden downturn in 2009, followed by a recovery after that year, albeit at a relatively slow and even a negative growth rate in 2012.

We have argued that Montenegro, as a nation, is looking forward to EU membership, cognizant that there are major advantages in joining the Union, and that there are some disadvantages as well. Opinion polls indicate that the population of Montenegro and political parties are in their vast majority in favour of joining the EU.

Montenegro expects to join the EU in the near future, but it is not there yet as there are still issues that need to be resolved through negotiations. Up to June 2015, the EU and Montenegro had opened 20 out of 35 negotiation chapters,[23] with Montenegro expected to improve its performance with regard to environments management, economic governance, the judiciary and control of crime.

This chapter has also briefly discussed features that Montenegro shares with other small states, notably its high exposure to external shocks and its limited ability to enjoy the benefits of economies of scale. The chapter argues that small size need not inhibit Montenegro from attaining economic growth, given the right policy mix, since there are other small states within the EU that have managed to attain economic success in spite of their vulnerabilities and constraints.

According to the IMF (2015), economic growth in Montenegro is expected to accelerate, aided by expenditures on infrastructural projects. However, due to its high exposure to external shocks, it is important for Montenegro to continue on the road of reform by drawing up credible long-term plans relating to fiscal policy and implementing them, so as to safeguard public debt sustainability and continue to upgrade the business environment, conducive to the attraction of investment.

Another challenge relates to the labour market, where structural reforms are called for to improve labour force participation rates so as to boost potential growth and at the same time increase the pool of tax revenue. In addition, with regard to the labour market, wages need to be aligned with productivity.

Compared with the dreary prospects at the beginning of the twenty-first century, the current outlook of the economy of Montenegro is not bleak and the prospects will be even better with the adoption of the EU policy that assigns importance to the rule of law, development of infrastructure, fiscal sustainability and structural reforms. This policy framework should lead to increasing productivity, rising competitiveness and the attainment of Montenegro's strategic goal – better quality of life for every Montenegrin citizen in the European Union (Government of Montenegro, 2013).

Notes

1 The authors would like to thank Sladjana Pavlovic, MSc, who helped in collecting data and material for this chapter.
2 For more information on the economic history of Montenegro see Marovic (2006).
3 The Serbia and Montenegro federation, formally titled Federal Republic of Yugoslavia (FRY) was created in 1992, made up of the two remaining republics of Yugoslavia after its disintegration in 1991. In 2003, the FRY was reconstituted as the State Union of Serbia and Montenegro.
4 International sanctions were imposed in the spring of 1992 and their implementation remained in force until 1996. These sanctions led to international political and economic isolation of the FRY, and the economy plunged into disarray, characterized by smuggling and crime.
5 UN data: http://data.un.org/Data.aspx?d=SNAAMA&f=grID%3A101%3BcurrID%3AUSD%3BpcFlag%3A1.
6 Inflation in the period from April 1992 to January 1994 was 65% on a daily basis. On the eve of the new 1994 banknotes with 11 zeros (nominal value of 500 billion dinars) were printed, which meant that on the day of issue one could buy a few litres of milk, and next day the same amount was almost worthless.
7 The NATO bombing of Yugoslavia was a military operation during the Kosovo War.
8 With the dissolution of SFRY and the ensuing wars in Croatia and Bosnia-Herzegovina, sanctions were imposed by the UN Serbia and Montenegro federation, which were considered as responsible for the wars.
9 World Bank data available at: http://data.worldbank.org/indicator/NY.GDP.PCAP.PP.CD/countries?display=default.
10 The Yugoslav dinar was considered the worst currency globally (Hanke, 2000). In 1999, the year when Montenegro opted to adopt the deutschmark as its currency, inflation in dinars amounted to over 40%.
11 However a section of the population of Montenegro also preferred keeping the dinar (Vukotić, 2010: 1–2).
12 Montenegro adopted the euro when Germany itself adopted the euro and the deutschmark ceased to exist. Initially there were no objections from the European Central Bank (ECB), but since then the European Commission and the ECB have expressed a degree of dissatisfaction on this matter, as the unilateral use of the euro as the national currency was not compatible with the condition that the country must spend at least two years in the Exchange Rate Mechanism (ERM) II before formal euro adoption.
13 Average of exports and imports.
14 See Stankovic and Lazovic (2014) for a discussion on the importance of structural reforms for building a competitive economy in Montenegro.

15 Their projections are available in Government of Montenegro (2016).
16 See Stankovic (2014) for details about the planning process and measurement of the impact of fiscal reforms in Montenegro.
17 The action plan is available at: http://www.opengovpartnership.org/sites/default/files/legacy_files/country_action_plans/Montenegro_Action%20plan.pdf.
18 This program is available at: http://www.gov.me/en/News/145783/Montenegro-Economic-Reform-Programme-2015-2017.html.
19 A summary of this agreement is available at: http://ec.europa.eu/world/agreements/prepareCreateTreatiesWorkspace/treatiesGeneralData.do?step=0&redirect=true&treatyId=7281.
20 The document is available at: http://ec.europa.eu/enlargement/pdf/key_documents/2010/package/mn_opinion_2010_en.pdf.
21 http://thecommonwealth.org/our-work/small-states.
22 http://www.worldbank.org/en/country/smallstates/overview.
23 Information is available at: http://www.consilium.europa.eu/en/press/press-releases/2015/06/22-accession-conference-montenegro/.

References

Andrijašević, Ž. (2010) *Crnogorska vlast i ekonomski problemi Crne Gore (1878–1912)* (The Montenegrin government and the economic problems of Montenegro (1878–1912)). Podgorica: Crnogorska akademija nauka i umjetnosti.

Andrijašević, Ž. and Rastoder, Š. (2006) *Istorija Crne Gore, od najstarijih vremena do 2003*. (History of Montenegro, from the earliest times to 2003). Podgorica: Centar za iseljenike Crne Gore.

Baldacchino, G. and Bertram, G. (2009) 'The Beak of the Finch: Insights into the Economic Development of Small Economies', *The Round Table*, 98(401): 141–160.

Bogetić, Z. (2000) 'Official Dollarization: Current Experiences and Issues', *Cato Journal*, 20(2): 179–213. Available at: www.researchgate.net/profile/Zeljko_Bogetic/publication/228317616_Official_Dollarization_Current_Experiences_and_Issues/links/0912f510fc369d6de4000000.pdf (accessed 23 January 2016).

Briguglio, L., Cordina, G., Vella, S. and Vigilance, C. (2010) *Profiling Vulnerability and Resilience: A Manual for Small States.* Commonwealth Secretariat and Islands and Small States Institute of the University of Malta.

Đurović, M. (1958) *Trgovački kapital u Crnoj Gori u drugoj polovini XIX i početkom XX vijeka* (Commercial capital in Montenegro in the second half of the nineteenth and early twentieth century). Cetinje: Istorijskiinstitut NR Crne Gore.

European Commission (2014) *Montenegro Progress Report*. Available at: http://ec.europa.eu/enlargement/pdf/key_documents/2014/20141008-montenegro-progress-report_en.pdf (accessed 23 January 2016).

Government of Montenegro (2013) *Directions of Development (2013–2016), Government of Montenegro.* Available at: http://www.gov.me/en/search/128212/Montenegro-Development-Directions-2013-2016.html (accessed 23 January 2016).

Government of Montenegro (2015) *Montenegro Economic Reform Program 2015–2017*. Available at: http://www.gov.me/en/News/145783/Montenegro-Economic-Reform-Programme-2015-2017.html (accessed 23 January 2016).

Government of Montenegro (2016) *Montenegro Economic Reform Program 2016–2018*. Available at: www.gov.me/ResourceManager/FileDownload.aspx?rid=229775&iType=2 (accessed 23 January 2016).

Hanke, S. (2000) *The Beauty of a Parallel Currency*, CATO Institute. Available at: http://www.cato.org/publications/commentary/beauty-parallel-currency (accessed 23 January 2016).

IMF (2009) *Republic of Montenegro: 2008 Article IV Consultation – Staff Report*. Available at: https://www.imf.org/external/pubs/ft/scr/2009/cr0988.pdf (accessed 23 January 2016).

IMF (2015) *IMF Article IV Consultation*. Available at: http://www.imf.org/external/pubs/ft/scr/2015/cr1526.pdf (accessed 23 January 2016).

Katnić, M. (2010), 'Fiskalna politika i ekonomski razvoj Crne Gore, Zbornik radova' (Fiscal policy and economic development of Montenegro), in *Crna Gora u XXI stoljeću – u eri kompetitivnosti, Knjiga 3 Ekonomski razvoj* (Montenegro in XXI century – the competitiveness era. Book 3: Economic Development). Podgorica: CANU.

Lukšić, I. (2012) *O strukturnim reformama u Crnoj Gori. Zbornik radova – Stanovništvo i razvoj* (Structural reforms in Montenegro, Proceedings – Population and Development). Beograd: Institut društvenih nauka.

Marovic, B. (2006), *Ekonomska istorija Crne Gore* (Economic history of Montenegro), Podgorica.

Schneider, F. (2009) 'The Size of the Shadow Economy for 25 Transition Countries over 1999/00 to 2006/07: What do we know?' Department of Economics, Johannes Kepler University of Linz. Available at: www.econ.jku.at/members/schneider/files/publications/latestresearch2010/shadecon_25transitioncountries.pdf (accessed 23 January 2016).

Stankovic, T. (2014) 'Case Study on Montenegro', in M. Mrak, R. Bauchmüller and P. McClure (eds), *Fiscal Impact Assessment of Structural Reforms, Case Studies on South East Europe*, Chapter 6: 127–146. Ljubljana: Center of Excellence in Finance. Available at: http://www.cef-see.org/assets/reports/FIASR_book_2014_web.pdf (accessed 23 January 2016).

Stankovic, T. and Lazovic, V. (2014) 'Structural Reforms as Competitiveness Instrument and Fiscal Cost', Proceedings of the IV International Conference on 'Entrepreneurship and Innovation as Precondition for Economic Development'. Available at: www.ekonomija.ac.me/sites/ekonomija.bild-studio.me/files/multimedia/fajlovi/vijesti/2014/06/iv_international_conference_-_the_book_of_absracts.pdf (accessed 23 January 2016).

Vukotić, V. (2010) 'Deset godina DEM/EURO' (Ten years of Deutsche Mark/Euro), *Kolumna En, Vijesti*. Available at: http://www.vukotic.net/files/publikacije/1294669427_7865.pdf (accessed 23 January 2016).

World Bank (2009) *Montenegro – Beyond the Peak: Growth Policies and Fiscal Constraints*. Available at: http://www.mf.gov.me/files/1229590787.pdf (accessed 23 January 2016).

10 The Slovenian economy

The road to European Union accession, the crisis and beyond

Mojmir Mrak

1 Introduction

The Republic of Slovenia is a sovereign state located in the southern part of Central Europe. It borders Italy on the west, Austria on the north, Hungary on the northeast, Croatia on the east and south, and has a short Adriatic coast on the southwest. The country covers close to 21,000 square km and has a population of around two million.

Its geographical location, at the crossroads of important European economic and cultural corridors, explains to a large extent why the current territory of Slovenia was, in its history, part of many different state formations. It formed part of the Austro-Hungarian Empire for several centuries until its collapse during the First World War. In 1918, the Slovenes became part of the Kingdom of Serbs, Croats and Slovenes that was in 1929 renamed the Kingdom of Yugoslavia. During the Second World War, the territory was occupied by German, Italian and Hungarian forces, after which it became an integral part of the Federal People's Republic of Yugoslavia. After the 1948 break with the Soviet Union, two specific interlinked concepts were introduced gradually into the Yugoslav system of market socialism. One was social ownership and the other was self-management. These systems were significantly different from the state ownership concept and in sharp contrast to the central planning system in the Soviet bloc countries.

During the 1980s, the Yugoslav economic experiment[1] started to show increasing signs of inability to solve its economic and political problems, similar to the situation in other socialist countries in Central and Eastern Europe. During the second half of the decade, the deterioration accelerated and precipitated the disintegration of the federation. In the same period, the European Community, after a decade of 'eurosclerosis' started a new wave of integration characterized by a path towards a single European market and monetary union.

Under these circumstances, and taking into account the unsuccessful attempts of the Slovene communist leadership to transform Yugoslavia into a loose confederation with membership in the European Communities as its strategic orientation, there was no other alternative for Slovenia but to take up its independence path.

The main objective of this chapter is twofold: first to present Slovenia's case study with respect to its transition from a planned to a market economy and from a one-party system to a democracy; second to discuss Slovenia's European Union (EU) and euro integration paths, including its performance during the recent economic and financial crisis.

The chapter is organized into five sections. Section 2, which follows this introductory section, discusses the economic challenges faced by the newly independent sovereign state. This section also describes the attempts undertaken to stabilize the economy after the transition recession associated with the loss of former Yugoslav markets. Section 3 presents key features of Slovenia's accession to the EU and the adoption of the euro, and discusses the advantages and disadvantages associated with the two processes. Section 4 starts with a discussion of the economic boom period Slovenia experienced in the early years of EU membership. It also explains why the recent crisis hit the country so strongly and how the authorities managed the crisis. Section 5 concludes the chapter with some lessons derived from the Slovenian experiences.

2 Independence and early transition period

2.1 Slovenia's economy at the time of 1991 independence

Slovenia was the wealthiest republic of the former Socialist Federal Republic of Yugoslavia. During the 1980s, with only 8% of the population of the federation, it generated 18% of its social product and 20% of its industrial production. It also had the lowest unemployment rate (3.2%) compared to 14.9% in the federation. Productivity was at a level at least twice as high as the country's average. With its geographical location and skilled human capital, Slovenia also acted as Yugoslavia's window to the West. During the 1970s and 1980s, it established extensive trade links with companies in the West based very often on long-term business contracts (World Bank, 1999: 2). In contrast to the socialist economies in the Soviet bloc, foreign trade in the former Republic of Yugoslavia was not centralized through state trading organizations.

As a consequence of these features of the Yugoslav economic system and of Slovenia's specificities within the federation, the country had the most favourable initial conditions for successful transition among all the former socialist countries. Slovenia had the highest per capita income among them and was also the most open, measured by exports and imports as a ratio of gross domestic product (GDP). Exports have traditionally been the most important growth and overall development engine of Slovenia.

As a small open economy, Slovenia was highly impacted by the crisis that followed the break-up of former SFRY. Slovenia had already been negatively affected in the late 1990s by the loss of traditional markets, both within other republics of the former SFRY as well as in Eastern European socialist countries. Another important reason for immediate post-independence recession was the high degree of economic instability inherited from the former SFRY, reflected in hyperinflation and in large external debt problems. Such a recession in the early transition period was felt in other socialist countries as well, and it was primarily a result of the change from socialist central planning to free market economies. In 1991, i.e. in the year when Slovenia declared independence, its GDP declined by as much as 8.9% followed by further 5.5% decline in 1992 as shown in Table 10.1.

2.2 *Post-independence stabilization of the economy*

Slovenia's authorities responded to the challenges of independence and transition with a strong adjustment programme aimed at stabilizing the economy. The key pillar of this programme was the introduction of the new currency, the Slovenian tolar, in October 1991, which actually delinked Slovenia's monetary system and policy from the federation and therefore from the former SFRY's hyperinflation trends. With coordinated monetary and fiscal policies the authorities succeeded in reducing inflation, while trade liberalization and broader integration into the international economy were instrumental for the country to redirect its trade flows away from a vanishing Yugoslav market.

Slovenia's economic turnaround began in 1993, rendering the country the second Central European country, after Poland, to recover from the severe output shock of the transition and in the case of Slovenia also from the independence shock. After initial GDP growth of 2.8% in 1993, growth increased to an average level of over 4.0% in the following three years, as shown in Table 10.1.

Successful macroeconomic stabilization during the transition period was accompanied by structural reforms. In contrast to several other transition economies that opted for a 'big-bang approach', typically reflected in quick privatization and therefore a rapid redefinition of the roles of the private and

Table 10.1 Main macroeconomic indicators, 1991–1996

	1991	*1992*	*1993*	*1994*	*1995*	*1996*
GDP per capita (US$)	6,331	6,275	6,366	7,205	9,431	9,481
Real GDP growth (%)	-8.9	-5.5	2.8	5.3	4.1	3.5
Inflation (%)	117.7	201.3	32.3	19.8	12.6	9.7
Unemployment (%)	n.a.	8.3	9.1	9.1	7.4	7.3
Fiscal balance (% of GDP)	2.6	0.2	0.3	-0.2	0.0	0.3
Export of goods and services (% of GDP)	n.a	63.1	58.5	58.9	55.3	55.6
Current account (% of GDP)	n.a.	7.4	1.5	3.8	-0.4	0.2

Source: Mrak, Rojec and Silva-Jauregui (2004).

the public sectors, Slovenia took a very gradualist approach in this regard. By 1996, private sector participation in GDP reached only 40%, i.e., well below the level observed at that period in other transition countries of Central and Eastern Europe (World Bank, 1999: 3). The high share of state ownership in the Slovenian economy was to an extent partly the result of the method of privatization which in fact de-stimulated private investors and reduced incentives for foreign direct investment (FDI).

During this period, wage pressures and tolar appreciation led to a deterioration of Slovenia's external position in the mid-1990s. In 1995, the trade deficit increased to 5.1% of GDP against 1.2% only two years earlier (World Bank, 1999: 5). However, Slovenia was able to keep sound public finances in these early years of the transition. In the 1991–1996 period, public finances were by and large in equilibrium (see Table 10.1) and public debt remained below 25% of GDP. This included a portion of the former SFRY's debt taken over by Slovenia in its successful negotiations with all three of the group of foreign creditors to which the former SFRY defaulted in the first half of the 1980s. By normalizing its relations with foreign creditors and after achieving a single A rating by the three major rating agencies in 1996,[2] Slovenia obtained full access to the international capital markets at very reasonable prices (on this subject, see Mrak, Rojec and Silva-Jauregui, 2004).

2.3 Three specific features of Slovenia's early transition period

As elaborated by Mrak, Rojec and Silva-Jauregui (2004), there are three main features that distinguish the transition process in Slovenia from that of other transition countries of Central and Eastern Europe. The first feature is the already mentioned gradualist approach to transition. In terms of its duration, it was not limited to the early transition period only, but continued all the way until the recent financial crisis. There are several reasons explaining why Slovenia opted for this approach instead of the 'shock therapy' approach which was preferred by the majority of transition economies. One reason was a relatively high level of pre-transition economic development, which reduced the urgency of the reforms. In less developed transition economies this option was simply not feasible, as their backwardness required a bolder approach. In addition, the pre-transition economic elites in Slovenia, again in contrast to other transition economies, were important agents of change even before the transition period. To a large degree these elites retained their position in the economy and society in the early transition period. A related reason for the gradualist approach during the transition period was a tradition of consensus building among stakeholders in connection with major reform decisions. (For a detailed elaboration of the gradualist approach to transition and differences among various authors on this subject see, for example, Mencinger (2004) and Rojec et al. (2004)).

The second distinguishing feature of Slovenia's transition related to the change from a regional economy to a fully-fledged national economy. With political independence, in 1992, Slovenia had to transform itself from being a part of a larger political entity into a sovereign state. The challenges faced by Slovenia as a result were not related exclusively to economic factors, but also to putting in place the institutions necessary for the functioning of a sovereign state, including the Central Bank with its own currency, the Ministry of Finance with entirely new fiscal and customs responsibility, and the Ministry of Foreign Affairs with the network of diplomatic representations. Another challenge for the authorities was how to tackle the loss of trade with other republics of the former SFRY which had been the backbone of Slovenia's economy when it was part of the federation. And finally, Slovenia had to address complex issues associated with its transformation from a republic forming part of the former SFRY to a sovereign state, including major external debt problems inherited from the federation. In addition Slovenia, as a sovereign state, had to undertake major governance changes in order to become member of major international organizations. It should be underlined that in contrast to what happened in the case of the orderly dissolution of Czechoslovakia, the dissolution of the former SFRY was very chaotic and violent, with no agreement among the former members of the federation. These factors had an important influence on the sequencing of reforms. For example, the creation of a national currency and of a customs system was the absolute priority in early independence days.

The third specific feature of Slovenia's transition is the political and economic legacy of the former SFRY. As already mentioned, the Yugoslav self-management socialist system was quite different from the centrally planned system in other former socialist economies. Its characteristics had positive implications on Slovenia at the time when it started the process of transition. As a consequence, the Slovenian managers had a pre-transition experience of being exposed to market conditions and especially to competition. Self-management was, however, also a negative legacy, as the system of internal ownership strongly influenced Slovenia's approach to privatization. This ownership structure proved to be an important obstacle to efficient corporate governance and enterprise restructuring, and may have worked against the attraction of FDI.

3 Slovenia accedes to the EU and adopts the euro

3.1 The delay in the institutionalization of the EU accession process

During the second half of the 1980s, independence emerged as a necessary solution for Slovenia as it became obvious that transformation of the former SFRY was not possible. During that period, the 'Europe now' slogan summarized the desires of the population in Slovenia not only for economic and political transformation but also for a European future. Euro-Atlantic integration, and within this framework membership in the EU, became the key strategic objective.

Political recognition of the Republic of Slovenia by the members of the European Community at the end of 1991 and in the first months of 1992 was a precondition for the institutionalization of relations between Slovenia and the European Community. Slovenia was, however, by far the last country, among the Central European countries aspiring for EU accession, to sign the Association Agreement. While other countries from the sub-region signed similar contracts in the first half of the 1990s, in the case of Slovenia this happened only in June 1996 (Potočnik *et al.*, 2007: 345).

There are several reasons that could explain the reasons for the delay in the institutionalization of the country's relationship with the EU. First, Slovenia became an independent sovereign state only in mid-1991 and was politically recognized by the EU member states a year later. Second, as one of the successors of the former SFRY, Slovenia inherited problems with all the three groups of its foreign creditors, i.e. multilateral financial institutions, commercial banks, and governments, of which many were EU member states. Third, the late signing of the Association Agreement was partly also due to the de facto veto position of neighbouring Italy. Italy claimed that the issue of property on the territory of Slovenia that had been owned by Italian citizens before they opted for Italy after the Second World War, had not been resolved.

The 'Italian' problem was resolved on the basis of the so-called 'Spanish compromise', whereby Slovenia agreed that citizens of EU member states who had permanently resided on the present territory of Slovenia for a period of three years would have a right to purchase the property from the day the Association Agreement came into force. The 'Spanish compromise' actually opened the door for Slovenia to start accession negotiations in December 1997, as part of the so-called 'Luxembourg group', which included four other Central European countries, namely the Czech Republic, Estonia, Hungary and Poland, and also Cyprus.

3.2 Slovenia's EU accession process and negotiations

While during the period between independence and the beginning of the EU accession negotiations the most pressing issue for Slovenia was associated with the creation of a sovereign state, in the years that followed the EU accession process took centre stage. The process itself became an extremely important vehicle for accelerating the reform agenda and implementing needed structural reforms. Meeting the economic criteria for EU membership set at the 1993 Copenhagen Council[3] coincided well with the transition objectives aimed at strengthening Slovenia's economic potential and its international competitiveness. Successful transition was thus seen in Slovenia as a precondition for EU accession, and conversely, the accession process was seen as instrument for speeding up the country's transition.

In the second half of the 1990s, Slovenia adopted several strategic reforms necessary for the second stage of its transition, as contained in two main strategy documents, namely the 1995 "Strategy for Economic Development of Slovenia" and the 1998 "Strategy of the Republic of Slovenia for Accession to the EU". The key objectives of these strategies were, first, to speed up economic growth of the country and thus allow its economic catching up with EU member states, and second, to improve the competitiveness of the Slovenian economy. The 1998 Strategy further on outlined a set of consistent medium-term economic and social policy measures that were required for Slovenia to harmonize its legal system with the *acquis communautaire* and to ensure its enforcement through adequate administrative and judiciary set-ups.

As in all EU candidate countries, Slovenia's EU accession process consisted of the harmonization of Slovenia's law with the EU body of laws, and of negotiations that focused primarily on transition periods for the adoption of EU regulations and directives. Negotiations also took place internally, within Slovenia, to prepare the country's position vis-à-vis the individual negotiation chapters. The final phase of the negotiations consisted of the talks on the financial package, that is, the funds to be paid by Slovenia into the EU budget and EU budget funds to be allocated to Slovenia primarily for agriculture and cohesion (Potočnik and Garcia Lombardero, 2004: 375).

Slovenia succeeded in achieving a strong political consensus with respect to its EU accession. It was supported by practically all major political parties, so it can be said that EU accession was an overall national project. A strong pro-EU orientation of the Slovene political and economic elites, as well as certain specific features of the country's legal framework, have contributed to a successful negotiation process.[4]

In Slovenia, parliament, or more precisely its Committee for International Relations, had to approve each individual negotiating position. Although this occasionally created logistical problems in running the negotiations, this procedure also guaranteed transparency of the process, eased the final decision making on EU accession in parliament and generated a favourable response in the accession referendum. Furthermore, Slovenia was the only one of the 12 candidate countries whose negotiation positions were publicly available immediately upon their adoption by the parliament. Strong pro-EU political consensus was reflected also in the structure of the EU negotiating team appointed by the government. The team, composed of experts, with each of them responsible for negotiations on one or more negotiating chapters, had remained unchanged throughout all the five years of the negotiations in spite of several changes in the government coalitions.

3.3 Advantages and disadvantages of EU membership

The process of EU accession negotiations for ten candidate countries, including Slovenia, was successfully completed at the December 2012 Copenhagen Council and the Treaty on EU Accession received a high level of Slovenian public support at the March 2003 referendum with 89% of votes cast in favour of EU membership.

Slovenia has always been a part of the European geographic and cultural space. As a consequence, historical factors and cultural tradition as well as geographic location and economic links with Europe have been driving forces that predetermined Slovenian aspirations for integration within the EU. These aspirations, though already present before the 1991 independence, became much more explicit at the time when Slovenia constituted itself as a sovereign state.

Being a small and open economy, economic arguments have always been considered as the crucial drivers supporting the accession of Slovenia to the EU, even though non-economic aspects, especially on security and political issues, were of importance as well. The long-term goal of EU accession for Slovenia was to increase the welfare and living standards of its population by catching up with the EU in terms of economic development. Participation in the huge internal EU market characterized by four freedoms was expected to lead towards an increased volume of trade, to larger inflow of foreign capital, to more employment and consequently to higher economic growth. An important contribution to stronger economic growth was expected also from significant net inflows of funds from the EU budget. Slovenia was at the same level of development, measured as GDP per capita, as Portugal and Greece, and therefore it was realistic to expect that the country would become eligible for substantial inflows of regional and cohesion funds on accession to the EU.

Among the non-economic benefits of being an EU member, the contribution towards political stability and formal participation in EU institutions were cited most frequently. It is true that under EU Treaties the voting power of small states in the EU is rather small, but in many respects it is still more than proportional to the share in the European population. Having the possibility to participate actively in the decision making of the EU, including having a veto power in politically sensitive areas, is a major advantage to a small country like Slovenia.

There were, of course, concerns associated with EU membership as well. The most important one was that a member state loses its full sovereignty in certain areas of its economic and political development, or more precisely, the country is obliged to transfer parts of its sovereignty to the EU institutions.

Other potential drawbacks of EU accession, raised during the negotiations, included non-economic ones, such as the concern that the Slovene language would be under pressure and could even disappear in the large multicultural EU. On the economic side, there was the fear that the free movement of capital would cause a large inflow of capital aimed at buying Slovenia's land and property.

Membership in the EU was also a challenge for Slovene public finances. The budget expenditure, equivalent to about 1% of GDP, was required to finance the harmonization of the country with the *acquis*, especially in the area of agriculture and environment, and to finance the introduction of the Schengen border. In addition, the revenue side of public finances was dented with the accession to EU as customs duties collected on Slovenian borders became part of an integral EU budget. (See Mrak (2005) for more details on the fiscal effects of EU accession.)

All in all, assessing the advantages and disadvantages of Slovenia's accession it seemed that benefits largely exceeded the costs. This view was supported by several academic studies carried out in the country and based on different methodologies (see, for example, Potočnik and Majcen, 1996; Majcen, 1999). Net benefits were expected particularly in the longer-run as the flow of benefits would continue over time while the adjustment was to have been largely accomplished prior to accession or in the first few years of the membership.

Benefits and costs associated with EU accession were, however, not distributed proportionally in time and space, as well as among different sectors of the economy and groups in the society. The winners of EU accession were definitely some exporters who in general benefited from liberalization of foreign trade and access to a large market. On the losing side were primarily those sectors and firms that were protected from foreign competition in the pre-EU membership and failed to restructure themselves in time (Lavrač and Majcen, 2006: 12–14). For example, the agro-industry had enjoyed protection from competing imports. In addition, due to free trade agreements with countries in the region, Slovenian agricultural products had a preferential status *vis-à-vis* competitors from the EU.

3.4 Economic performance during the EU accession period

Although Slovenia signed the Association Agreement last among the 12 candidate countries, the overall process of Slovenia's integration in the negotiations was smooth and successful. By the end of 2001, the country provisionally closed all negotiating chapters except those related to the financial package which had to be negotiated jointly with all candidate countries. Slovenia was the only candidate country that met fully the timetable set in the 'road map' for the negotiations adopted at the Nice Council in December 2001. The fact that Slovenia was considered at that time as one of the best prepared candidate countries for accession to the EU was later confirmed by the fact that Slovenia was asked to preside the EU Council in the first half of 2008 – the first among the new EU member states.

The political credibility of Slovenia at the time of its EU accession was accompanied by solid economic standing. As shown in Table 10.2, the country grew at an average annual growth rate of over 3.4% between 2000 and 2004, a rate significantly over the EU average. Measured in purchasing power parity (PPP) terms, Slovenia's GDP per capita was, in 1995, 68% of the EU-25 average while in 2004, in the year of EU accession, this figure increased to 80% and was equivalent to that of Greece and Portugal.

The annual inflation rate decreased from a two-digit figure in the mid-1990s to below 2.5% in the early 2000s and the unemployment rate stabilized at level just below 7%. Even though public finances slipped into a deficit in 1997

Table 10.2 Main macroeconomic indicators, 2000–2005*

	2000	*2001*	*2002*	*2003*	*2004*	*2005*
GDP per capita (in PPP terms) (% of EU-25)	73	74	75	77	80	82
Real GDP growth (%)	4.1	2.7	3.5	2.7	4.2	3.9
Inflation (%)	2.5	2.0	2.4	2.0	2.3	2.2
Unemployment (%)	6.7	6.2	6.3	6.7	6.3	6.3
General government balance (% of GDP)	−3.9	−4.3	−2.7	−2.8	−2.2	−2.8
Current account (% of GDP)	0.6	0.6	0.6	0.4	0.1	0.2
Public debt (% of GDP)	26	28	30	29	29	28

Source: *Development Report*, IMAD (several annual issues).

and had remained there since then, these deficits were rather small until the year of accession and the public debt remained below 30% of GDP. With the continuation of the managed float exchange rate policy and in close cooperation with supporting fiscal policy, the central bank succeeded in maintaining external balance. The current account of Slovenia showed a small surplus in the first years of the 2000s.

In terms of structural reforms, Slovenia's performance was much less impressive during the accession negotiation period (Peternelj, 2005: 3–5; Mrak, Rojec and Silva-Jauregui, 2004: xxix–xxxiii). Slovenia continued with its gradual approach to the transition, in particular with respect to trade liberalization and privatization. The country basically applied a strategy that gave economic agents sufficient time to adapt to the changing international environment without excessive pressure to restructure or to close down unsustainable enterprises.

In the enterprise sector, the emphasis on privatization by internal buy-outs de facto served to maintain the status quo by avoiding massive layoffs, but at the cost of subdued enterprise performance. In the financial sector, the largest banks remained firmly under majority state ownership while the capital market never established itself as a credible intermediator of long-term savings. One reason was that capital market development was strongly and negatively influenced by the adopted concept of mass privatization. On the other hand, capital market development was constrained also by monetary policy considerations including the tolar appreciation pressure caused by net capital inflows. Relatively slow and limited privatization with at least implicit preference given to domestic investors, under the protection of national interest argument, kept FDI inflows at very low levels. As observed by various surveys, including the World Bank's annual *Doing Business* reports, Slovenia was doing relatively poorly *vis-à-vis* other Central European countries in terms of reducing or eliminating obstacles in the business environment.

There were moderate reforms in the labour and health sectors as well as in pension schemes during the 1997–2004 period. Although these modifications had a positive fiscal impact, they were far from sufficient to guarantee long-term stability of public finances in the country, especially taking into account its ageing population.

3.5 Why Slovenia opted for early adoption of the euro

The political credibility and solid economic performance, especially on its macroeconomic side, that Slovenia enjoyed during the accession process, encouraged the Slovenian authorities to enter the euro area as quickly as possible. There were at least five specific arguments that were used to support early adoption of the euro. First, there was a high degree of trade integration of Slovenia with the EU and a high degree of similarity of the country's economic structure with other members of the euro area. Second, with entrance into the EU, Slovenia had already lost some of its monetary sovereignty. Third, Slovenia had a relatively strong fiscal position. Fourth, Slovenia, as a small economy, was highly exposed to external shocks, and membership of the euro area could provide some shelter against financial vulnerability. And fifth, real convergence of the country was already at a relatively advanced stage – Slovenia's GDP per capita, in PPP terms, was around 80% of the EU-25 average (Mrak, 2010a). Of course, the decision was also influenced by the fact that each of the new EU member states was legally obliged to adopt the euro once it was able to meet the Maastricht criteria.

A political decision for early adoption of the euro in Slovenia was made in November 2003 when the government and the Central Bank signed a Programme on ERM II Entry and Adoption of the Euro (Government of Slovenia and Bank of Slovenia, 2003). It should be underlined that the document also had the support of social partners. Key elements of the Programme included the reform of the wage indexation mechanism in the public and private sector, commitment to control increases of administered prices, pressure to improve efficiency in sectors shielded from competition, further stabilization of the tolar–euro exchange rate, and further progress in fiscal consolidation. In line with the Programme, Slovenia entered into the ERM II mechanism in June 2004, that is less than two months after the country became an EU member, and the authorities successfully met the challenges associated with its mechanism (Bole and Mramor, 2006). In spring 2006, the European Commission and the European Central Bank prepared the convergence reports, indicating that Slovenia met all the five Maastricht criteria. On this basis the June 2006 European Council took the decision that Slovenia was to become a euro zone member, with the exchange rate set at 239.64 tolar per €. With the changeover that happened in January 2007, Slovenia became the 13th euro zone member state and the first among the countries that joined the EU in 2004.

4 The crisis

4.1 Systemic weaknesses of Slovenia's transition surfaces after accession to the EU

There was a close interrelationship between Slovenia's transformation into a sovereign state and its integration into the EU. Membership in the EU associated with a vision of prosperity had *de facto* become the highest priority not only for political and economic elites but also for the population at large. On the institutional side, though being somewhat late with structural reforms, Slovenia was perceived as a country with a stable economy and pragmatic economic policy. This view about Slovenia as a 'success story' of transition and a country that positioned itself as a candidate for EU accession was shared also by many in Slovenia and elsewhere.

There was, however, also a negative side of Slovenia's overconcentration on EU membership issues, which could be summarized with the word 'complacency'. It was believed that in Slovenia, if not explicitly at least implicitly, that the EU policies and the *acquis* would provide a basis for the country's economic development and transformation in the future. While concentrating on EU membership, Slovenia continued with its very gradual transition in all those areas that were not strictly governed by the *acquis* (Türk, 2013). As a consequence, the country delayed further transformation with respect to the economic institutions, technological development and industrial structures, and remained sceptical towards the need for FDI. In addition, Slovenia continued to have problems in developing professional and well-functioning institutions related to the judiciary and public administration in particular, which are key for the successful completion of the transition.

Another important political problem resurfaced following EU accession. Historically, the Slovenian population was traditionally politically divided between the left and the right. During the Second World War and in the period immediately after the war, this division was further deepened with the left by and large joining or at least supporting the Tito communists and at least one part of the right *de facto* collaborated with the occupation forces. At the time of the fall of the Berlin Wall, when the window of opportunity to become an independent state opened, Slovenia's political elite succeeded in uniting the population under the vision of a sovereign state fully integrated in the prosperous Europe. This unity of the population remained more or less stable throughout the European integration processes, but the divisions emerged again soon after the strategic objective for the country was achieved. On the political scene, these divisions have been reflected in various forms, such as ideological intolerance between certain political parties, often leading to deadlocks in dialogues between the government and the opposition, difficulties in building a constitutional majority required to adopt some major decisions, and abuse of the referendum as the most democratic form of decision making.

Strong political divisions have had their impact on economic development as well. Over the last ten years, Slovenia has been in a kind of a vacuum with respect to the preparation and adoption of strategic development documents. In contrast to the previous period when EU membership was the key and undisputed objective, in the more recent period Slovenia has failed to articulate a longer-term vision of the country and to define economic development objectives. The last economic development strategy for Slovenia dates back to 2005 and had the time horizon of 2013, when the last EU medium-term financial perspective expired. There were several attempts in recent years to prepare a new development strategy but with no success.

4.2 Overheating of the economy

The deadly cocktail of complacency, unfinished transition and cheap money available on international markets resulted in a growth model leading to the overheating of the economy (Mrak, 2010b: 1–2). Under this model, the main engine of growth was high domestic demand generated both by private consumption and inward oriented investment and financed by large net capital inflows. As Slovenia was rather restrictive on FDI, these inflows were entering into the country primarily in the form of debt financing, more precisely of commercial bank loans raised either from parent banks domiciled in the old EU member states or borrowed directly from the market. In 2007 alone, net capital inflow to Slovenia through the banking sector amounted to €3.4 billion, equivalent to around 10% of GDP (Bank of Slovenia, 2012: II-56).

Strong net capital inflows had a counter effect on the growing current account deficits. An important negative consequence of large capital inflows, intermediated by banks, led to rapid increases in domestic demand, exacerbating Slovenia's external vulnerabilities in the form of rising current account deficit. In contrast to the whole pre-EU accession period, when the current account of Slovenia was by and large balanced, in the following years its external account worsened significantly between 2006 and 2008, as shown in Table 10.3.

In the period 2006–2008, the average annual economic growth of Slovenia amounted to 5%, which was significantly higher than its potential, long-term growth, so the country was experiencing a significant positive output gap. Unfortunately, this was not addressed with a counter cyclical fiscal policy. On the contrary, fiscal policy was actually pro-cyclical in that period, contributing to even stronger overheating of the economy. It is more than obvious that policy makers in Slovenia at that time had either not understood properly or had at least strongly underestimated the dramatic changes the entrance of the country into the monetary union would have on its overall macroeconomic policy mix.

By transferring monetary and therefore exchange rate policy to the euro zone, it was only the fiscal policy that remained under full sovereignty of national authorities. As a consequence, fiscal policy became, in a monetary

Table 10.3 Main macroeconomic indicators, 2006–2015*

	2006	*2007*	*2008*	*2009*	*2010*	*2011*	*2012*	*2013*	*2014*
GDP per capita (in PPP terms) (% of EU-28)	86	87	89	85	83	83	82	82	83
Real GDP growth (%)	5.8	6.9	3.3	−7.8	1.2	0.6	−2.6	−1.0	2.6
Inflation (%)	2.3	2.8	5.6	2.1	1.9	2.0	2.7	0.7	0.2
Unemployment (%)	6.0	4.9	4.4	5.9	7.1	7.7	8.2	10.4	9.3
General government balance (% of GDP)	−1.4	0.0	−1.8	−6.1	−5.6	−6.6	−4.0	−14.9	−4.9
Current account (% of GDP)	−2.5	−4.2	−5.4	−0.6	−0.1	0.2	2.7	5.6	5.8
Public debt (% of GDP)	26	26	22	35	38	47	54	70	81

Source: *Development Report*, IMAD (several annual issues).

union environment, much more important in relative terms than in an environment where the country continues to have its own national currency. And of course, fiscal policy mistakes tend to be costly and have longer-term negative implications on the economy forming part of a monetary union.

In spite of warnings coming from different sources, Slovenia's fiscal policy in the 2006–2008 'boom period' was highly inappropriate for the euro zone's environment which was characterized by a very low level of inflation. This was a period when the inflation rate in Slovenia was twice as high as that of the euro zone and when, as a consequence of inflation rate differentials, real interest rates in Slovenia were actually negative. It is not surprising that this cheap money was used for investment, mostly in physical infrastructure, property and construction, and also for financing highly leveraged management buy-outs.

Overheating of the Slovenian economy was closely associated with the growing pressure on wages, which were increasing faster than productivity. This negatively affected the international competitiveness of the country and as a result Slovenia's export sector, traditionally the most vital part of the economy, lost shares on the global markets.

4.3 'Bust period': economic crisis and its management

In the last quarter of 2008, and after a long period of rapid economic growth, Slovenia entered into a deep crisis with a fall in GDP of close to 8% in 2009 (see Table 10.3). Economic growth in Slovenia was affected more drastically by the crisis than other new EU central European member states. This could be attributed to the fact that overall vulnerability of the country's growth model was much higher than in other countries in the region. Given that Slovenia was in the euro zone, it could not react with its own foreign exchange adjustment.

The dramatic decline of economic growth in Slovenia after the outbreak of the crisis interrupted its almost two decades-long period of strong real economic convergence towards the EU average. After achieving per capita GDP (in PPP terms) equivalent to 89% of EU-28 average in 2008, it declined to 83% in 2010 and remained at a more or less unchanged level in the following years (see Table 10.3).

In 2014, Slovenia was the only Central European transition economy worse off than it was at the time it joined the EU, given that in 2004, the corresponding figure was 86% of the EU-28 average. This indicated a kind of a lost decade for Slovenia. Although other Central European countries experienced an interruption in their real economic convergence path, their overall record for the 2004–2014 period was not a decline when comparing 2014 with 2004. In the case of Poland and Slovakia, the convergence record was impressive since they respectively converged from 49% to 68% and from 57% to 76% of the EU average. The Czech Republic and Hungary made smaller steps forward, respectively converging from 79% to 84% and from 62% to 68%, which can be explained by the fact that they started from a relatively high level of development (Eurostat, 2015).

The poor performance in economic growth and real convergence of Slovenia in recent years can be only partially attributed to the 2008/2009 economic crisis. Perhaps even more important for the prolonged recession was the inappropriate policy response of the authorities in the following years, especially in the period 2010–2012. Under an implicit assumption that the crisis was to be of a short-term character and following the tradition of gradual transition with all important economic decisions to be based on a consensus among social partners, the authorities were postponing the highly needed fiscal consolidation. Instead of cutting public expenditures in line with the reduced volume of revenues available, Slovenia entered into a prolonged period of high public finance deficits. In the four-year period between 2009 and 2012, the deficit amounted, on average, to more than 5% of GDP (see Table 10.3).

Weakness in the banking sector was another source of the significant deterioration of Slovenia's public finances in the post-crisis period. As has been mentioned already, the pre-crisis boom in Slovenia was largely based on foreign banking loans. As the interbank market collapsed during the crisis, this form of inflow dried up completely. The banks, which in their majority were state owned, lost market access to cover refinancing needs, and in order to prevent their bankruptcy the government had no other alternative but to step in with several rounds of bank recapitalizations. The capital account figures from Slovenia's balance of payments statistics reflect clearly these dramatic changes. While in 2007, i.e. in the peak year of the 'boom' period, Slovenia registered a net capital inflow in the form of banking loans of €5.6 billion (equivalent to around 15% of GDP), in 2009, i.e., in the peak year of the 'bust' period, there was a net capital outflow of banking loans of €4.0 billion (again more than 10% of GDP). As banks would collapse under these circumstances, the government stepped in with its financial support generated by borrowing abroad in the form of bonds issued on international financial markets. In 2009 alone, Slovenia issued more than €4 billion worth of bonds on international financial markets (IMF, 2011: 36).

As a consequence of the need to address the public finance deficits and the bank recapitalizations, the public debt of Slovenia skyrocketed. From a comfortable level of below 30% of GDP it increased to over 80% of GDP as shown in Table 10.3. In contrast to the two-decade long pre-crisis record of sound public finances, during the post-crisis period public finance turned into a major liability.

Another important constraint which hampered speedy recovery of the Slovenian economy was the high rate of indebtedness in the enterprise sector. Due to the method of privatization applied in Slovenia, associated with weak corporate governance structures, it is not surprising that external funding of the corporate sector in the pre-crisis period was largely based on debt-financing from banks, while equity funding from either domestic or foreign owners was largely missing. This funding model collapsed with the crisis as the banks ceased to finance companies that were overleveraged. As a consequence, many of the companies were put into bankruptcy, causing a significant increase in unemployment (see Table 10.3). This has also resulted in a growing proportion of so-called non-performing loans in the banks' portfolio, which in turn required further recapitalizations.

This toxic nexus of the sovereign and private debt in Slovenia, coupled with the inability of the Slovene authorities to address the crisis effectively, in turn had a negative effect on the capital market. The rating of Slovenia was downgraded several times and the spreads for its borrowing on the international capital markets capital started to widen. From a country that was long considered by the markets as a part of the euro-zone's core and a possible contributor to the solution of the crisis, Slovenia was transferred into one of the problematic, peripheral euro-zone countries. Immediately after the Cyprus crisis, in spring 2013, Slovenia was even considered to be the next candidate for 'troika' assistance. This was a period when the financial credibility of Slovenia was at its lowest.

4.4 Recent return to the economic stability path

With a decisive programme of measures taken under the threat of a default in the second half of 2013, Slovenia avoided the need for EU–IMF funding and the policy conditionality associated with these funds. The key features of this programme were the following: first, based on extensive asset quality reviews of bank portfolios accompanied by stress tests, non-performing loans from state-owned banks were transferred into a 'bad bank'. Balance sheets of banks were recapitalized, with funds equivalent to roughly 10% of GDP, under EU state aid rules, where Slovenia agreed to privatize these banks by 2017. Second, there followed an intensification of privatization based on the list of 15 state-owned companies. Some of these – Airport Ljubljana or Telekom Slovenia for example – were considered to be in high demand by foreign investors. Third, parliament introduced the fiscal rule into the constitution, which in fact meant that over the business cycle public finances of the country have to remain in equilibrium. And fourth, the authorities started to act decisively on the expenditure side of public finances in order to bring the deficit at a level below 3% of GDP, expecting that this would happen in 2015.

Ambitious and deep rooted 'home based' reforms accompanied with an improved economic environment within the EU resulted in the return of Slovenia to the growth path by 2014, when its growth rate was 2.6% (see Table 10.3), one of the highest in EU, and a similar rate was expected in 2015. Improved growth figures, positive developments in bank rehabilitation, declining indebtedness of the corporate sector and improved export performance have bolstered the confidence of international capital markets in Slovenia and significantly reduced the spreads for Slovenia's borrowing on these markets. These lower spreads should, of course, be judged in the context of lower borrowing costs for all peripheral euro-zone countries in the more recent period.

5 Conclusion

This chapter has shown that following its independence, Slovenia passed through three distinct phases. The first phase was characterized by the transition from a region of a federation to a sovereign state. The key feature of the second phase was preparation of the country for accession to the EU and adoption of the euro, while the third phase was dominated by the boom and bust sub-periods associated with the recent crisis. Throughout its whole post-independence period Slovenia was characterized as a champion of the gradualist approach with a strong tradition of consensus building among stakeholders having an important role within the process of major policy and structural reform decisions.

Many lessons can be derived from the Slovene economic changes during the past 20 years or so, with the most important one being that good economic governance is essential for stability. Even though economic reforms should not be excessively rushed, procrastination in this regard may lead to missed opportunities. In the case of Slovenia, the institutional set ups were not upgraded to match the rapid economic growth of the country. This, of course, requires political will and commitment. Support of the social partners is essential as well. But here again, consensus should not lead to overdue delays in decision taking. Another important lesson to be learned is that being a member of the EU and of the euro group does not guarantee stability.

It is up to individual countries to ensure fiscal prudence and to create an overall environment that will strengthen the international competitiveness of the country and will be conducive to entrepreneurship development.

Notes

1 The federation was in the meantime renamed Socialist Federal Republic of Yugoslavia (SFRY).
2 This was the highest country rating among the transition economies at that time.
3 The Copenhagen economic accession criteria approved in 1993 specify that acceding countries must have (1) a functioning market economy and (2) the capacity to cope with competition and market forces within the EU.
4 On this subject see Potočnik et al. (2007: 347–350).

References

Bank of Slovenia (2012) *Monthly Bulletin*, November 2012 (in Slovene).

Bole, V. and Mramor, D. (2006) 'Soft Landing in the ERM II: Lessons from Slovenia', in J. Prašnikar, (ed.). *Competitiveness, Social Responsibility and Economic Growth*, Nova Science Publishers.

Eurostat (2015) Table with data on GDP per capita in PPS. Available at: http://ec.europa.eu/eurostat/tgm/table.do?tab=table&init=1&language=en&pcode=tec00114&plugin=1 (accessed 23 January 2016).

Government of Slovenia and Bank of Slovenia (2003) *Program on ERM II Entry and Adoption of the Euro*. Retrieved from https://www.bsi.si/library/includes/datoteka.asp?DatotekaId=1243 (accessed 23 January 2016).

IMAD (various annual issues). *Development Report*. Institute of Macroeconomic Analysis and Development of the Republic of Slovenia. Available at: http://www.umar.gov.si/en/publications/development_report/?no_cache=1 (accessed 23 January 2016).

IMAD (1995) *Strategy for Economic Development of Slovenia*. Institute of Macroeconomic Analysis and Development of the Republic of Slovenia. Available at: www.umar.gov.si/fileadmin/user_upload/projects/slovenia_development_strategy.pdf (accessed 23 January 2016).

IMAD (1998) *Strategy of the Republic of Slovenia for Accession to the European Union: Economic and Social Part*. Institute of Macroeconomic Analysis and Development of the Republic of Slovenia.

IMF (2011) *Article IV Consultation – Staff Report*. Available at: https://www.imf.org/external/pubs/ft/scr/2011/cr11121.pdf (accessed 23 January 2016).

Lavrač, V. and Majcen, B. (2006) *Economic Issues of Slovenia's Accession to the EU*. Working Paper No. 1, IER.

Majcen, B. (1999) *Measurement of Costs and Benefits of Accession to the EU for Selected CEECs. Country Report: Slovenia*. Vienna: The Vienna Institute for Comparative Studies (WIIW), Research Report No. 256.

Mencinger, J. (2004) 'Transition to National and Market Economy: A Gradualist Approach', in M. Mrak, M. Rojec, and C. Silva-Jauregui (eds). *Slovenia: From Yugoslavia to the European Union*. World Bank.

Mrak, M. (2004) 'Succession Issues in Allocating the External Debt of SFR Yugoslavia and Achieving Slovenia's Financial Independence', in M. Mrak, M. Rojec, and

C. Silva-Jauregui (eds). *Slovenia: From Yugoslavia to the European Union.* World Bank.

Mrak, M. (2005) 'Slovenia: European Union Related Medium Term Public Finance Challenges', *Ekonomicky časopis*, 53.

Mrak, M. (2010a). *Euro Adoption in Slovenia: Lessons Learned and Challenges Ahead.* Presentation at the Forum Observatory on the New Eurozone, Budapest, 6 June.

Mrak, M. (2010b). 'Redefining Growth Models for Eastern European countries after the Crisis: Can Eastern Europe Grow Again at a Faster Rate than Western Europe?' Presentation at the 6th Annual Meeting of Senior Budget Officials in Budva, Montenegro, 23–24 September. Available at: www.oecd.org/gov/budgeting/6thannualmeetingofseniorbudgetofficialsfromcentraleasternandsouth-easterneuropeancountries23-24september2010.htm (accessed 23 January 2016).

Mrak, M., Rojec, M. and Silva-Jauregui, C. (2004) 'Introduction', in M. Mrak, M. Rojec, and C. Silva-Jauregui (eds). *Slovenia: From Yugoslavia to the European Union.* World Bank.

Peternelj, M. (2005) 'Slow is Beautiful: Slovenia's Approach to Transition', *European Commission, ECFIN Country Focus*, 10(2).

Potočnik, J. and Majcen, B. (1996) *Possible Effects of Slovenian Integration into the EU: CGE Approach.* Ljubljana: IMAD.

Potočnik, J., Černe, F., Erjavec, E. and Mrak, M. (2007) 'The Accession of Slovenia to the EU', in G. Vassiliou (ed.). *The Accession Story*, Oxford: Oxford University Press.

Potočnik, J. and Garcia Lombardero, J. (2004) 'Slovenia's Road to Membership in the European Union', in M. Mrak, M. Rojec, and C. Silva-Jauregui (eds). *Slovenia: From Yugoslavia to the European Union.* World Bank.

Rojec, M., Šušteršič, J., Vasle, B., Bednaš, M. and Jurančič, S. (2004) 'The Rise and Decline of Gradualism in Slovenia', *Post-Communist Economies*, 16(4) December.

Türk, D. (2013) 'Slovenia and the European Union'. Address by Dr Danilo Türk, Former President of the Republic of Slovenia at the Sarajevo Business Forum, Sarajevo, B&H, 17 May.

World Bank (1999) *Slovenia: Economic Transformation and EU Accession, Volume II: Main Report.* A World Bank Country Study. Available at: www-wds.worldbank.org/external/default/WDSContentServer/WDSP/IB/1999/07/29/000094946_99041505302542/Rendered/PDF/multi_page.pdf (accessed 23 January 2016).

Index